TUNISIA

T0295691

INTERNET, E-COMMERCE
INVESTMENT AND BUSINESS
GUIDE

STRATEGIC INFORMATION, REGULATIONS,
OPPORTUNITIES

International Business Publications, USA
Washington DC, USA - Tunisia

TUNISIA
INTERNET, E-COMMERCE INVESTMENT AND BUSINESS GUIDE
STRATEGIC INFORMATION, REGULATIONS, OPPORTUNITIES

UPDATED ANNUALLY

Cover Design: International Business Publications, USA

We express our sincere appreciation to all government agencies and international organizations which provided information and other materials for this guide

International Business Publications, USA. has used its best efforts in collecting, analyzing and preparing data, information and materials for this unique guide. Due to the dynamic nature and fast development of the economy and business environment, we cannot warrant that all information herein is complete and accurate. IBP does not assume and hereby disclaim any liability to any person for any loss or damage caused by possible errors or omissions in the guide.
This guide is for individual use only. Use this guide for any other purpose, included but not limited to reproducing and storing in a retrieval system by any means, electronic, photocopying or using the addresses or other information contained in this guide for any commercial purposes requires a special written permission from the publisher.

2018 Edition Updated Reprint International Business Publications, USA
ISBN 1-4387-4871-X

This guide provides basic information for starting or/and conducting business in the country. The extraordinary volume of materials covering the topic, prevents us from placing all these materials in this guide. For more detailed information on issues related to any specific investment and business activity in the country, please contact
Global Investment Center, USA
Please acquire the list of our business intelligence and marketing reports and other business publications. We constantly update and expand our business intelligence and marketing materials. Please contact the center for the updated list of reports on over 150 countries.

For additional analytical, business and investment opportunities information,
please contact Global Investment & Business Center, USA
at (703) 370-8082. Fax: (703) 370-8083. E-mail: ibpusa3@gmail.com
Global Business and Investment Info Databank - www.ibpus.com

Printed in the USA

For additional analytical, business and investment opportunities information,
please contact Global Investment & Business Center, USA
at (703) 370-8082. Fax: (703) 370-8083. E-mail: ibpusa3@gmail.com
Global Business and Investment Info Databank - www.ibpus.com

TUNISIA
INTERNET, E-COMMERCE INVESTMENT AND BUSINESS GUIDE
STRATEGIC INFORMATION, REGULATIONS, OPPORTUNITIES

TABLE OF CONTENTS

For additional analytical, business and investment opportunities information,
please contact Global Investment & Business Center, USA
at (703) 370-8082. Fax: (703) 370-8083. E-mail: ibpusa3@gmail.com
Global Business and Investment Info Databank - www.ibpus.com

For additional analytical, business and investment opportunities information,
please contact Global Investment & Business Center, USA
at (703) 370-8082. Fax: (703) 370-8083. E-mail: ibpusa3@gmail.com
Global Business and Investment Info Databank - www.ibpus.com

**For additional analytical, business and investment opportunities information,
please contact Global Investment & Business Center, USA
at (703) 370-8082. Fax: (703) 370-8083. E-mail: ibpusa3@gmail.com
Global Business and Investment Info Databank - www.ibpus.com**

**For additional analytical, business and investment opportunities information,
please contact Global Investment & Business Center, USA
at (703) 370-8082. Fax: (703) 370-8083. E-mail: ibpusa3@gmail.com
Global Business and Investment Info Databank - www.ibpus.com**

For additional analytical, business and investment opportunities information,
please contact Global Investment & Business Center, USA
at (703) 370-8082. Fax: (703) 370-8083. E-mail: ibpusa3@gmail.com
Global Business and Investment Info Databank - www.ibpus.com

BUSINESS AND DEVELOPMENT PROFILES

STRATEGIC PROFILE

Capital and largest city	Tunis 36°49′N 10°11′E
Official languages	Arabic[2]
Spoken languages	• Tunisian Arabic • Berber • French (commercial and educational)
Ethnic groups	Arab (<40% – 98%, Berber (1%[10] – >60%), European (1%),[9] Turkish, Jewish and other (1%)
Religion	Islam (state religion; 99.1% Sunni others (1%; including Christian, Jewish, Shia, Bahá'í)[9]
Demonym	Tunisian
Government	Unitary semi-presidential republic
• President	Beji Caid Essebsi
• Head of Government	Youssef Chahed
Legislature	Assembly of the Representatives of the People
Formation	
• Husainid Dynasty inaugurated	15 July 1705
• Independence from France	20 March 1956
• Republic declared	25 July 1957
• Revolution Day	14 January 2011
Area	
• Total	163,610 km^2 (63,170 sq mi) (91st)
• Water (%)	5.0
Population	
• 2016 estimate	11,304,482 (79th)
• Density	63/km^2 (163.2/sq mi) (133rd)
GDP (PPP)	2017 estimate
• Total	$136.797 billion
• Per capita	$12,065
GDP (nominal)	2017 estimate
• Total	$40.289 billion
• Per capita	$3,553
Gini (2010)	36.1 medium
HDI (2016)	▲ 0.725[17] high · 97th
Currency	Tunisian dinar (TND)
Time zone	CET (UTC+1)
Drives on the	right
Calling code	+216
ISO 3166 code	TN
Internet TLD	.tn

Tunisia is the northernmost country in Africa and, at almost 165,000 square kilometres (64,000 sq mi) in area, the smallest country in the Maghreb region of North Africa. It is bordered by Algeria to the west, Libya to the southeast and the Mediterranean Sea to the north and east. As of 2013, its population is estimated at just under 10.8 million. Its name is derived from its capital city, Tunis, located on the country's northeast coast.

Geographically, Tunisia contains the eastern end of the Atlas Mountains and the northern reaches of the Sahara desert. Much of the rest of the country's land is fertile soil. Its 1,300 kilometres (810 mi) of coastline includes the African conjunction of the western and eastern parts of the Mediterranean Basin and, by means of the Sicilian Strait and Sardinian Channel, features the African mainland's second and third nearest points to Europe after Gibraltar.

Tunisia has a high human development index. It has an association agreement with the European Union and is a member of La Francophonie, the Arab Maghreb Union, the Arab League and the African Union. Close relations with Europe – in particular with France and with Italy – have been forged through economic cooperation, privatisation and industrial modernization.

In 2011, a revolution resulted in the overthrow of the autocratic President Zine El Abidine Ben Ali followed by the country's first free elections. Since then, Tunisia has been consolidating democracy. The country held its first Presidential elections since the 2011 Arab Spring on November 23, 2014

GEOGRAPHY

Location: Northern Africa, bordering the Mediterranean Sea, between Algeria and Libya

Geographic coordinates: 34 00 N, 9 00 E

Map references: Africa

Area:
total: 163,610 sq km
land: 155,360 sq km
water: 8,250 sq km

Area—comparative: slightly larger than Georgia

Land boundaries:
total: 1,424 km
border countries: Algeria 965 km, Libya 459 km

Coastline: 1,148 km

Maritime claims:
contiguous zone: 24 nm
territorial sea: 12 nm

Climate: temperate in north with mild, rainy winters and hot, dry summers; desert in south

Terrain: mountains in north; hot, dry central plain; semiarid south merges into the Sahara

Elevation extremes:
lowest point: Shatt al Gharsah -17 m
highest point: Jabal ash Shanabi 1,544 m

Natural resources: petroleum, phosphates, iron ore, lead, zinc, salt

For additional analytical, business and investment opportunities information,
please contact Global Investment & Business Center, USA
at (703) 370-8082. Fax: (703) 370-8083. E-mail: ibpusa3@gmail.com
Global Business and Investment Info Databank - www.ibpus.com

Land use:
arable land: 19%
permanent crops: 13%
permanent pastures: 20%
forests and woodland: 4%
other: 44%

Irrigated land: 3,850 sq km

Natural hazards: NA

Environment—current issues: toxic and hazardous waste disposal is ineffective and presents human health risks; water pollution from raw sewage; limited natural fresh water resources; deforestation; overgrazing; soil erosion; de-certification

Environment—international agreements:
party to: Biodiversity, Climate Change, De-certification, Endangered Species, Environmental Modification, Hazardous Wastes, Law of the Sea, Marine Dumping, Nuclear Test Ban, Ozone Layer Protection, Ship Pollution, Wetlands
signed, but not ratified: Marine Life Conservation

Geography—note: strategic location in central Mediterranean

PEOPLE

Population: 9,380,404

Age structure:
0-14 years: 32% (male 1,526,743; female 1,433,503)
15-64 years: 63% (male 2,933,487; female 2,947,189)
65 years and over: 5% (male 275,411; female 264,071) (July 1998 est.)

Population growth rate: 1.43%

Birth rate: 20.07 births/1,000 population

Death rate: 5.06 deaths/1,000 population

Net migration rate: -0.73 migrant(s)/1,000 population

Sex ratio:
at birth: 1.08 male(s)/female
under 15 years: 1.07 male(s)/female
15-64 years: 1 male(s)/female
65 years and over: 1.04 male(s)/female

Infant mortality rate: 32.64 deaths/1,000 live births

Life expectancy at birth:
total population: 73.1 years
male: 71.72 years
female: 74.58 years

Total fertility rate: 2.44 children born/woman

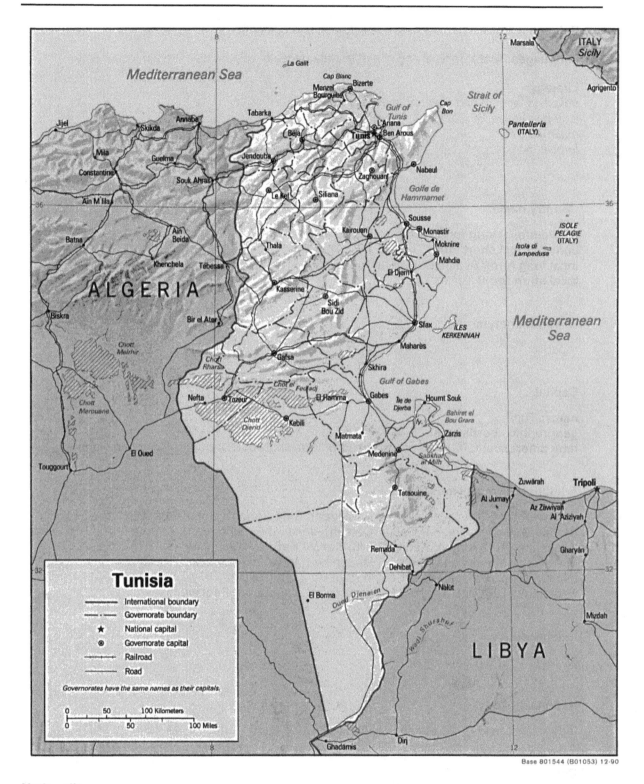

Nationality:
noun: Tunisian(s)
adjective: Tunisian

Ethnic groups: Arab 98%, European 1%, Jewish and other 1%

For additional analytical, business and investment opportunities information,
please contact Global Investment & Business Center, USA
at (703) 370-8082. Fax: (703) 370-8083. E-mail: ibpusa3@gmail.com
Global Business and Investment Info Databank - www.ibpus.com

Religions: Muslim 98%, Christian 1%, Jewish and other 1%

Languages: Arabic (official and one of the languages of commerce), French (commerce)

Literacy:
definition: age 15 and over can read and write
total population: 66.7%
male: 78.6%
female: 54.6%

GOVERNMENT

Country name:

conventional long form: Tunisian Republic
conventional short form: Tunisia
local long form: Al Jumhuriyah at Tunisiyah
local short form: Tunis

Government type:

republic

Capital:

name: Tunis
geographic coordinates: 36 48 N, 10 11 E
time difference: UTC+1 (6 hours ahead of Washington, DC, during Standard Time)

Administrative divisions:

24 governorates (wilayat, singular - wilayah); Beja (Bajah), Ben Arous (Bin 'Arus), Bizerte (Banzart), Gabes (Qabis), Gafsa (Qafsah), Jendouba (Jundubah), Kairouan (Al Qayrawan), Kasserine (Al Qasrayn), Kebili (Qibili), Kef (Al Kaf), L'Ariana (Aryanah), Mahdia (Al Mahdiyah), Manouba (Manubah), Medenine (Madanin), Monastir (Al Munastir), Nabeul (Nabul), Sfax (Safaqis), Sidi Bouzid (Sidi Bu Zayd), Siliana (Silyanah), Sousse (Susah), Tataouine (Tatawin), Tozeur (Tawzar), Tunis, Zaghouan (Zaghwan)

Independence:

20 March 1956 (from France)

National holiday:

Independence Day, 20 March (1956); Revolution and Youth Day, 14 January (2011)

Constitution:

several previous; latest approved by Constituent Assembly 26 January 2014 (2014)

Legal system:

mixed legal system of civil law, based on the French civil code, and Islamic law; some judicial review of legislative acts in the Supreme Court in joint session

International law organization participation:

has not submitted an ICJ jurisdiction declaration; non-party state to the ICCt

Suffrage:

18 years of age; universal except for active government security forces (including the police and the military), people with mental disabilities, people who have served more than three months in prison (criminal cases only), and people given a suspended sentence of more than six months

Executive branch:

chief of state: President Beji CAID ESSEBSI (since 31 December 2014)
head of government: Prime Minister Youssef CHAHED (since 27 August 2016)
cabinet: selected by the prime minister and approved by the Assembly of the Representatives of the People

elections/appointments: president directly elected by absolute majority popular vote in 2 rounds if needed for a 5-year term (eligible for a second term); election last held on 23 November and 21 December 2014 (next to be held in 2019); following legislative elections, the prime minister is selected by the majority party or majority coalition and appointed by the president

election results: Beji CAID ESSEBSI elected president in second round; percent of vote - Beji CAID ESSEBSI (Call for Tunisia) 55.7%, Moncef MARZOUKI (CPR) 44.3%
Legislative branch:
description: unicameral Assembly of the Representatives of the People or Majlis Nuwwab ash-Sha'b (Assemblee des representants du peuple) (217 seats; members directly elected in multi-seat constituencies by proportional representation vote; members serve 5-year terms)

elections: initial election held on 26 October 2014 (next to be held in 2019)
election results: percent of vote by party - Call for Tunisia 37.6%, Ennahdha 27.8%, UPL 4.1%, Popular Front 3.6%, Afek Tounes 3.0%, CPR 2.1%, other 21.8%; seats by party - Call to Tunisia 86, Nahda 69, UPL 16, Popular Front 15, Afek Tounes 8, CPR 4, other 17, independent 2

Judicial branch:
highest court(s): Court of Cassation or Cour de Cassation (organized into 1 civil and 3 criminal chambers); Constitutional Court (consists of 12 members)
note: the new Tunisian constitution of January 2014 called for the creation of a constitutional court by the end of 2015; the court will consist of 12 members - 4 each appointed by the president, the Supreme Judicial Council or SJC (an independent 4-part body consisting mainly of elected judges and the remainder legal specialists), and the Chamber of the People's Deputies (parliament); members will serve 9-year terms with one-third of the membership renewed every 3 years; in late 2015, the International Commission of Jurists called on Tunisia's parliament to revise the draft on the Constitutional Court to ensure compliance with international standards; as of spring 2018 the court had not been appointed

judge selection and term of office: Supreme Court judges nominated by the SJC; judge tenure based on terms of appointment; Constitutional Court members appointed 3 each by the president of the republic, the Chamber of the People's Deputies, and the SJC; members serve 9-year terms with one-third of the membership renewed every 3 years
subordinate courts: Courts of Appeal; administrative courts; Court of Audit; Housing Court; courts of first instance; lower district courts; military courts

Political parties and leaders:
Afek Tounes [Yassine BRAHIM]
Al Badil Al-Tounisi (The Tunisian Alternative) [Mehdi JOMAA]
Call for Tunisia (Nidaa Tounes) [Hafedh CAID ESSEBSI]
Congress for the Republic or CPR [Imed DAIMI]
Current of Love [Hachemi HAMDI] (formerly the Popular Petition party)
Democratic Alliance Party [Mohamed HAMDI]
Democratic Current [Mohamed ABBOU]
Democratic Patriots' Unified Party [Zied LAKHDHAR]
Free Patriotic Union or UPL (Union patriotique libre) [Slim RIAHI]
Green Tunisia Party [Abdelkader ZITOUNI]
Machrou Tounes (Tunisia Project) [Mohsen MARZOUK]
Movement of Socialist Democrats or MDS [Ahmed KHASKHOUSSI]
Nahda Movement (The Renaissance) [Rachid GHANNOUCHI]
National Destourian Initiative or El Moubadra [Kamel MORJANE]
Party of the Democratic Arab Vanguard [Ahmed JEDDICK, Kheireddine SOUABNI]
People's Movement [Zouheir MAGHZAOUI]
Popular Front (coalition includes Democratic Patriots' Unified Party, Workers' Party, Green Tunisia, Tunisian Ba'ath Movement, and Party of the Democratic Arab Vanguard)
Republican Party [Maya JRIBI]
Tunisian Ba'ath Movement [OMAR Othman BELHADJ]
Tunisia First (Tunis Awlan) [Ridha BELHAJ]
Workers' Party [Hamma HAMMAMI]

Political pressure groups and leaders:
Tunisian Association of Women Democrats or ATFD
Tunisian League for Human Rights or LTDH [Jamel MSALLEM]
Tunisian General Labor Union or UGTT [Noureddine TABOUBI]
Tunisian Women's Association for Research and Development or AFTURD
International organization participation:
ABEDA, AfDB, AFESD, AMF, AMU, AU, BSEC (observer), CAEU, CD, EBRD, FAO, G-11, G-77, IAEA, IBRD, ICAO, ICC (national committees), ICCt, ICRM, IDA, IDB, IFAD, IFC, IFRCS, IHO, ILO, IMF, IMO, IMSO, Interpol, IOC, IOM, IPU, ISO, ITSO, ITU, ITUC (NGOs), LAS, MIGA, MONUSCO, NAM, OAS (observer), OIC, OIF, OPCW, OSCE (partner), UN, UNCTAD, UNESCO, UNHCR, UNIDO, UNOCI, UNWTO, UPU, WCO, WFTU (NGOs), WHO, WIPO, WMO, WTO

Diplomatic representation in the US:
chief of mission: Ambassador Faycal GOUIA (since 18 May 2015)
chancery: 1515 Massachusetts Avenue NW, Washington, DC 20005
telephone: [1] (202) 862-1850
FAX: [1] (202) 862-1858

Diplomatic representation from the US:
chief of mission: Ambassador Daniel H. RUBINSTEIN (since 26 October 2015)
embassy: Zone Nord-Est des Berges du Lac Nord de Tunis 1053

mailing address: Zone Nord-Est des Berges du Lac Nord de Tunis 1053
telephone: [216] 71 107-000
FAX: [216] 71 107-090

Flag description:

red with a white disk in the center bearing a red crescent nearly encircling a red five-pointed star; resembles the Ottoman flag (red banner with white crescent and star) and recalls Tunisia's history as part of the Ottoman Empire; red represents the blood shed by martyrs in the struggle against oppression, white stands for peace; the crescent and star are traditional symbols of Islam
note: the flag is based on that of Turkey, itself a successor state to the Ottoman Empire

National symbol(s):

encircled red star and crescent

National anthem:

name: "Humat Al Hima" (Defenders of the Homeland)

ECONOMY

Tunisia's diverse, market-oriented economy has long been cited as a success story in Africa and the Middle East, but it faces an array of challenges during the country's ongoing political transition. Following an ill-fated experiment with socialist economic policies in the 1960s, Tunisia embarked on a successful strategy focused on bolstering exports, foreign investment, and tourism, all of which have become central to the country's economy. Key exports now include textiles and apparel, food products, petroleum products, chemicals, and phosphates, with about 80% of exports bound for Tunisia's main economic partner, the European Union.

Tunisia's liberal strategy, coupled with investments in education and infrastructure, fueled decades of 4-5% annual GDP growth and improving living standards. Former President (1987-2011) Zine el Abidine BEN ALI continued these policies, but as his reign wore on cronyism and corruption stymied economic performance and unemployment rose among the country's growing ranks of university graduates. These grievances contributed to the January 2011 overthrow of BEN ALI, sending Tunisia's economy into a tailspin as tourism and investment declined sharply. During 2012 and 2013, the Tunisian Government's focus on the political transition led to a neglect of the economy that resulted in several downgrades of Tunisia's credit rating. As the economy recovers, Tunisia's government faces challenges reassuring businesses and investors, bringing budget and current account deficits under control, shoring up the country's financial system, bringing down high unemployment, and reducing economic disparities between the more developed coastal region and the impoverished interior.

GDP (purchasing power parity):

$108.4 billion
country comparison to the world: 72
$105.4 billion (2012 est.)
$101.8 billion (2011 est.)
note: data are in 2013 US dollars

For additional analytical, business and investment opportunities information, please contact Global Investment & Business Center, USA at (703) 370-8082. Fax: (703) 370-8083. E-mail: ibpusa3@gmail.com Global Business and Investment Info Databank - www.ibpus.com

GDP (official exchange rate):

$48.38 billion

GDP - real growth rate:

2.8%
country comparison to the world: 124
3.6% (2012 est.)
-1.9% (2011 est.)

GDP - per capita (PPP):

$9,900
country comparison to the world: 119
$9,800 (2012 est.)
$9,500 (2011 est.)
note: data are in 2013 US dollars

Gross national saving:

26.1% of GDP
country comparison to the world: 43
25.4% of GDP (2012 est.)
24.1% of GDP (2011 est.)

GDP - composition, by end use:

household consumption: 66.5%
government consumption: 18.4%
investment in fixed capital: 22.6%
investment in inventories: 3.5%
exports of goods and services: 49.2%
imports of goods and services: -60.1%

GDP - composition, by sector of origin:

agriculture: 8.6%
industry: 30.4%
services: 61%

Agriculture - products:

olives, olive oil, grain, tomatoes, citrus fruit, sugar beets, dates, almonds; beef, dairy products

Industries:

petroleum, mining (particularly phosphate, iron ore), tourism, textiles, footwear, agribusiness, beverages

For additional analytical, business and investment opportunities information,
please contact Global Investment & Business Center, USA
at (703) 370-8082. Fax: (703) 370-8083. E-mail: ibpusa3@gmail.com
Global Business and Investment Info Databank - www.ibpus.com

Industrial production growth rate:

3%
country comparison to the world: 104

Labor force:

3.974 million
country comparison to the world: 91

Labor force - by occupation:

agriculture: 18.3%
industry: 31.9%
services: 49.8% (2009 est.)

Unemployment rate:

17.2%
country comparison to the world: 151
17.4% (2012 est.)

Population below poverty line:

3.8% (2005 est.)

Household income or consumption by percentage share:

lowest 10%: 2.3%
highest 10%: 31.5% (2000)

Distribution of family income - Gini index:

40 (2005 est.)
country comparison to the world: 59
41.7 (1995 est.)

Budget:

revenues: $12.16 billion
expenditures: $15.8 billion

Taxes and other revenues:

25.1% of GDP
country comparison to the world: 128

Budget surplus (+) or deficit (-):

-7.5% of GDP
country comparison to the world: 188

Public debt:

51.1% of GDP
country comparison to the world: 64
46.1% of GDP (2012 est.)

Fiscal year:

calendar year

Inflation rate (consumer prices):

6.1%
country comparison to the world: 176
5.6% (2012 est.)

Central bank discount rate:

5.75% (31 December 2010 est.)

Commercial bank prime lending rate:

7.31% (31 December 2012 est.)
country comparison to the world: 126
6.76% (31 December 2011 est.)

Stock of narrow money:

$13.08 billion (31 December 2013 est.)
country comparison to the world: 71
$13.44 billion (31 December 2012 est.)

Stock of broad money:

$29.8 billion (31 December 2013 est.)
country comparison to the world: 74
$30.72 billion (31 December 2012 est.)

Stock of domestic credit:

$35.59 billion (31 December 2013 est.)
country comparison to the world: 67
$36.09 billion (31 December 2012 est.)

Market value of publicly traded shares:

$8.887 billion (31 December 2012 est.)

For additional analytical, business and investment opportunities information,
please contact Global Investment & Business Center, USA
at (703) 370-8082. Fax: (703) 370-8083. E-mail: ibpusa3@gmail.com
Global Business and Investment Info Databank - www.ibpus.com

country comparison to the world: 67
$9.662 billion (31 December 2011)
$10.68 billion (31 December 2010 est.)

Current account balance:

-$4.556 billion
country comparison to the world: 165
-$3.773 billion (2012 est.)

Exports:

$17.46 billion
country comparison to the world: 74
$17.07 billion (2012 est.)

Exports - commodities:

clothing, semi-finished goods and textiles, agricultural products, mechanical goods, phosphates and chemicals, hydrocarbons, electrical equipment

Exports - partners:

France 26.2%, Italy 16%, Germany 9.4%, Libya 7.6%, US 4.3% (2012)

Imports:

$24.95 billion
country comparison to the world: 73
$23.1 billion (2012 est.)

Imports - commodities:

textiles, machinery and equipment, hydrocarbons, chemicals, foodstuffs

Imports - partners:

France 19.8%, Italy 16.7%, Germany 7.3%, China 6%, Spain 5.3%, Algeria 4.4% (2012)

Reserves of foreign exchange and gold:

$8.113 billion (31 December 2013 est.)
country comparison to the world: 78
$8.36 billion (31 December 2012 est.)

Debt - external:

$26.95 billion (31 December 2013 est.)
country comparison to the world: 75
$24.6 billion (31 December 2012 est.)

Stock of direct foreign investment - at home:

$34.64 billion (31 December 2013 est.)
country comparison to the world: 59
$33.4 billion (31 December 2012 est.)

Stock of direct foreign investment - abroad:

$295 million (31 December 2013 est.)
country comparison to the world: 82
$285 million (31 December 2012 est.)

Exchange rates:

Tunisian dinars (TND) per US dollar -
1.638
1.5619 (2012 est.)
1.4314 (2010 est.)
1.3503 (2009)
1.211 (2008)

ENERGY

Electricity - production:

15.14 billion kWh
country comparison to the world: 81

Electricity - consumption:

13.29 billion kWh
country comparison to the world: 82

Electricity - exports:

0 kWh
country comparison to the world: 204

Electricity - imports:

19 million kWh
country comparison to the world: 106

Electricity - installed generating capacity:

3.652 million kW
country comparison to the world: 83

Electricity - from fossil fuels:

For additional analytical, business and investment opportunities information,
please contact Global Investment & Business Center, USA
at (703) 370-8082. Fax: (703) 370-8083. E-mail: ibpusa3@gmail.com
Global Business and Investment Info Databank - www.ibpus.com

96.8% of total installed capacity
country comparison to the world: 65

Electricity - from nuclear fuels:

0% of total installed capacity
country comparison to the world: 190

Electricity - from hydroelectric plants:

1.7% of total installed capacity
country comparison to the world: 139

Electricity - from other renewable sources:

1.5% of total installed capacity
country comparison to the world: 79

Crude oil - production:

68,310 bbl/day
country comparison to the world: 56

Crude oil - exports:

77,980 bbl/day
country comparison to the world: 42

Crude oil - imports:

3,680 bbl/day
country comparison to the world: 80

Crude oil - proved reserves:

425 million bbl
country comparison to the world: 52

Refined petroleum products - production:

11,170 bbl/day
country comparison to the world: 103

Refined petroleum products - consumption:

88,380 bbl/day
country comparison to the world: 82

Refined petroleum products - exports:

For additional analytical, business and investment opportunities information,
please contact Global Investment & Business Center, USA
at (703) 370-8082. Fax: (703) 370-8083. E-mail: ibpusa3@gmail.com
Global Business and Investment Info Databank - www.ibpus.com

3,391 bbl/day
country comparison to the world: 96

Refined petroleum products - imports:

80,980 bbl/day
country comparison to the world: 56

Natural gas - production:

1.93 billion cu m
country comparison to the world: 58

Natural gas - consumption:

3.28 billion cu m
country comparison to the world: 69

Natural gas - exports:

0 cu m (2011 est.)
country comparison to the world: 194

Natural gas - imports:

1.78 billion cu m
country comparison to the world: 51

Natural gas - proved reserves:

65.13 billion cu m
country comparison to the world: 60

Carbon dioxide emissions from consumption of energy:

20.52 million Mt

COMMUNICATIONS

Telephones - main lines in use:

1.105 million
country comparison to the world: 71

Telephones - mobile cellular:

12.84 million
country comparison to the world: 68

For additional analytical, business and investment opportunities information,
please contact Global Investment & Business Center, USA
at (703) 370-8082. Fax: (703) 370-8083. E-mail: ibpusa3@gmail.com
Global Business and Investment Info Databank - www.ibpus.com

Telephone system:

general assessment: above the African average and continuing to be upgraded; key centers are Sfax, Sousse, Bizerte, and Tunis; telephone network is completely digitized; Internet access available throughout the country
domestic: in an effort to jumpstart expansion of the fixed-line network, the government has awarded a concession to build and operate a VSAT network with international connectivity; rural areas are served by wireless local loops; competition between the two mobile-cellular service providers has resulted in lower activation and usage charges and a strong surge in subscribership; a third mobile, fixed, and ISP operator was licensed in 2009 and began offering services in 2010; expansion of mobile-cellular services to include multimedia messaging and e-mail and Internet to mobile phone services also leading to a surge in subscribership; overall fixed-line and mobile-cellular teledensity has reached about 125 telephones per 100 persons
international: country code - 216; a landing point for the SEA-ME-WE-4 submarine cable system that provides links to Europe, Middle East, and Asia; satellite earth stations - 1 Intelsat (Atlantic Ocean) and 1 Arabsat; coaxial cable and microwave radio relay to Algeria and Libya; participant in Medarabtel; 2 international gateway digital switches

Broadcast media:

broadcast media is mainly government-controlled; the state-run Tunisian Radio and Television Establishment (ERTT) operates 2 national TV networks, several national radio networks, and a number of regional radio stations; 1 TV and 3 radio stations are privately owned and report domestic news stories directly from the official Tunisian news agency; the state retains control of broadcast facilities and transmitters through L'Office National de la Telediffusion; Tunisians also have access to Egyptian, pan-Arab, and European satellite TV channels

Internet country code:

.tn

Internet hosts:

576
country comparison to the world: 180

Internet users:

3.5 million
country comparison to the world: 60

TRANSPORTATION

Airports:

29
country comparison to the world: 118

Airports - with paved runways:

total: 15
over 3,047 m: 4
2,438 to 3,047 m: 6
1,524 to 2,437 m: 2
914 to 1,523 m: 3

Airports - with unpaved runways:

total: 14
1,524 to 2,437 m: 1
914 to 1,523 m: 5
under 914 m:
8

Pipelines:

condensate 68 km; gas 3,111 km; oil 1,381 km; refined products 453 km

Railways:

total: 2,165 km (1,991 in use)
country comparison to the world: 69
standard gauge: 471 km 1.435-m gauge
narrow gauge: 1,694 km 1.000-m gauge (65 km electrified)

Roadways:

total: 19,418 km
country comparison to the world: 112
paved: 14,756 km (includes 357 km of expressways)
unpaved: 4,662 km

Merchant marine:

total: 9
country comparison to the world: 116
by type: bulk carrier 1, cargo 2, passenger/cargo 4, roll on/roll off 2

Ports and terminals:

major seaport(s): Bizerte, Gabes, Rades, Sfax, Skhira

MILITARY

Military branches:

Tunisian Armed Forces (Forces Armees Tunisiens, FAT): Tunisian Army (includes Tunisian Air Defense Force), Tunisian Navy, Republic of Tunisia Air Force (Al-Quwwat al-Jawwiya al-Jamahiriyah At'Tunisia)

Military service age and obligation:

20-23 years of age for compulsory service, one year service obligation; 18-23 years of age for voluntary service; Tunisian nationality required (2012)

Manpower available for military service:

males age 16-49: 2,846,572
females age 16-49: 2,952,180

Manpower fit for military service:

males age 16-49: 2,397,716
females age 16-49: 2,484,097

Manpower reaching militarily significant age annually:

male: 90,436
female: 87,346

Military expenditures:

1.55% of GDP
country comparison to the world: 58
1.34% of GDP (2011)
1.55% of GDP (2010)

INTERNATIONAL ISSUES

Disputes - international:

Trafficking in persons:

current situation: Tunisia is a source, destination, and possible transit country for men, women, and children subjected to forced labor and sex trafficking; Tunisia's increased number of street children, children working to support their families, and migrants who have fled unrest in neighboring countries are vulnerable to human trafficking; Tunisian women recruited into Lebanon's entertainment industry are forced into prostitution on arrival and other Tunisian women are forced into prostitution in Jordan; some Tunisian girls employed in domestic work are held in conditions of forced labor
tier rating: Tier 2 Watch List - Tunisia does not fully comply with the minimum standards for the elimination of trafficking; however, it is making significant efforts to do so; the government continues to maintain that human trafficking is not a widespread problem in Tunisia, which undermines awareness campaigns and does not differentiate human trafficking from migrant smuggling; prior commitments to enact draft anti-trafficking legislation were not fulfilled, and the government has not developed or implemented procedures to identify proactively trafficking victims; the government has assisted an unidentified number of trafficking victims in its shelters for vulnerable groups

IMPORTANT INFORMATION FOR UNDERSTANDING TUNISIA

PROFILE

OFFICIAL NAME: Tunisian Republic

GEOGRAPHY

Area: 163,610 sq. km. (63,378 sq. mi.), slightly smaller than Missouri.
Cities: *Capital*--Tunis; Greater Tunis urban area: pop. 2,083,000 (includes Tunis, Ariana, Ben Arous, and Manouba governorates) Sfax (pop. 820,100).
Terrain: Arable land in north and along central coast; south is mostly semiarid or desert.
Climate: Hot, dry summers and mild, rainy winters.

PEOPLE

Nationality: *Noun and adjective*--Tunisian(s).
Population : 9.9 million.
Annual growth rate : 1.14%.
Ethnic groups: Arab-Berber 98%, European 1%, other 1%.
Religions: Muslim 98%, Christian 1%, Jewish less than 1%.
Languages: Arabic (official), French.
Education: *Years compulsory*--9. *Literacy*--66.7% (male 78.6%; female 54.6%).
Health : *Infant mortality rate*--25.8/1,000. *Life expectancy*--70.1 years male, 74.2 years female.
Work force (3.4 million) *Services*--44.1%; *industry*--33.2%; *agriculture*--22%.

GOVERNMENT

Type: Republic.
Constitution: June 1, 1959; amended July 12, 1988, June 29, 1999, and June 1, 2002.
Independence: March 20, 1956.
Branches: *Executive*--chief of state President Zine El Abidine BEN ALI (since November 7, 1987) head of government, Prime Minister Mohamed GHANNOUCHI (since November 17, 1999) cabinet, Council of Ministers appointed by the president; president elected by popular vote for a 5-year term; election last held October 24, 1999 (next to be held in October 2004); prime minister appointed by the president. Election results: President Zine El Abidine BEN ALI reelected for a third term; candidates from opposition: Mohamed Belhaj Amor (PUP) and Abderrahmene Tlili (UDU); percent of vote--Zine El Abidine BEN ALI 99.44% (officially).
Legislative--unicameral Chamber of Deputies or Majlis al-Nuwaab (182 seats; 5-year terms; 148 seats are elected by popular vote for party lists on a winner-take-all basis). An additional 34 seats (20% of the total) are distributed to opposition parties on a proportional basis as provided for in 1999 constitutional amendments; a referendum in 2002 created a second chamber. Elections last held October 24, 1999 (next to be held in October 2004).
Election results: percent of vote by party--RCD 92%; seats by party-- RCD 148, MDS 13, UDU 7, PUP 7, Al-Tajdid 5, PSL 2. Note: The opposition increased number of seats from 19 to 34. *Judicial*--independent District Courts, Courts of Appeal, Highest Court (Cour de

Cassation). Judges of the highest court are appointed by the President.

Political parties: Et-Tajdid Movement (Mohamed Harmel); Constitutional Democratic Rally Party (Rassemblement Constitutionnel Democratique) or RCD President Zine El Abidine BEN ALI (official ruling party); Democratic Forum for Labor and Liberties or FDTL (Mustapha Ben Jaafar); Liberal Social Party or PSL (Mounir Beji); Movement of Democratic Socialists or MDS (Ismail Boulahia); Popular Unity Party or PUP (Mohamed Bouchiha); Unionist Democratic Union or UDU (vacant); Democratic Progressive Party or PDP (Nejib Chebbi).

Political pressure groups and leaders: Legal--Tunisian Human Rights League or LTDH (Mokhtar Trifi). Outlawed--An-Nahda (Renaissance) the Islamic fundamentalist party (Rached El Ghanouchi); National Council for Liberties in Tunisia or CNLT (Sihem Ben Sedrine); Congress for the Republic or CPR (Moncef Marzouki); Tunisian Communist Labor Party or POCT (Hamma Hammami); Tunisian Green Party or PVT (Abdelkader Zitouni).

Administrative divisions: 24 governorates--Ariana, Beja, Ben Arous, Bizerte, EL Kef, Gabes, Gafsa, Jendouba, Kairouan, Kasserine, Kebili, Mahdia, Manouba, Medenine, Monastir, Nabeul, Sfax, Sidi Biu Zid, Siliana, Sousse, Tataouine, Tozeur, Tunis, Zaghouan.

Suffrage: Universal at 20 (Active duty members of the military may not vote.).

PEOPLE

Modern Tunisians are the descendents of indigenous Berbers and of people from numerous civilizations that have invaded, migrated to, and been assimilated into the population over the millenia. Recorded history in Tunisia begins with the arrival of Phoenicians, who founded Carthage and other North African settlements in the 8th century BC. Carthage became a major sea power, clashing with Rome for control of the Mediterranean until it was defeated and captured by the Romans in 146 B.C. The Romans ruled and settled in North Africa until the 5th century when the Roman Empire fell and Tunisia was invaded by European tribes, including the Vandals. The Muslim conquest in the 7th century transformed Tunisia's and the make-up of its population, with subsequent waves of migration from around the Arab and Ottoman world, including significant numbers of Spanish Moors and Jews at the end of the 15th century. Tunisia became a center of Arab culture and learning and was assimilated into the Turkish Ottoman Empire in the 16th century. It was a French protectorate from 1881 until independence in 1956, and retains close political, economic, and cultural ties with France.

Nearly all Tunisians (98% of the population) are Muslim. There has been a Jewish population on the southern island of Djerba for 2000 years, and there remains a small Jewish population in Tunis which is descended from those who fled Spain in the late 15th century. There is no indigenous Christian population. Small nomadic indigenous minorities have been mostly assimilated into the larger population.

GOVERNMENT AND POLITICAL CONDITIONS

Tunisia is a republic with a strong presidential system dominated by a single political party. President Zine el-Abedine Ben Ali has been in office since 1987 when he deposed Habib Bourguiba, who had been President since Tunisia's independence from France in 1956. The ruling party, the Constitutional Democratic Assembly (RCD), was the sole legal party for 25 years--when it was known as the Socialist Destourian Party (PSD)--and still dominates political life. The President is elected to 5-year terms--with virtually no opposition--and appoints a Prime Minister and cabinet, who play a strong role in the execution of policy. Regional governors and local administrators also are appointed by the central government; largely consultative mayors and municipal councils are elected. There is a unicameral legislative body, the Chamber of Deputies, which has 182 seats, 20% of which are reserved for the opposition. It plays a growing role as an arena for debate on national policy but never originates legislation and virtually always passes bills presented by the executive with only minor changes. The judiciary is nominally independent but responds to executive direction especially in political cases. The military is professional and does not play a role in politics.

Tunisia's independence from France in 1956 ended a protectorate established in 1881. President Bourguiba, who had been the leader of the independence movement, declared Tunisia a republic in 1957, ending the nominal rule of the former Ottoman Beys. In June 1959 Tunisia adopted a Constitution modeled on the French system, which established the basic outline of the highly centralized presidential system that continues today. The military was given a defined defensive role, which excluded participation in politics. Starting from independence, President Bourguiba placed strong emphasis on economic and social development, especially education, the status of women, and the creation of jobs, policies continued under the Ben Ali administration. The results were strong social indicators--high literacy and school attendance rates, low population growth rates, and relatively low poverty rates--and generally steady economic growth rates. These pragmatic policies have contributed to social and political stability.

Progress toward full democracy has been slow. Over the years President Bourguiba stood unopposed for re-election several times and was named "President for life" in 1974 by a constitutional amendment. At the time of independence, the Neo-Destourian Party (later the PSD)--enjoying broad support because of its role at the forefront of the independence movement--became the sole legal party when opposition parties were banned until 1981.

When President Ben Ali came to power in 1987 he promised greater democratic openness and respect for human rights, signing a "national pact" with opposition parties. He oversaw constitutional and legal changes, including abolishing the concept of president for life, the establishment of presidential term limits, and provision for greater opposition party participation in political life. But the ruling party, renamed the Democratic Constitutional Assembly (RCD), continued to dominate the political scene because of its historic popularity and the advantage it enjoyed as the ruling party. Ben Ali ran for re-election unopposed in 1989 and 1994, and won 99.44% of the vote in 1999 when he faced two weak opponents. The RCD won all seats in the Chamber of Deputies in 1989, and won all of the directly elected seats in the 1994 and 1999 elections. However, constitutional amendments in those years provided for the distribution of additional seats to the opposition parties in 1999. Currently, five opposition parties share 33 of the 182 seats in the Chamber. A May 2002 referendum approved constitutional changes proposed by Ben Ali to allow him to run for a fourth term in 2004, created a second parliamentary chamber, and provided for other changes.

There are currently seven legal opposition parties, the Social Democratic Movement (MDS), the Popular Unity Party (PUP), the Union of Democratic Unionists (UDU), Ettajdid (also called the Renewal Movement), the Social Liberal Party (PSL), plus the Democratic Progressive Party (PDP) and the Democratic Forum for Labor and Liberties or FDTL, the only two not represented in the Chamber of Deputies. Most accept the basic economic and social policies of the government but are critical of the pace of democratization in the country--and focus considerable attention on support for Arab causes. The parties are generally weak and divided and face considerable restrictions on their ability to organize. The Islamist opposition party, An-Nadha, was allowed to operate openly in the late 1980s and early 1990s despite a ban on religiously based parties. The government outlawed An-Nadha as a terrorist organization in 1991 and arrested its leaders and thousands of party members and sympathizers, accusing them of plotting to overthrow the President. The party is no longer openly active in Tunisia, and its leaders operate from exile in London. There are several pro-democracy activists who have been denied permission to establish other opposition political parties.

While there are thousands of nominally established non-governmental organizations, civil society also is weak. The Tunisian Human Rights League (LTDH), the first such organization in the Arab world, operates under restrictions and suffers from internal divisions. The Tunisian Association of Democratic Women (ATFD), the Young Lawyers Association, and the Bar Association also are active. The government has denied legal status to a handful of other human rights advocacy groups who, nonetheless, attempt to gather and publicize information on the human rights situation in the country.

Although Tunisia states it is committed to making progress toward a democratic system, citizens still do not have full political freedom. There are curbs on the press and on freedom of speech. Many critics have called for clearer, effective distinctions between executive, legislative, and judicial powers. The foreign press and foreign-based satellite television channels have criticized the Tunisian Government and demanded more freedom of speech and greater respect for human rights. There are frequent reports of widespread torture and abuse of prisoners, especially political prisoners, by security officers.

Trade unions have played a key role in Tunisia's history since the struggle for independence, when the 1952 assassination of labor leader Farhat Hached was a catalyst for the final push for against French domination. The General Union of Tunisian Workers (UGTT), the country's sole labor confederation, has generally focused on bread-and-butter issues but at some critical moments in Tunisia's history has played a decisive role in the nation's political life. Despite a drop in union membership from 400,000 to about 250,000 as the structure of the Tunisian economy changed, the UGTT continues to hold a prominent place in Tunisia's political and social life, and negotiates with government and the umbrella employer group for higher wages and better benefits. The current leadership, headed by Abdessalem Jerad, was elected at an extraordinary congress in February 2002, held to reset the union's direction after its former long-time leader was removed for embezzlement in 2000. The current board of directors includes some former dissidents and has pledged to reinvigorate the union and increase its role in the country's political life.

Tunisia is a leader in the Arab world in promoting the legal and social status of women. A Personal Status Code was adopted shortly after independence in 1956 which, among other things, gave women full legal status (allowing them to run and own businesses, have bank accounts, and seek passports under their own authority) and outlawed polygamy. The government required parents to send girls to school, and today more than 50% of university students are women. Rights of women and children were further enhanced by 1993 reforms, which included a provision to allow Tunisian women to transmit citizenship even if they are married to a foreigner and living abroad. The government has supported a remarkably successful family planning program that has reduced the population growth rate to just over 1% per annum, contributing to Tunisia's economic and social stability.

Tunisia's judiciary is headed by the Court of Cassation, whose judges are appointed by the president. The country is divided administratively into 23 governorates. The president appoints all governors.

PRINCIPAL GOVERNMENT OFFICIALS

Pres., **Moncef MARZOUKI**
Prime Min., **Hamadi JEBALI**
Min. of Agriculture, **Mohamed BEN SALEM**
Min. of Culture, **Mehdi MABROUK**
Min. of Education, **Abdellatif ABID**
Min. of Environment, **Mamiya EL BANNA**
Min. of Equipment & Housing, **Mohamed SALMANE**
Min. of Finance, **Houcine DIMASSI**
Min. of Foreign Affairs, **Rafik ABDESSALEM**
Min. of Higher Education & Scientific Research, **Moncef BEN SALEM**
Min. of Human Rights & Govt. Spokesman, **Samir DILOU**
Min. of Industry & Trade, **Mohamed Amine CHAKHARI**
Min. of Information Technology & Communications, **Mongi MARZOUK**
Min. of Interior, **Ali LAAREYDH**
Min. of Investment & International Cooperation, **Riadh BETTAIEB**
Min. of Justice, **Noureddine BHIRI**
Min. of Labor & Professional Training, **Abdelwahab MAATAR**
Min. of National Defense, **Abdelkarim ZBIDI**
Min. of Public Health, **Abellatif MEKKI**
Min. of Regional Development & Planning, **Jameleddine GHARBI**
Min. of Religious Affairs, **Nourredine KHADMI**
Min. of Social Affairs, **Khalil ZAOUIA**
Min. of State Property & Real Estate, **Slim BEN HMIDANE**
Min. of Tourism, **Ilyes FAKHFAKH**
Min. of Transport, **Karim HAROUNI**
Min. of Women's Affairs & the Family, **Silhem BADI**
Min. of Youth & Sports, **Tarik DIAB**
Min.-Del. for Administrative Reform, **Mohamed ABBOU**
Min.-Del. for Economic Issues, **Ridha SAADI**

For additional analytical, business and investment opportunities information, please contact Global Investment & Business Center, USA at (703) 370-8082. Fax: (703) 370-8083. E-mail: ibpusa3@gmail.com Global Business and Investment Info Databank - www.ibpus.com

Min.-Del. for Governance & Combating Corruption, **Abderahmane LADGHAM**
Min.-Del. for Relations With the Constituent Assembly, **Abderrazak KILANI**
Pres., Constituent Assembly, **Mustapha Ben JAAFAR**
Governor, Central Bank, **Mustapha Kamel NABLI**
Ambassador to the US, **Mohamed Salah TEKAYA**
Permanent Representative to the UN, New York, **Ghazi JOMAA**

Tunisia's embassy in the United States is located at 1515 Massachusetts Avenue NW, Washington, DC 20005 (tel. 1-202-862-1850, fax 1-202-862-1858).

ECONOMY

GDP	$47.13 billion Nominal
GDP growth	2.81%
GDP per capita	$4329
GDP by sector	agriculture: 11%; industry: 35.3%; services: 53.7%
Inflation (CPI)	6.04%
Population below poverty line	15.5%
Gini coefficient	36.1
Labour force	3.315 million
Labour force by occupation	agriculture: 18.3%; industry: 31.9%; services: 49.8%
Unemployment	15.2%
Main industries	petroleum, mining (particularly phosphate and iron ore), tourism, textiles, footwear, agribusiness, beverages
Ease-of-doing-business rank	50th
	External
Exports	$17.06 billion
Export goods	clothing, semi-finished goods and textiles, agricultural products, mechanical goods, phosphates and chemicals, hydrocarbons, electrical equipment
Main export partners	France 26.3% Italy 16.0% Germany 9.4% Libya 7.9% United States 4.3%
Imports	$24.31 billion
Import goods	textiles, machinery and equipment, hydrocarbons, chemicals, foodstuffs
Main import partners	France 20.2% Italy 16.9% Germany 7.5% China 6.1% Spain 5.4% Algeria 4.4%
FDI stock	$31.86 billion
Gross external debt	$20.13 billion
	Public finances

Public debt	44.32% of GDP
Revenues	$10.05 billion
Expenses	$16.22 billion
Credit rating	• Standard & Poor's: BBB (Domestic) BBB- (Foreign) BBB (T&C Assessment) Outlook: Negative • Moody's: Baa3 Outlook: Negative • Fitch: BBB Outlook: Negative
Foreign reserves	US$9.269 billion

Tunisia is in the process of economic reform and liberalization after decades of heavy state direction and participation in the economy. Prudent economic and fiscal planning have resulted in moderate but sustained growth for over a decade. Tunisia's economic growth historically has depended on oil, phosphates, agri-food products, car parts manufacturing, and tourism. In the World Economic Forum 2008/2009 Global Competitiveness Report, the country ranks first in Africa and 36th globally for economic competitiveness, well ahead of Portugal (43), Italy (49) and Greece (67). With a GDP (PPP) per capita of $9795 Tunisia is among the wealthiest countries in Africa. Based on HDI, Tunisia ranks 5th in Africa.

Tunisia is in the process of economic reform and liberalization after decades of heavy state direction and participation in the economy. Prudent economic and fiscal planning have resulted in moderate sustained growth for over a decade. Tunisia's economic growth historically has depended on oil, phosphates, agriculture, and tourism. The government's economic policies had limited success during the early years of independence. During the 1960s, a drive for collectivization caused unrest, and farm production fell sharply. Higher prices for phosphates and oil and growing revenues from tourism stimulated growth in the 1970s, but an emphasis on protectionism and import substitution led to inefficiencies. Tunisia received considerable economic assistance during this period from the United States and European and Arab countries and is one of the few developing countries in the region to have moved into the "middle income" category.

An overvalued dinar and a growing foreign debt sparked a foreign exchange crisis in the mid-1980s. In 1986, the government launched a structural adjustment program to liberalize prices, reduce tariffs, and reorient Tunisia toward a market economy.

Tunisia's economic reform program has been lauded as a model by international financial institutions. The government has liberalized prices, reduced tariffs, lowered debt-service-to-exports and debt-to-GDP ratios, and extended the average maturity of its $10 billion foreign debt. Structural adjustment brought additional lending from the World Bank and other Western creditors. In 1990, Tunisia acceded to the General Agreements on Tariffs and Trade (GATT) and is a member of the World Trade Organization (WTO).

For additional analytical, business and investment opportunities information, please contact Global Investment & Business Center, USA at (703) 370-8082. Fax: (703) 370-8083. E-mail: ibpusa3@gmail.com Global Business and Investment Info Databank - www.ibpus.com

In 1996 Tunisia entered into an "Association Agreement" with the European Union (EU) which will remove tariff and other trade barriers on most goods by 2008. In conjunction with the Association Agreement, the EU is assisting the Tunisian Government's Mise A Niveau (upgrading) program to enhance the productivity of Tunisian businesses and prepare for competition in the global marketplace.

The government has totally or partially privatized about 160 state-owned enterprises since the privatization program was launched in 1987. Although the program is supported by the UGTT, the government has had to move carefully to avoid mass firings. Unemployment continues to plague Tunisia's economy and is aggravated by a rapidly growing work force. An estimated 55% of the population is under the age of 25. Officially, 14.3% of the Tunisian work force is unemployed, but the real numbers of jobless or underemployed are higher.

In 1992, Tunisia reentered the private international capital market for the first time in 6 years, securing a $10-million line of credit for balance-of-payments support. In January 2003 Standard and Poor affirmed its investment grade credit ratings for Tunisia. The World Economic Forum 2002-03 ranked Tunisia 34th in the Global Competitiveness Index Ratings (two places behind South Africa, the continent's leader). In April 2002, Tunisia's first dollar-denominated sovereign bond issue since 1997 raised U.S.$458 million, with maturity in 2012.

The stock exchange is under the control of the state-run Financial Market Council and lists nearly 50 companies. The government offers substantial tax incentives to encourage companies to join the exchange, but expansion is still slow.

The Tunisian Government adopted a unified investment code in 1993 to attract foreign capital. More than 1,600 export-oriented joint venture firms operate in Tunisia to take advantage of relatively low labor costs and preferential access to nearby European markets. Economic links are closest with European countries, which dominate Tunisia's trade. Tunisia's currency, the dinar, is not traded outside Tunisia. However, partial convertibility exists for bonafide commercial and investment transaction. Certain restrictions still limit operations carried out by Tunisian residents.

In October 2002 the U.S. and Tunisia signed a Trade and Investment Framework Agreement (TIFA) designed to provide a forum for discussions on expanding trade and investment between the two countries. The first U.S.-Tunisia Council on Trade and Investment envisioned under the agreement took place in Washington DC in October 2003, and the second is scheduled for Fall 2004. TIFA's can be the first step towards a Free Trade Agreement (FTA) and the Government of Tunisia has expressed interest in concluding an FTA with the United States at some point in the future.

FOREIGN RELATIONS

President Ben Ali has maintained Tunisia's long-time policy of seeking good relations with the West, including the United States, while playing an active role in Arab and African regional bodies. President Bourguiba took a nonaligned stance but emphasized close relations with Europe and the United States.

Tunisia has long been a voice for moderation and realism in the Middle East. President Bourguiba was the first Arab leader to call for the recognition of Israel in a speech in Jericho in 1965. Tunisia served as the headquarters of the Arab League from 1979 to 1990 and hosted the Palestine Liberation Organization's (PLO) headquarters from 1982 to 1993, when the PLO Executive Committee relocated to Jericho and the Palestinian Authority was established after the signing of the Oslo Agreement. (The PLO Political Department remains in Tunis.) Tunisia consistently has played a moderating role in the negotiations for a comprehensive Middle East peace. In 1993, Tunisia was the first Arab country to host an official Israeli delegation as part of the Middle East peace process and maintained an Interests Section until the outbreak of the 2000 Intifada. Israeli citizens of Tunisian descent may travel to Tunisia on their Israeli passports.

Wedged between Algeria and Libya, Tunisia has sought to maintain good relations with its neighbors despite occasionally strained relations. Tunisia and Algeria resolved a longstanding border dispute in 1993 and have cooperated in the construction of a natural gas pipeline through Tunisia that connects Algeria to Italy. Tunisia recently signed an agreement with Algeria to demarcate the maritime frontier between the two countries.

Tunisia's relations with Libya have been erratic since Tunisia annulled a brief agreement to form a union in 1974. Diplomatic relations were broken in 1976, restored in 1977, and deteriorated again in 1980, when Libyan-trained rebels attempted to seize the town of Gafsa. In 1982, the International Court of Justice ruled in Libya's favor in the partition of the oil-rich continental shelf it shares with Tunisia. Libya's 1985 expulsion of Tunisian workers and military threats led Tunisia to sever relations. Relations were normalized again in 1987. While supporting the UN sanctions imposed following airline bombings, Tunisia has been careful to maintain positive relations with her neighbor. Tunisia supported the lifting of UN sanctions against Libya in 2003, and Libya is again becoming a major trading partner.

Tunisia has supported the development of the Arab Maghreb Union (UMA), which includes Algeria, Morocco, Mauritania, and Libya. Progress on Maghreb integration remains stymied, however, as a result of bilateral tensions between some member countries.

U.S.-TUNISIAN RELATIONS

The United States has very good relations with Tunisia, which date back more than 200 years. The United States has maintained official representation in Tunis almost continuously since 1797, and the American treaty with Tunisia was signed in 1799. The two governments are not linked by security treaties, but relations have been close since Tunisia's independence. U.S.-Tunisian relations suffered briefly after the 1985 Israeli raid on PLO headquarters in Tunis, after the 1988 assassination of PLO terrorist Abu Jihad, and in 1990 during the Gulf War when Tunisia objected to U.S. intervention following Iraq's invasion of Kuwait. In each case, however, relations warmed again quickly, reflecting strong bilateral ties. The United States and Tunisia have an active schedule of joint military exercises. U.S. security assistance historically has played an important role in cementing relations. The U.S.-Tunisian Joint Military Commission meets annually to discuss military cooperation, Tunisia's defense modernization program, and other security matters.

For additional analytical, business and investment opportunities information, please contact Global Investment & Business Center, USA at (703) 370-8082. Fax: (703) 370-8083. E-mail: ibpusa3@gmail.com Global Business and Investment Info Databank - www.ibpus.com

The United States first provided economic and technical assistance to Tunisia under a bilateral agreement signed March 26, 1957. The U.S. Agency for International Development (USAID) managed a successful program until its departure in 1994, when Tunisia's economic advances led to the country's "graduation" from USAID funding. Tunisia enthusiastically supported the U.S.-North African Economic Partnership (USNAEP) designed to promote U.S. investment in, and economic integration of the Maghreb region. The program provided over $4 million between 2001 and 2003 in assistance to Tunisia. The Middle East Partnership Initiative (MEPI) was launched in 2002 and incorporated the former USNAEP economic reform projects while adding bilateral and regional projects for education reform, civil society development and women's empowerment. On 18 August 2004, the MEPI Regional Office opened in Embassy Tunis. The Regional Office is staffed by both American diplomats and regional specialists. It is responsible for coordinating MEPI activities in Algeria, Egypt, Lebanon, Morocco and Tunisia in close coordination with the American Embassies in those countries.

American private assistance has been provided liberally since independence by foundations, religious groups, universities, and philanthropic organizations. The U.S. Government has supported Tunisia's efforts to attract foreign investment. The United States and Tunisia concluded a bilateral investment treaty in 1990 and an agreement to avoid double taxation in 1989. In October 2002, the U.S. and Tunisia signed a Trade and Investment Framework Agreement (TIFA), and in October 2003 held the first TIFA Council Meeting in Washington, DC.
American firms seeking to invest in Tunisia and export to Tunisia can receive insurance and financing for their business through U.S. Government agencies, including the Overseas Private Investment Corporation (OPIC) and the Export-Import Bank. The best prospects for foreigners interested in the Tunisian market are in high technology, energy, agribusiness, food processing, medical care and equipment, and the environmental and tourism sectors.

PRINCIPAL U.S. OFFICIALS
chief of mission: Ambassador Daniel H. RUBINSTEIN (since 26 October 2015)

Deputy Chief of Mission--Marc Desjardins (arrives in August 2007)
Political/Economic Counselor--Dorothy C. Shea
Commercial Attaché--Beth Mitchell
The U.S. Embassy in Tunisia is located in Zone Nord-Est des Berges du Lac, Nord de Tunis, 2045 La Goulette, Tunisie (tel: 216-71-107-000, fax: 216-71-962-115)

TRAVEL AND BUSINESS INFORMATION
The U.S. Department of State's Consular Information Program provides Consular Information Sheets, Travel Warnings, and Public Announcements.

Consular Information Sheets exist for all countries and include information on entry requirements, currency regulations, health conditions, areas of instability, crime and security, political disturbances, and the addresses of the U.S. posts in the country.

For additional analytical, business and investment opportunities information,
please contact Global Investment & Business Center, USA
at (703) 370-8082. Fax: (703) 370-8083. E-mail: ibpusa3@gmail.com
Global Business and Investment Info Databank - www.ibpus.com

Travel Warnings are issued when the State Department recommends that Americans avoid travel to a certain country.

Public Announcements are issued as a means to disseminate information quickly about terrorist threats and other relatively short-term conditions overseas that pose significant risks to the security of American travelers. Free copies of this information are available by calling the Bureau of Consular Affairs at 202-647-5225 or via the fax-on-demand system: 202-647-3000. Consular Information Sheets and Travel Warnings also are available on the Consular Affairs Internet home page: http://travel.state.gov. Consular Affairs Tips for Travelers publication series, which contain information on obtaining passports and planning a safe trip abroad, are on the Internet and hard copies can be purchased from the Superintendent of Documents, U.S. Government Printing Office, telephone: 202-512-1800; fax 202-512-2250.
Emergency information concerning Americans traveling abroad may be obtained from the Office of Overseas Citizens Services at (202) 647-5225. For after-hours emergencies, Sundays and holidays, call 202-647-4000.

The National Passport Information Center (NPIC) is the U.S. Department of State's single, centralized public contact center for U.S. passport information. Telephone: 1-877-4USA-PPT (1-877-487-2778). Customer service representatives and operators for TDD/TTY are available Monday-Friday, 8:00 a.m. to 8:00 p.m., Eastern Time, excluding federal holidays.
Travelers can check the latest health information with the U.S. Centers for Disease Control and Prevention in Atlanta, Georgia. A hotline at 877-FYI-TRIP (877-394-8747) and a web site at http://www.cdc.gov/travel/index.htm give the most recent health advisories, immunization recommendations or requirements, and advice on food and drinking water safety for regions and countries. A booklet entitled Health Information for International Travel (HHS publication number CDC-95-8280) is available from the U.S. Government Printing Office, Washington, DC 20402, tel. (202) 512-1800.

Information on travel conditions, visa requirements, currency and customs regulations, legal holidays, and other items of interest to travelers also may be obtained before your departure from a country's embassy and/or consulates in the U.S. (for this country, see "Principal Government Officials" listing in this publication).

U.S. citizens who are long-term visitors or traveling in dangerous areas are encouraged to register their travel via the State Department's travel registration web site at https://travelregistration.state.gov or at the Consular section of the U.S. embassy upon arrival in a country by filling out a short form and sending in a copy of their passports. This may help family members contact you in case of an emergency.

INTERNET AND E-COMMERCE IN TUNISIA - STRATEGIC INFORMATION AND DEVELOPMENTS

BASIC INFORMATION

Tunisia has been among the first African countries to implement an ICT-based national strategy aimed at:

> modernizing the telecommunications infrastructure throughout the country;

> formulating a regulatory framework for the digital economy that supports the private sector and fosters corporate competitiveness;

> developing human resources through the restructuring of education, training, and research institutions; and

> enhancing international cooperation and partnerships in the ICT field.

Since 2002, the telecommunications sector in Tunisia has been deregulated, a national telecommunications agency created, and an electronic signature and electronic document exchange adopted. The World Summit on the Information Society (WSIS), started by the United Nations in 1998 on Tunisia's proposal and hosted by the country in its second phase in 2005, boosted the role of ICT in the country's economic and

As early as 1999, Tunisia formulated a national cyber-security strategy aimed at increasing information systems' security in the country and fostering electronic commerce and online services, as well as protecting users against cyber-threats. A first measure was the adoption in 1999 of a law defining cybercrime and specifying sanctions against IT hackers.

Subsequent measures included the establishment of the National Agency for Computer Security (ANSI) and the Tunisian Computer Emergency Response Team (TunCERT).[13] ANSI's mission is to raise governmental and business organizations' awareness and assist them to implement actions to ensure the security of their information systems. Through its TunCERT, ANSI is the first operational center in Africa recognized by the worldwide network Forum of Incident Response and Security Teams. It is a member of the Network of Centers of Excellence of the United Nations Conference on Trade and Development (UNCTAD), and also serves as Vice President of the Organization of the Islamic Conference-Computer Emergency Response Team.

The deployment of broadband networks has resulted in a significant expansion, mainly through the rapid deployment of digital subscriber line (DSL) and fiber optic technologies. The number of Internet users has grown over the past few years to reach one-third of the population, stimulated by the reduction in DSL subscription costs that makes subscription affordable to most citizens (See Figure 1). More specifically, the cost of a 1 Mb connection was reduced by 25 percent in 2008 and by an additional 45 percent in 2009, to reach almost US$27 per month, compared with a cost of US$61.5 in 2007.

For international connectivity and as part of the "Hannibal system,"Tunisia has just laid out its own submarine cable to Europe, with a capacity of 3.2 terabits per second (Tb/s).

Added to this is the capacity provided by the Keltra cable (which links Tunisia to Italy) and by the South East Asia-Middle East-Western Europe 4 (SEA-ME-WE4) submarine fiber-optic cable consortium. International connectivity using several submarine cables, the national IP/MPLS, and multiple technology access networks has enabled operators to offer reliable national and international links at an affordable price. The international Internet reached 27.5 Gb/s in November 2009, up from only 11.25 Gb/s

Tunisia has one of the most developed telecommunications infrastructures in North Africa with broadband prices among the lowest in Africa. Internet access is available throughout the country using a fibre-optic backbone and international access via submarine cables, terrestrial and satellite links. Tunisia's international bandwidth reached 37.5 Gbit/s in 2010, up from 1.3 Gbit/s in 2006.

Over the last decades, higher education in Tunisia has evolved at a quickening pace.The country today has 14 universities and 200 institutions of higher education covering all parts of Tunisia and providing students with over 1,000 study programs or career paths. Total university enrollment has increased from 40,000 students (37 percent of them women) in the academic year 1986–87 to more than 350,000 students (59 percent of them women) in the academic year 2007–08. Students enrolled in sciences and engineering increased from 10 percent in 1992–93 to 25 percent in 2007–08.Also,the number of higher-education graduates increased 12-fold within two decades, from 5,200 in 1987–88 to more than 60,000 in 2007–08, significantly contributing to the country's economic development.[19]

Faced with the dual challenge of integrating the country into the global economy while ensuring employment for the growing number of university graduates, Tunisia has implemented some major reforms.These include increased deregulation of several economic sectors, enhanced research and development (R&D) efforts through sustained public investment, the development of new technology parks across the country, and higher awareness in the public and private sectors about the country's move toward a knowledge-based economy.

Since the government introduced a law enacting new research policy guidelines in 1996,Tunisia's scientific research has advanced at a steady pace. In addition to 30 specialized research centers and institutes, the country today has 140 laboratories and 630 research units (mainly located within universities) grouping together some 20,000 researchers, including faculty members, PhD candidates,and Master-level students.Tunisia's budget for scientific research and technological innovation currently represents 1.25 percent of its GDP and is expected to reach 1.5 percent of GDP by 2014.[21] In order to reinforce science-industry links and bolster R&D and innovation, the country's infrastructure also includes technical centers, high-tech enterprises, and incubators, mostly located within a network of 10 technology parks spread all over the country. Furthermore, the government established the Research and Innovation Promotion Agency in 2009 with the aim of promoting and transferring research results across different sectors of the economy.

TECHNOLOGY PARKS

Tunisia's transition toward a knowledge-based economy represents a key pillar of the country's 10th and 11th development plans (for the 2002–06 and 2007–11 periods, respectively), thus extending the national effort, begun in the 1990s, to restructure the higher-education and research sectors. Within this framework, the government set up a dozen technology parks (three of which are devoted to ICT) countrywide, in order to create the interdisciplinary innovation and synergies needed for sustainable economic development.

In March 2010 there were 3,600,000 Internet users, 33.9% of the population, up from 9.3% in 2006.[3] This compares favorably with the world average of 30.2%, the African average of 11.4%, and the Middle East average of 31.7%.[4] There were 114,000 broadband subscriptions. 84% of Internet users accessed the Internet at home, 75.8% at work, and 24% use public Internet cafés.[5] There were 2,602,640 Facebook users in June 2011 for a 24.5% penetration rate. This compares well with the 10.3% rate for the world as a whole, 3.0% for Africa, and the 7.5% rate for the Middle East.[3]

This approach enables technology-based development and provides solid foundations for a high-tech industry. These technology parks host science and technology education and training programs as well as R&D projects.

Such activities are aimed at enhancing Tunisia's value-added products and services and the country's attractiveness for FDI. The success of the technology parks' strategy requires having a minimum critical mass (through the effective onsite presence of several stakeholders); a good experimentation, learning, and adaptation approach; and an institutional and organizational proximity, which enables sharing experiences and best practices.

NATIONAL STRATEGY FOR OFFERING STATE-OF-THE-ART IT SERVICES

Tunisia's ICT development strategy aims at making this sector a catalyst for economic growth and international competitiveness. Determined to stay at the cutting edge of the ICT field, the country pays special attention to the continuous improvement of the installed infrastructure. The use of ICT in the public sector enhances its adoption in all economic sectors and in society at large. Thanks to this effective utilization, ICT's contribution to GDP has increased from 7 percent in the last three years to 11 percent at present.

Several major initiatives have been undertaken over the last decade to develop ICT-based value-added services. These were either fully supported by the government or made possible through public-private partnerships. Examples of such e-services, which received international recognition and in some cases were adopted and used by other countries, include Tunisie TradeNet, TrainPost, and financial e-clearance (detailed information on these services is available in Box 3).

Furthermore, the new US$3 billion project, called Tunis Telecom City, will position Tunisia as a key international destination in the telecommunications sector. It will offer state-of-the-art education, research, and training in the telecommunications field and a business incubator for telecommunications startups, as well as venture capital and financing (see Box 4).

- 40 -

Tunisia has faced several challenges in implementing its national ICT strategy. In particular:

There has been insufficient innovation in software and application development in spite of the government's offer to companies of financial support and tax incentives.

Competition from other IT offshoring, BPO, and IT service destinations in the region (such as Morocco and Egypt) has been stiff.

Enhancing the country's technology platform remains a challenge, although several projects have been launched to develop software for telecommunications and industrial systems, machine-to-machine solutions, embedded software, mobile services and content, digital media, and security for information systems and infrastructure.

Notwithstanding government efforts to improve online service quality and expand the use of ICT in educational institutions, public-sector agencies, and with cybercafés throughout the country, the digital divide has not been completely bridged yet.

In spite of government incentives to boost R&D activities in the ICT sector, many ICT firms faced difficulties in international competition.This is because of their limited financial resources and the lack of private investment in the sector.

The Ministry of Communication Technologies established the Tunisian Internet Agency (ATI) to regulate the country's Internet and domain name system (DNS) services. The ATI is also the gateway from which all of Tunisia's eleven Internet service providers (ISPs) lease their bandwidth. Six of these ISPs are public (ATI, INBMI, CCK, CIMSP, IRESA and Defense's ISP); the other five — 3S Global Net, HEXABYTE, TopNet, Tunisia Telecom, Ooredoo Tunisia, and Orange Tunisia — are private.[6]

The government has energetically sought to expand internet access. The ATI reports 100% connectivity in the education sector (universities, research laboratories, primary and secondary schools). Government-brokered "free Internet" programs provide web access for the price of a local telephone call and increased competition among ISPs has lowered costs and significantly reduced economic barriers to Internet access. Those for whom personal computers remain prohibitively expensive may also access the internet from more than 300 cybercafés set up by the authorities

The Information and Communications Technology (ICT) sector is a priority sector in Tunisia, both as a as a dynamic sector of innovation and as a vehicle for the development of other economic sectors. Tunisia's ICT sector is open to international interests through export, foreign investment, partnership, and outsourcing with both developed and developing countries, particularly with other African countries.

According to the National Institute of Statistics (NIS), the ICT sector makes up 7.2% of Tunisia's GDP, and employs approximately 80,000 people (2016). According to the NIS, the ICT sector is made up of 1,800 private companies, 219 shared service centers, eight development centers serving multinational companies, a telephone density of 98.8 lines per 100 inhabitants, and more than 3 million Internet users with an annual evolution of 38% a year.

Tunisia now has three ICT-oriented technoparks, as well as 18 cyberparks entirely dedicated to training and scientific and technological research. This is part of Tunisia's ambitious "Tunisie Digitale 2020" plan, which aims to make the country an international player in the digital world by developing a network of competitive and innovative companies.

According to the Ministry of Communication Technologies and Digital Economy, the Tunisian telecommunication network is among the most modern in the Mediterranean area, composed of seven nodes nationwide, equipped with multiservice broadband switches, integrating telephone traffic, internet, and multimedia traffic.

Tunisia's information technology sector offers a number of promising investment opportunities.

These investment opportunities include:

Tunisian engineering and IT companies have made remarkable progress in the field of software development.

Software production is a high-value-added business, it has a favorable legal and financial framework, and the Tunisian market has real comparative advantages.

The **Tunisian Government's** *2016-2020 Development Plan* will support a large number of projects in the ICT sector spread across Tunisia, including:

The generalization and development of broadband Internet access;

The digitization of government administration services;

The promotion of services for export as part of a public-private partnership (online purchase, e-health, e-commerce, etc...); and

Offshoring (*Smart Tunisia*), encouraging foreign companies to hire Tunisians.

Tunisia, which intends to become a production platform in this field and an attractive destination for international partners (despite the difficult situation that followed the 2011 revolution), is actively seeking investment and partnership initiatives.

The Tunisian environment is a favorable destination for ICT companies to establish themselves or carry out privileged exchanges. It is an ideal hub platform to access neighboring markets, such as Algeria or Libya, as well as other African and Middle East markets.

MINISTRY OF INFORMATION AND COMMUNICATION TECHNOLOGIES

Agency overview	
Agency executives	Mohamed Naceur Ammar, Minister of Communication Technologies
	Lamia Cheffai Sghaier, Secretary of State responsible for Information , Internet and Free software

Website	www.infocom.tn/ 13 Avenue Jugurtha, Tunis 1002, Tunisie Phone: (+216) 71 846 100 Fax: (+216) 71 846 600 Email: com@ati.tn

The **Ministry of Communication Technologies and Digital Economy of Tunisia** is a cabinet-level governmental agency in Tunisia in charge of organizing the sector, planning, control and supervision of activities directed at acquiring new technology and improving the communications sector in Tunisia.

LEGAL FRAMEWORK

The Tunisian telecommunications sector has undergone legal reforms since the late 1990s. The *Telecommunications Code*(TC) is set in Law No. 2001-1 (15 January 2001), Law No. 2002-46 (May 2002), Law No. 2008-1 (8 January 2008), and Law No. 2013-10 (12 April 2013)

The purpose of this *Telecommunications Code* is to organize the telecommunications sector. This organization includes:

The installation and operation of telecommunications networks;

The provision of universal telecommunications services;

The provision of telecommunications services;

The provision of television broadcasting services; and

The management of rare telecommunications resources.

Tunisia also implemented a series of measures in order to modernize the legal and regulatory framework for telecommunications, which included:

The creation of the National Telecommunications Authority (NTA) to regulate interconnection, numbering, and other matters, as well as to resolve disputes between operators;

The creation of the National Frequency Agency (NFA) to manage the radio spectrum; and

Increasing the financial independence of the NTA.

For additional analytical, business and investment opportunities information,
please contact Global Investment & Business Center, USA
at (703) 370-8082. Fax: (703) 370-8083. E-mail: ibpusa3@gmail.com
Global Business and Investment Info Databank - www.ibpus.com

ICT SECTOR DEVELOPMENTS - IMPORTANT INFORMATION

THE ICT - BASIC DATA

- More than 1 800 private firms.
- 219 centers of shared services employing more than 17 500 people.
- 3,000-4,000 jobs created each year.
- 12 internet service providers.
- 8 development centers serving multinationals.
- A telephone density of 98.8 lines per 100 inhabitants.
- Over 3 million internet users with an annual growth of 38%.
- 184 certified auditors in the field of computer security.
- 7 Cyber Parks spread over several regions and 7 others nearing completion.

GROWTH OF ICT

Communication technologies is a priority sector in Tunisia. It is one of the most dynamic sectors, with one of the highest growth rates (15% in 2009).

The sector is experiencing significant growth, it currently contributes by 10% to the GDP as against only 2.5% in 2002 and 9% of employment positions across the country.

ICT SECTOR STRUCTURE

Since the 1980s, Tunisia aimed at boosting the ICT sector as a full-fledged economic sector, creating wealth and high value-added jobs, while also developing ICTs in order to modernize other economic sectors and improve their competitiveness.

The telecommunications network is fully digitized in and offers a variety of different data transmission techniques and services, including Videotex, X25 Package, Frame Relay, ATM, ISDN, DSL, GPRS, as well as various specialized links, and of course the Internet. The Internet provides 34 Mbps Nx2Mbit access to several Internet Service Providers (ISPs), seven of which are private (see Annex 1.2).

According to the publication "Tunisia in Figures"[Footnote2] of 'Statistics Tunisia', the number of subscribers to the Internet in Tunisia is estimated at 1.8 million for the year 2015-2016 (against, 1.1 million in 2012, 1.4 million in 2013 and 1.7 million in 2014). According to the same source, the number of websites in Tunisia is estimated for 2015-2016 at 29,938 (against 15,938 in 2012, 19,303 in 2013 and 24,673 in 2014).

TUNISIAN STRATEGY IN ICT

"Digital Tunisia 2020" is a five-year strategy targeting ICT technologies in order to significantly increase the number of jobs and export earnings within the ICT sector. This strategy aims to make Tunisia an international digital reference, and make ICT an important lever for socio-economic development[Footnote3].

Through this strategy, Tunisia aims to:

Ensure social inclusion and reduce the digital divide;

Generalize the use of ICT within Tunisia;

Evolve towards a transparent e-Administration;

Create employment;

Create value added by encouraging innovation; and

Improve business competitiveness through the development of ICTs.

The implementation of the 2020 digital is intended to achieve as results:

To create TND 11 billion in additional value after 5 years (by 2020);

To reach TND 6 billion in export after 5 years;

To create 95,000 jobs in 5 years; and

To provide internet connectivity to 3000 families[Footnote4].

In addition to the "Digital Tunisia 2020" strategy, which focuses on the entire sector, the **"Smart Tunisia"** program is intended for companies in the offshoring sector. The main objective of this program is to create 50,000 information technology jobs in five years (2016-2020). Tunisia is aware of the economic potential of this sector, and has allocated, for five years, CAD $ 750 million for incentives to support international and local actors in growing and developing their activities in the ICT field.[Footnote5]
In summary, the objectives of "Smart Tunisia" are to:

Create 50,000 jobs in the ICT sector over 5 years;

Act as a single point of contact for the program's beneficiary companies and foreign investors;

Make Tunisia an important interlocutor of Francophone offshoring; and

Raise Tunisia as a hub and a platform of skills for Europe, Africa, and the Middle East.

INVESTMENTS

It has benefited from the high level of investment, amounting to some 3.9 billion dinars over the period 2007-2011 vs. just 430 million dinars over the period 1992-1996. Such strong growth is attributable to better infrastructure, especially telecommunications infrastructure, involving active and motivated participation by private companies operating in this field.

SUPPORT BODIES

The National Computer and Office Automation Union Chamber, Fedelec–UTICA. Ministry of Communication Technologies.

MASTERING TECHNOLOGY

Architecture: subject oriented, client-server, web, third party architecture.

Mastery of environments: Unix (Solaris, HP UX, Linux, Aix, Sun OS, Irix), Windows (2000, XP, Vista).

Application servers: Apache, Weblogic, Windows NT Server, JBoss.

→**Mastery of databases**: Oracle, Developper, Designer, My SQL, Microsoft SQL, Sybase, Informix, Paradox, Microsoft Access.

Mastery of languages: Perl-CGI, C/C++, Action X, Java, Java script, Corba, ASP, HTML, DHTML, XML, Visual Basic,PHP, PYTHON, SQL.

Mastery of graphic tools: OSF-Motif, Dataview, X-Windows.

AREAS OF EXPERTISE

→ Offshore development of new technologies for international clients.
→ Banks, insurance and trade solutions.
→ ERP, SCM solutions and services to companies.
→ CRM, business intelligence, solutions for storing documents and services.
→ Solutions and software for management and services.
→ The integration of information or communication systems
→ The integration of real time systems and embedded systems
→ Real time industrial systems.
→ Fleet and navigational system management.
→ Telecommunications systems: tailored developments, added value services, billing, installation, networks.
→ E-business, e-commerce, e-learning, e-government solutions.
→ Development of websites and services.
→ Management of information systems, IT systems & software...
→ Solutions and services for tourism.
→ All kinds of tailored developments for the public sector (electricity, gas transport...).
→ Offshore computer services.
→ Call centers serving the local market and clients abroad.

INFRASTRUCTURE

A communication technology park in El Ghazala, which has a state of the art infrastructure to meet the needs of leading firms in the sectors of new information and communication technology.
The extension works are underway to provide this city with 100 000 sqm of additional outfitted areas.

Sfax has a technopole devoted to informatics and multi media, an attractive opportunity for foreign investors.

Seven cyberparks in El Kef, in Siliana, in Monastir, in Kasserine, in Gafsa, in Kairouan and in Sousse. Seven more parks are underway in other regions (Kebili, Tataouine, Medenine, Zaghouan, Beja, Jendouba and Sidi Bouzid).

→ A technological evolution in terms of communication infrastructure which is among the most up to date in the Mediterranean basin. Indeed, the Tunisian telecommunications network is equipped with a multifunction broadband switch ensuring the traffic of voice, internet and multimedia at the same time.

It is also composed of two international gateways, of connections by submarine cable and of digital spatial links. Satellite telecommunication projects like the project Thouraya at the level of the Arab world, the RASCOM project in Africa and SEAMEWE4 project at an international level cover the goal of providing total connectivity for Tunisia.

⁺ A digital culture throughout the Tunisian territory with a network of fully digitized telephone, an Internet network covering 100% of the country and an internet bandwidth for international connection reaching 17.5 Gb/s.

This techonological level is confirmed by the latest ranking of Tunisia in the 'Global Information Technology Report 2008-2009'.

Rank	Country	Score
19	France	5.17
38	**Tunisia**	**4.34**
45	Italy	4.16
46	China	4.15
54	India	4.03
55	Greece	4.00
58	Rumania	3.97
76	Egypt	3.76
86	Morocco	3.59

2008-2009 Global Information Technology Report, Davos World Economic Forum

Comparative costs

Human resources

Tunisia has a large number of young graduates with skills and qualifications in various branches that meet the needs of businesses. In 2008 there were more than 9,500 graduates holding degrees in computer sciences and communications, compared to 1,769 in 2002.

Trends in the number of students registered in ICT training courses

A SUITABLE REGULATORY FRAMEWORK

Telecommunications code.
Legislation governing e-commerce and e-signature.
Legislation on high technology and multipurpose complexes.
Legislation on computer security.
Protection of copyrights.
Protection of personal data guaranteed by the Constitution.
The creation of the Supreme Council of the Digital Economy.
A regulatory and technical framework for the telephone service through Voice over IP 'VoIP'.

(1= nonexistent, 7 = well developed and enforced)

Rank	Country	Score
16	France	5.4
29	Belgium	4.9
30	**Tunisia**	**4.9**

35	Spain	4.8
39	Czech Republic	4.6
52	Italy	4.2
55	Turkey	4.0
73	Romania	3.7
76	Greece	3.6
87	Poland	3.4
97	Morocco	3.1
Rank	**Country**	**Score**
16	France	5.4
29	Belgium	4.9
30	**Tunisia**	**4.9**
35	Spain	4.8
39	Czech Republic	4.6
52	Italy	4.2
55	Turkey	4.0
73	Romania	3.7
76	Greece	3.6
87	Poland	3.4
97	Morocco	3.1

For additional analytical, business and investment opportunities information,
please contact Global Investment & Business Center, USA
at (703) 370-8082. Fax: (703) 370-8083. E-mail: ibpusa3@gmail.com
Global Business and Investment Info Databank - www.ibpus.com

DIGITAL TUNISIA 2020

BASIC INFORMATION

According to the objectives assigned to the digital economy sector within the National Development Plan (PND) 2016-2020, the Government requested Bank support to finance the Support Project for Implementation of the "Digital Tunisia 2020" National Strategic Plan (PNS). The project comprises: (i) the establishment of the main ministerial information systems (IS) (e-finance, e-justice, e-local government, etc.); and (ii) all the platforms that guarantee an e-government (interoperability, public cloud, Government intranet, etc.).. Furthermore, it provides for institutional support that includes feasibility studies to prepare for the rest of the project, support actions (legal assistance, management change, communication, etc.) and implementation of various project activities. The project will be implemented over a four-year (2018-2021) period for an estimated total of EUR 134,96 million as follows: (i) an ADB window loan of EUR 71.56 million; and (ii) a national counterpart contribution of EUR 63.4 million from the national budget.

The digital sector presents a major source of growth for the Tunisian economy, not to mention its role in improving business competitiveness and contributing to the social inclusion of the population.

The state has therefore devised a strategy to put in place the infrastructure and the framework necessary for the development of this sector of the future.

The development of this sector will raise the level of skills and innovation in the Tunisian economy and provide opportunities for graduates of the university.

unisian authorities have raised ICTs into a national priority, given the sector performance generated in recent years by substantial public and private investments in infrastructure. The outcomes of such a bold policy are the creation of many technological centres (El Ghazala in Tunis, Sfax, etc.); the establishment of many underwater connections with Europe in particular; the creation of call centres; and the establishment of regional and national offices of large multinationals like Alcatel, Ericsson, Sofrecom, etc.

PNS TD2020 FOCUSES ON THE FOLLOWING FOUR PILLARS:

✓Pillar 1: Infrastructure - aimed at generalizing access to broadband internet and knowledge and developing ultra-high-speed internet.

Pillar 2: e-Gov -aimed at transforming administrative services through the use and adoption of digital technology to enhance the efficiency and transparency of operations for citizens and the business community.

Pillar 3: e-Business - aimed at transforming businesses through digital technology to enhance competitiveness, productivity and integration and making innovation the driving force of the digital industry by developing creative and functional solutions that support all sectors of activity and entrepreneurship.

Pillar 4: Smart Tunisia -geared towards placing Tunisia among the top three countries in Offshoring and making it the Leader in IT Offshoring in the Africa-Middle

East region.

The execution of "Smart Gov 2020" will lay the foundation for an effective and open administration that provides accessible, simple and high-quality services to users and businesses, and actively contributes to Tunisia's development.

PNS TD2020 contributes to the drive to transform the country from a low-cost economy, especially in the digital technology sector, to an economic hub thanks to Tunisia's location on the intersection between Europe, the MENA (Middle East and North Africa) region and Sub-Saharan Africa. To that end, Tunisia can leverage the comparative advantages of the above-mentioned three regions to expand its digital production for export. These include: (i) the quality of its educational system (higher education, in particular); (ii) competitive labour costs; and (iii) the digital environment (which is generally satisfactory albeit perfectible).

"Tunisia Digital 2020" is a five-year strategy targeting ICT technologies in order to significantly increase the number of jobs and export earnings within the ICT sector. This strategy aims to make Tunisia an international digital reference and make ICT an important lever for socio-economic development.

Tunisia Digital 2020 is a strategy that has 4 axes:
Infrastructures: development of high and very high speed
e-Gov infrastructures : Migration towards IPV6, private national public sector cloud, framework of interoperability of the governmental IS, electronic identifier of the citizen and the companies , modernization of major state applications, e-service to the citizen, trust mark for online
e-Business services: e-Education, e-Health, digital innovation
Offshoring: Smart Tunisia program

Through this strategy, Tunisia would like to create **employment, value added by innovation and improve business competitiveness by the development of ICTs**.

The various projects defined in the framework of the program will be carried out either under public funding or within the framework of a public-private partnership. Some components will be financed by the French Development Agency

EXPECTED IMPACTS

Broaden access to high and very high speed internet

Improve the services of the administration

Place Tunisia in the top 3 offshoring and as a leader in IT offshoring in the MENA region

Make digital and innovation the drivers of new growth

Bridging the digital divide

The main objectives of this project:

• To create TND 11 billion in additional value after 5 years (by 2020);
• To reach TND 6 billion in export after 5 years;
• To create 95,000 jobs in 5 years;
• To provide internet connectivity to 3000 families.

In addition to the "Digital Tunisia 2020" strategy, which focuses on the entire sector, **the "Smart Tunisia" program intends to become an attractive destination for international partners and for companies in the offshoring sector.**

The Tunisian parliament has approved an agreement with the African Development Bank (ADB) worth €71.56 million ($85.1 million) on a loan to fund the Digital Tunisia 2020 project.

On 21 December the Tunisian government signed a loan agreement with the ADB to contribute to the Digital Tunisia 2020 project.

The aim of the project is to move towards electronic management, which offers quality digital services and contributes to the creation of job opportunities in the digital field and the transfer of services.

The Assembly of People's Representatives (ARP) began, on the morning of Wednesday, July 11, the examination of the draft law on the approval of a credit granted by the African Development Bank (ADB) to Tunisia to contribute to the financing of the project of establishment of the national strategic plan "Digital Tunisia 2020".

The plenary session was chaired by the Vice President of the ARP, Faouzia Ben Fodha Chaâr, in the presence of the Minister of Communication Technologies and Digital Economy, Anouar Mâarouf.

On December 21, 2017, Tunisia and the ADB signed a loan agreement totaling 71.56 million euros, the equivalent of 180 million dinars (MDT).

Tunisia plans, through this project, to narrow the digital divide and facilitate access to communication technologies. The overall cost of this project, implemented by the Ministry of ICT, amounts to 135 million euros, or 357 MTD, which is provided to 53% by the ADB and the rest by the Tunisian government.

The project "Digital Tunisia 2020" aims to develop electronic governance (electronic portal, digitization of the Post, information system for the industrial and commercial sector ...) for the cost of 109.9 million euros, in addition to the setting up the Open Data system worth 5.95 million euros.

The interest rate on this loan is estimated at 0.44%, which will be repaid over 19 years with a grace period of 6 years. The project will be carried out over the period 2018-2022.

SMART TUNISIA

The new e-government strategy, "Smart Gov 2020", has been unveiled. Funded by the AfDB to the tune of 500 million dinars, this system is structured around 5 main pillars, Minister of Information Technologies and the Digital Economy,

The first pillar targets the re-engineering of administrative processes in the service of the citizens. The second pillar concerns programs comprising the various information systems of the administration and all that relates to the flow of information between different administrations, such as the electronic management of correspondence.

The third pillar focuses on the reform of the information systems of all sectors in order to integrate the e-government system, while the fourth pillar is linked to the new services that e-government will provide to citizens. The last pillar obviously affects the Open-Gov, which will allow Tunisia to climb on the scale of the main destinations for investment.

The main objective of the program is to create **50,000 information technology jobs in five years** (2016-2020), to become a unique contact for foreign investors and important interlocutor of francophone **offshoring**and act as a hub for Africa, Europe, and the Middle East.

Investment opportunities in new information technology sector are:

• Software development's field;
• Software production;
• The generalization and development of broadband Internet access;
• The digitization of government administration services;
• The promotion of services for export as part of a public-private partnership (online purchase, e-health, e-commerce, etc...);
• Offshoring, encouraging foreign companies to hire Tunisians.

A paperless administration by 2020

Through this project, Tunisia aims to digitize the Tunisian administration through e-service with a goal of "zero paper" by 2020, added the minister. He highlighted the efforts made at this level to eradicate the complexity and slowness of current administrative procedures favoring certain forms of corruption.

How? Through an efficient and open administration, by providing accessible, simple and high quality services to citizens and businesses, the Minister replied.

Towards the realization of development projects

This opinion is shared by his colleague Abid Briki, who took the opportunity to insist on this policy.

For, the reform of the Tunisian administration and its modernization are becoming more and more a requirement and an important step to begin the major reforms. "The objectives of the Five-year Development Plan 2016-2020 can never be achieved without modernizing the administration or improving its performance by adopting the new information technologies," assured the minister.

As justification, he highlighted the current state of administration which does not favor investment and the achievement of the objectives of post-revolutionary Tunisia, especially in this economic situation marked by an abysmal budget deficit that would to rise to 6 pc at the end of 2016, accentuated by the worsening of public debt, at around 64 pc of GDP, against just over 40 pc in 2010.

This is important for a government that relies on these reforms in terms of governance and integrity and legislation that is supposed to facilitate administrative processes. The aim is to enable the implementation of development policies.

These reforms come at an opportune moment when Tunisia is trying to revive its economy, to stimulate growth and to initiate a new economic dynamic, thanks to the organization of the "Tunisia 2020" conference. It is an unavoidable event that proves confidence in the Tunisia, with the numerous commitments announced.

Between donations, aid and credits, this event made it possible to garner a total financing amount of 34 billion dinars.

INVESTMENT AND BUSINESS OPPORTUNITIES

In the ICT sector, Tunisia is considered ahead of other similar countries. The Government of Tunisia has, among other initiatives:

Developed an electronic dinar platform (e-Dinar);

Developed electronic procurement;

Diffusion of ICT through trade facilitation policies and programs (Tunisia TradeNet); and

Supported PubliNets.

Tunisia, through its legislation and development policy, allows foreign investors to invest up to 100% in non-resident companies in a number of sectors, including manufacturing, tourism, communications, computers, and consulting.

The creation of "Offshore" companies in Tunisia makes it possible to for foreign investors to optimize their productivity and benefit from opportunities presented by the Tunisian business climate. In addition, the Tunisian banking network provides freedom and security in the management and the transfer of investments, in the investor's currency of choice.

The low cost of wages, as well as Tunisia's system of payroll social contributions, make an attractive hiring environment for investors. In addition, Tunisia is party to a number of international conventions to prevent double-taxation, including with Canada.

One of the development strategies put in place by local authorities as an important vehicle for boosting and attracting foreign direct investments (FDI) is the 'concession', as is the case for Global System of Mobile Telecommunication (GSM) licenses.

The country has great potential to position itself as a regional leader in hosting ICT investments, thanks to a business environment that encourages investment, in both in general and in the ICT field in particular. Tunisia's New Investment Code, which came into effect in April 1, 2017, regulates investment and provides new incentives to sectors that generate wealth and jobsFootnote 10.

Attractive features of the Tunisian Market and the ICT Sector

Qualified human resources, including the availability of engineers and scientists;

Well-developed infrastructure;

A quality ICT platform;

A competitive price-performance ratio;

Foreign companies that have chosen Tunisia as their location have been able to expand their scope of activities by moving towards higher value-added activities;

Locating offices in Tunisia has enabled companies to:

Improve the competitiveness of their parent companies by reducing their operating costs;

Compensate for a lack of human resources in ICT in their country of origin; and

Maintain and strengthen jobs in the country of origin while making Tunisia a backward baseFootnote 11.

Business opportunities in the ICT Sector

R & D and design engineering: The availability of developed infrastructure and the quality of local human resources have attracted a number of international companies to locate research and development activities in Tunisia.

E-health and telemedicine: Tunisia has many specialized doctors able to carry out remote diagnostics and to perform medical analysis, such as X-ray analysis and electrocardiograms. Studies have shown that performing such remote medical activities from Tunisia can help compensate for a shortage of doctors in northern countries, providing services of equivalent quality at much lower costs.

Software development and maintenance: Companies based in Tunisia are active in a number of software-related activities, including design, development, testing, validation, consulting, installation, technical support, and maintenance.

Business Process Outsourcing (BPO): A number of companies have located BPO activities in Tunisia, in areas such as data entry and information processing.

Analysis, data extraction, decision-making, assistance and consulting: This included activities in a number of fields such as banking, insurance, finance, accounting, health, and human resources.

The development of 'technology parks': Tunisia is seeking strategic partners for the development of tech-based industrial zones. These projects are intended to strengthen synergies between education, research, and industryFootnote 12; as well as to provide ICT companies with hosting facilities that meet international standardsFootnote

E-COMMERCE SEVELOPMENT

The Tunisian postal service operates an electronic payment system called the e-dinar. Customers establish an account and replenish it by purchasing credit at a post office. Many public services in Tunisia can be paid using e-dinars.

Tunisian credit cards are not convertible to hard currency and thus cannot be used for purchases made on foreign commercial internet sites. Debit and credit cards can be used for domestic internet payment for a few services, such as public utilities, telecommunication, and university registration.

Most Tunisian banks allow account holders to use bank-affiliated credit and debit cards to make domestic on-line purchases denominated in dinars. The Tunisian dinar is a non-convertible currency, however, so on-line purchases in foreign currency are not allowed, and few Tunisians make cross-border purchases via eCommerce. In recognition of this limitation, the Ministry of Communication, Technology, and Digital Economy launched a Digital Technology Charge Card in May 2015 for Tunisians with college degrees, which allows these card holders to make on-line purchases of software, mobile applications, web services, and publications in support of entrepreneurial activities. Individual users are limited to 1,000 dinars (about $467) in annual purchases. The program has been expanded to include Tunisian IT companies, which are allotted up to 10,000 dinars (about $4,670) annually to purchase on-line services, including server hosting and freelance programming services. As of May 2017, the Ministry of Communication, Technology, and Digital Economy recorded approximately 8,500 active users of this program, with 70% of users identified as individual college graduates and 30% identified as IT enterprises.

DOMESTIC ECOMMERCE (B2C)

Due to the general lack of credit cards and on-line payment systems, Tunisia's domestic eCommerce markets are underdeveloped. Most Tunisian banks offer account holders bank-affiliated credit and debit cards which can be used on domestic websites only. General purpose eCommerce retail sites similar to Amazon do not exist in Tunisia, but rather individual retailers and service providers offer their own on-line checkout systems tailored to Tunisian credit and debit cards. According to media, the Central Bank generally opposes allowing other on-line payment systems, which it views as a threatening capital flight route from the country. The lack of government support for cross-border flows in eCommerce also retards further development of the domestic eCommerce market.

CROSS-BORDER ECOMMERCE

Given the Tunisian dinar's status as a non-convertible currency, cross-border eCommerce purchases are not possible apart from specific allowances granted from the Tunisian Central Bank, which has historically opposed such transactions. Consequently, cross-border eCommerce purchases are negligible.

B2B ECOMMERCE

Due to the general lack of credit cards and on-line payment systems, Tunisia's domestic B2B eCommerce markets are significantly underdeveloped.

ECOMMERCE SERVICES

Due to the general lack of credit cards and on-line payment systems, Tunisia's eCommerce markets –- including those supporting eCommerce service providers –- are significantly underdeveloped.

Tunisia's National Institute for Standardization and Industrial Property (INNORPI) recognizes and enforces foreign patents registered in Tunisia, including those directed to eCommerce. Tunisian law affords foreign businesses treatment equal to that afforded Tunisian nationals. Tunisia has also updated its legislation to meet the requirement of the WTO agreement on Trade-Related Aspects of Intellectual Property (TRIPS). For the ".TN" country-specific top level domain name, the Tunisian Internet Authority (ATI) responds to complaints of cybersquatting from trademark owners and will transfer domain registrations to complainants upon demonstration that the accused website is used to pass off counterfeit goods.

ECOMMERCE SITES

Due to the general lack of credit cards and on-line payment systems, Tunisian consumers do not typically use B2B, B2C, and B2G eCommerce platforms.

ONLINE PAYMENT

Tunisian law mandates that only certified financial institutions with banking licenses are allowed to manage financial transactions. Consequently, electronic payment platforms require participation from at least one Tunisian bank, and the current regulatory framework allows payments only between existing Tunisian bank accounts. For example, BIAT, a leading Tunisian bank, has launched a mobile payment system called Via Mobile which allows electronic payments, but only between account holders at the bank. In view of this limitation, no significant eCommerce platform has emerged in Tunisia, and online payments remain a rarity.

MOBILE ECOMMERCE

The mobile eCommerce ecosystem is virtually nonexistent in Tunisia due to the general lack of on-line payment systems. Several mobile phone network providers, e.g., Ooredoo and Tunisie Telecom, have created on-line accounts through which users can purchase data and phone services using domestic bank accounts and pre-paid mobile cards. Funds can also be moved from one user's account to another within the same network. While these systems allow a form of on-line payment between users, the fact that funds can only be used to purchase data and phone services limits their utility.

For additional analytical, business and investment opportunities information, please contact Global Investment & Business Center, USA at (703) 370-8082. Fax: (703) 370-8083. E-mail: ibpusa3@gmail.com Global Business and Investment Info Databank - www.ibpus.com

Digital Marketing

Tunisia's Digital Technology Charge Card program, launched by the Ministry of Communication, Technology, and Digital Economy in May 2015, allows users to purchase digital marketing services on-line. Business contacts note that this program has allowed them to purchase targeted "key word" advertising services directly from companies such as Google and Facebook. The program remains limited, however, as participating marketing companies within Tunisia quickly exceed their yearly allowances of 1,000 dinars per individual or 10,000 dinars per IT company. Permission to exceed this amount requires a formal request to the Ministry of Communication, Technology, and Digital Economy and final approval from the Tunisian Central Bank, which is rare.

There are no significant consumer "buying holidays" for eCommerce in Tunisia. During the month of Ramadan, Tunisian consumption increases by 25% across all consumer categories. Given the paucity of eCommerce, however, there is no discernible coincident rise in on-line purchases during this period.

Tunisia's social media climate is open, voluminous, and lively. Facebook enjoys a dominant market position, with most Tunisian businesses and individuals maintaining an active on-line presence through the free platform to promote their goods and services and connect with customers rather than hosting their own websites. Twitter is popular amongst the intelligentsia and closely followed by political and media operatives. In March 2017, Facebook and Google reached a deal with leading Tunisian Internet provider TOPNET to host content on Tunisian servers, which will allow the companies to more quickly serve the growing content demands of Tunisia's Internet users.

IMPORTANT BUSINESS AND INVESTMENT CONTACTS

AGENCY FOR THE PROMOTION OF INDUSTRY AND INNOVATION

Address: 63, rue de Syrie, 1002 Tunis Belvedere - Tunisia
Tel: (216) 71 792 144
Fax: (216) 71 782 482
E-mail: apii@apii.tn

Created in 1972
Public institution under the supervision of the Ministry of Industry and SMEs
Implements government policy on promoting the industrial sector and innovation as a support structure for businesses and developers.
Offers services and products in the form of information, support, assistance, partnership and studies

THE API, ORGANIZED INTO 5 INTERVENTION CENTERS, OFFERS SERVICES FROM HEADQUARTERS AND ITS 24 REGIONAL OFFICES.

CFGA - CENTER FOR FACILITATION AND BENEFITS MANAGEMENT

The Center for Facilitation and Benefits Management (CFGA) implements rapid and simplified procedures through:

- **The One Stop Shop: it is ISO 9001 certified for:**

  o Issuance of certificates of deposit of declaration of investment projects

  o Completion of the formalities of formation of companies

  o Assisting the formation of companies

  o The realization of other types of services in connection with the creation of investment projects.

  o Assistance and information on the investment environment in Tunisia.

- **Single Window Services are located in Tunis, Sousse and Sfax**

  o Managing the benefits of code and FOPRODI for the benefit of businesses.

  o Decentralized processing of declaration certificates.

- **Products**

Corporate formation and benefits management:

  o Declaration and assistance to the constitution of companies

  o Benefits Management

CDII - CENTER FOR DOCUMENTATION AND INDUSTRIAL INFORMATION

- Monitor industrial and service projects and update the IDB by supporting a team of 50 investigators in 24 regional directorates

- Allows Tunisian companies to benefit from the services of the virtual salon of the Tunisian industry via internet: www.tunisieindustrie.nat.tn to make themselves known internationally.

- Periodically publishes notes and reports on the industrial situation and news and watch reports.

CEPI - CENTER FOR INDUSTRIAL STUDIES AND PROSPECTS

The Center for Industrial Studies and Prospects (CEPI) ensures a permanent strategic watch by realizing:

- **Different types of studies:**

  o strategic positioning studies of branches or industrial sectors where competitiveness factors and development perspectives are analyzed,

  o concerning the industrial environment,

- o   monographic studies of the Tunisian industry.

- o   project studies in the context of a Tunisian-Belgian partnership.

- **National seminars presenting the studies carried out.**

Products

- Strategic positioning studies

- Monographs

- o   A Monograph of manufacturing industries in Tunisia.

- o   8 Sector monographs

- Professional profiles of the API

- Project Briefs

CIDT - THE CENTER FOR INNOVATION AND TECHNOLOGICAL DEVELOPMENT
CIDT is made up of 3 structures and a Europe Enterprise Network:

- **A Partnership and Technological Development Structure**

- **A structure for promoting and disseminating the culture of innovation**

- **A business support task force in the field of innovation**

- **The Network Europe Enterprise Network EEN-Tunisia**

Partnership and Technology Development Structure
Mission:

- Identification of the subcontracting potential of Tunisian companies;

- Organization of international sectoral partnerships in Tunisia and abroad;

- Search for foreign partners for Tunisian companies based on the proposed cooperation profiles;

Structure for promoting and spreading the culture of innovation
Mission:

- Disseminate the culture of innovation in SMEs (training, seminars, thematic days, ...)

- Strengthen innovation management capabilities

- Support for setting up the R & D function in companies

- Promote innovation financing funds

Business support task force in the field of innovation

Mission:

- Canvassing companies with innovation potential

- Diagnosis to identify the company's needs for innovation and technological development

- Follow-up, coordination and support of companies in innovation actions

THE NETWORK EUROPE ENTERPRISE NETWORK EEN-TUNISIA

EEN-Tunisia is a network to offer services to SMEs on 3 axes:

Assistance and advice, feedback, cooperation between companies and internationalization

Services for INNOVATION AND TECHNOLOGICAL TRANSFER

Encouraging SMEs to participate in the RESEARCH AND DEVELOPMENT framework program.

CSCE - SUPPORT CENTER FOR BUSINESS CREATION

The Center offers:

information on all aspects of your project

training on topics related to business creation (15 training sessions)

the realization of the study of your project by an expert (coach)

support through personalized expertise (financial, technical, accounting, etc ...)

seeking funding from funding institutions

hosting your business in a nursery for a period of 2 years

the support of the company after leaving the nursery

In addition, the CSCE manages the National Network of Business Nurseries "RNPE" composed of 19 business incubators installed in the Higher Institutes of Technological Studies (ISET), the engineering schools of Tunis and Sfax, the universities (INSAT and EPT) and Technopoles (Ghazala, Borj Cedria, Sousse and Sfax).

THE NATIONAL NETWORK OF BUSINESS ENTERPRISE NURSERIES OFFERS YOU:

Personalized expertise (Coach)

Accounting

Financial expertise of the project

International expertise

swarming

Documentation- Website

To benefit from the services offered by the nursery, return the **registration form** to the local nursery belonging to **the National Network of Business Nurseries** .

24 REGIONAL DIRECTORATES

API in the regions

Ariana

Address	11, Rue Bel Hassine Jrad - Ariana 2080
Such	(216) - 71,716,064
Fax	(216) - 71 709 437
E-mail	dr.ariana@api.com.tn

Tunis

Address	Imm. N ° 3 - Bardo Center - 2000 the Bardo
Such	(216) - 71,519,852
Fax	(216) - 71,519,964
E-mail	dr.tunis@api.com.tn

Ben Arous

Address	59, Av. Of France - 2013 Ben Arous
Such	(216) - 71,388,755
Fax	(216) - 71,389,091
E-mail	dr.benarous@api.com.tn

Manouba

Address	48, Ave Habib Bourguiba 2010 The Manouba.
Such	(216) - 70,615,878
Fax	(216) - 70,615,884
E-mail	dr.manouba@api.com.tn

Beja

Address	Av. Habib Bourguiba - Imm. CTAMA - 9000 Beja
Such	(216) - 78,457,205
Fax	(216) - 78 456 522
E-mail	dr.beja@api.com.tn

Bizerte

Address	7, Rue du Nord - 7000 Bizerte
Such	(216) - 72 433 556
Fax	(216) - 72,433,667
E-mail	dr.bizerte@api.com.tn

Gabes

Address	18, Al Maârifa Street - 6001 Gabes
Such	(216) - 75,272,855
Fax	(216) - 75,272,855
E-mail	dr.gabes@api.com.tn ;

Gafsa

Address	6, Bagdad Street BP 214 - 2100 Gafsa
Such	(216) - 76,228,818
Fax	(216) - 76,221,535
E-mail	dr.gafsa@api.com.tn

Jendouba

Address	1, Avenue Habib Bourguiba corner - El Farabi Street, PO Box 195, 8100 Jendouba
Such	(216) - 78 601 577
Fax	(216) - 78 601 577
E-mail	dr.jendouba@api.com.tn

The Kef

Address	Mongi Slim Avenue - Imm Housing Bank - 2 nd floor BP210 - 7100 Le Kef
Such	(216) - 78 224 463 - 78 226 942

Fax	(216) - 78,227,419
E-mail	dr.kef@api.com.tn

Kairouan

Address	El Manar City, Av. Of the Environment - 3100 Kairouan
Such	(216) - 77,271,692
Fax	(216) - 77,271,355
E-mail	dr.kairouan@api.com.tn

Kasserine

Address	Building Rahmouni Avenue Habib Bourguiba in front of the Central Bank - 1200 Kasserine
Such	(216) - 77,474,772
Fax	(216) - 77,472,499
E-mail	dr.kasserine@api.com.tn

Kebili

Address	Road of Gabes - BP 34 - 4200 Kebili
Such	(216) - 75,490,234
Fax	(216) - 75,490,234
E-mail	dr.kebeli@api.com.tn

Mahdia

Address	1, Av. 2 March; Imm. Ben Abdallah 2 nd floor - 5100 Mahdia
Such	(216) - 73,680,527
Fax	(216) - 73,695,006
E-mail	dr.mehdia@api.com.tn

Medenine

Address	Sym South building 3rd floor - Ave Mansour El Houch 4100 Medenine
Such	(216) - 75,640,102
Fax	(216) - 75,640,838
E-mail	dr.mednine@api.com.tn

Monastir

Address	City Essada - Borj Khafacha Imm. Municipality [1st] floor 5060 Monastir
Such	(216) - 73,907,855
Fax	(216) - 73,907,694
E-mail	dr.monastir@api.com.tn

Nabeul

Address	80, Avenue Ali Belhouène - 8000 Nabeul
Such	(216) - 72,286,973
Fax	(216) - 72,286,963
E-mail	dr.nabeul@api.com.tn

Sfax

Address	Av. January 14, Ahmed Aloulou Street Imm. Local Loans and Support Fund - 3027 Sfax
Such	(216) - 74,416,019
Fax	(216) - 74,416,018
E-mail	dr.sfax@api.com.tn

Sousse

Address	Bd of Rabat - Imm. CNRPS - BP 24 - 4059 Sousse
Such	(216) - 73 222 404
Fax	(216) - 73,227,809
E-mail	dr.sousse@api.com.tn

Sidi Bouzid

Address	Habib Bourguiba Avenue - BP 95 - 9100 Sidi Bouzid
Such	(216) - 76,633,890
Fax	(216) - 76,634,802
E-mail	dr.sidibouzid@api.com.tn

Siliana

Address	4, Av. Taieb M'hiri - BP 34 - 6100 Siliana
Such	(216) - 78 871 463
Fax	(216) - 78 871 463
E-mail	dr.siliana@api.com.tn

Tataouine

Address	Av. Hédi Chaker Imm. Doukali - 2nd floor BP 410 - 3200 Tataouine
Such	(216) - 75 860 647
Fax	(216) - 75 860 647
E-mail	dr.tataouine@api.com.tn

Tozeur

Address	Av. El Hajij- BP 202 - 2200 Tozeur
Such	(216) - 76,470,919
Fax	(216) - 76,470,919
E-mail	dr.tozeur@api.com.tn

Zaghouan

Address	17, Independence Avenue - BP 36- 1100 Zaghouan
Such	(216) - 72,675,855
Fax	(216) - 72,676,263
E-mail	dr.zaghouan@api.com.tn

POTENTIAL BUSINESS PARTNERS

Société Nationale des Télécommunications « Tunisie Télécom »
actel.virtuelle@ttnet.tn
Tunisie Telecom, Jardins du Lac II, 1053, Tunis, Tunisie
(+216) 71 139 700

l'Office National des Postes « La Poste Tunisienne »
brc@poste.tn
Rue Hédi Nouira – 1030 Tunis, Tunisie
(+216) 71 839 000

Office National de la Télédiffusion
ont@telediffusion.net.tn
Cite Ennassim 1 Montplaisir BP 399 1080 Tunis
(+216) 71 180 000

Agence Nationale des Fréquences
com@anf.tn

39, Rue Asdrubal.La Fayette.Tunis.1002
(+216) 71 121 900

Agence Nationale de Certification Electronique
ance@certification.tn
Parc Technologique El Ghazala – Route de Raoued Km 3,5 – 2088 Ariana
(+216) 71 834 600

Agence Nationale de la Sécurité Informatique
ansi@ansi.tn
49 avenue Jean Jaurès, 1000 Tunis
(+216) 71 846 020

Centre d'Etudes et des Recherches des Télécommunications
cert@cert.mincom.tn
Parc Technologique El Ghazala – Route de Raoued Km 3,5 – 2088 Ariana
(+216) 71 835 000

Centre National de l'Informatique
webcni@cni.tn
17 Rue Belhassen Ben Chaabane 1005 El-Omrane
(+216) 71 783 055

Centre d'Information, de Formation, de Documentation et d'Etudes en Technologies des Communications
cidodecom@cifodecom.com.tn
Parc Technologique El Ghazala – Route de Raoued Km 3,5 – 2088 Ariana
(+216) 71 856 180

Pôle Elgazala des Technologies de la Communication « Elgazala Technopark »
contact@elgazala.tn
Elgazala Technopark, Raoued, Gouvernorat de l'Ariana, 2088 Ariana - Tunisie
(+216) 71 856 600

Ecole supérieure des communications de Tunis
courriel@supcom.rnu.tn
Cité Technologique des Communications - Rte de Raoued Km 3,5 - 2083, Ariana Tunis
(+216) 71 857 000

Institut Supérieur des Etudes Technologiques en Communications de Tunis
courriel@isetcom.rnu.tn
Route de Raoued, Km 3.5 – 2083 Cité EL Ghazala Ariana
(+216)71 857 000

National Agency for Electronic Certification (NAEC)
ance@certification.tn
www.certification.tn

For additional analytical, business and investment opportunities information,
please contact Global Investment & Business Center, USA
at (703) 370-8082. Fax: (703) 370-8083. E-mail: ibpusa3@gmail.com
Global Business and Investment Info Databank - www.ibpus.com

National Agency of Frequencies (NAF)
com@anf.tn
www.anf.tn

National Agency for Computer Security (NACS)
ansi@ansi.tn
www.ansi.tn

Tunisian Internet Agency (TIA)
com@ati.tn
www.ati.tn

Tunisie Télécom (TT)
info.entreprises@tunisietelecom.tn
www.tunisietelecom.tn

National Authority of Telecommunications (NAT)
contact@intt.tn
www.intt.tn

National Broadcasting Office (NBO):
Ont@telediffusion.net.tn
www.telediffusion.net.tn

Center for Studies and Research on Telecommunications (CSRT)
karim.wakil@cert.mincom.tn
www.cert.nat.tn

Ministry of Communication Technologies and Digital Economy
www.mincom.tn

SELECTED COMPANIES

Groupe WEVIOO
Technopark El Ghazela 2088 Tunis- Tunisie
Tél: 216 31 340 000
Fax: 216 70 721 163
contact@wevioo.com
www.wevioo.com
(It is an international consulting and IT services group in innovation, performance improvement and international development projects. Wevioo offers consulting solutions and specialized expertise to meet the challenges of strategic transformation and outsourcing).

VERMEG
Rue du Lac Neuchatel, Les Berges du Lac
1053 Tunis
Tél : 216 71 964 459
Fax : 216 71 963 878
info@vermeg.com
www.vermeg.com
(VERMEG is a private IT services company specializing in the development of innovative solutions for global securities markets, VERMEG also specializes in the

administration of funds and securities treatment favoring the standard practices of the international market).

ST2i (Société Tunisienne d'Informatique pour l'Ingénierie)
Résidence Sidi Mansour III Bloc A
1, Avenue du Dollar
Les Jardins du Lac - 1053 Tunis – Tunisie
Tél: 216 71 195 300   Fax: 216 71 195 301
st2i@st2i.com.tn
www.st2i.com.tn
(It is an integrator of IT and telecommunications solutions with high added value. ST2i offers its customers a support relationship for a successful realization of their projects, through a wide range of services covering the entire life cycle computer project).

Progress Engineering (PE)
Parc Technologique El Ghazala
BP 9 Cedex 2088 Tunisie
Tel: 216 71 85 63 60   Fax: 216 71 85 68 20
contact@progress.com.tn
www.progress.com.tn
(PE is an IT services company specializing in the study, consulting and computer development. Present on the IT services sector since 2000, the company has participated in the success of several IT projects across Tunisia and its customers in Europe).

CYNAPSYS
Park El Ghazala des technologies de communication
BP 105 Ariana, 2088 - TUNISIE
Tél. : 216 71 857 899
Fax : 216 71 858 794
info@cynapsys.de
www.cynapsys.de
(Founded in 2004, Cynapsys is a multidisciplinary DSC (Digital Service Company) with experience in the field of consulting and computer engineering, its main mission is to support its customers and partners in the development of efficient and innovative solutions. mainly oriented towards the sectors: E-gov, Telecom, Finance / Insurance, Industrial, publishers, services, NGOs, associations, DSC).

IBL EGINEERING
Route de Mateur Km3.5
Bizerte, Tunisie
Tél : 21672510011
Fax : 21672510033
contact@ibl-engineering.com
www.ibl-engineering.com
(IBL has set up a multidisciplinary consulting firm to support its clients throughout their electronic and IT projects, from feasibility studies to implementation, operation, maintenance and upgrading. IBL's staff is qualified to support all kind of customers through a wide range of services in information systems, web development, embedded software and electronic design).

MEDIANET
Avenue Hédi Nouira
Résidence Maya D1 Ennasr II, Tunis Tunisie
Tél : 216 71 827 484
Fax: 216 71 827 464
info@medianet.com.tn
www.medianet.com.tn
(Computer Services and Engineering Company (CSEC) active in the field of ICT,
operating in Tunisia and internationally, MEDIANET is a potential partner for the
implementation of personalized interactive web solutions).

Open Source Software Solutions Technology (O3STech)
129 Avenue de la Liberté
1002 Tunis Tunisie
Tél. : 216 71 703 485
Fax : 216 71 94 05 66
contact@o3stech.com
www.o3stech.com
(O3ST is an IT services company specializing in computer engineering, the development
of specific solutions, the development of e-business websites and the integration of
'Open Source' solutions adapted to the needs of customers according to their specific
projects).

SIGA – Système Informatique et Gestion Automatisée
(CSAM - Computer System and Automated Management)
Rue du Lac Malaren, Les Berges du Lac Tunis
Tél : 216 71 960 281
Fax : 216 71 960 336
contact@siga.com.tn
www.siga.com.tn
SIGA is a software engineering company was founded in 1996 to meet the growing
needs of organizations in the management of computer resources and use of advanced
technologies.

TSI (Tunisie Systèmes d'Information)
38, rue Kaboul
Ariana - Tunisie 2037
Tél : 216 71 827 745
Fax : 216 71 827 700
info@tsi.com.tn
www.tsi.com.tn
(TSI is a service company and computer engineering, whose mission is to design and
develop management applications by implementing the best technological solutions.
Since its inception, TSI has been designed to be a partner of choice for its customers,
especially for the realization of quality software products).

IDEE Informatique
35, rue Hédi Karray Centre Urbain Nord, 1082 – Tunis Tunisie
Tél : 216 71 230 011 Fax : 216 71 238 386
info@idee.com.tn
www.idee.com.tn

For additional analytical, business and investment opportunities information,
please contact Global Investment & Business Center, USA
at (703) 370-8082. Fax: (703) 370-8083. E-mail: ibpusa3@gmail.com
Global Business and Investment Info Databank - www.ibpus.com

(IDEE Informatique is a software publisher in Tunisia, covering all banking, post office, securities and social security coverage).

DIGINOV DIGITAL INNOVATION
Rue Yasser Arafat, Sahloul, Sousse 4054, Tunisie.
(+216) 73 82 00 24
(+216) 58 40 12 63
oessaddi@diginov.tech
www.diginov.tech
(DIGINOV helps its customers to improve their activities thanks to the high competence of its engineers, deep technology expertise and a complete package of services (web design, digital applications) DIGINOV adopts the emerging technologies dedicated "excellence" to exploit the latest technologies in order to provide customers with innovative business capabilities.

INTERNET SERVICE PROVIDERS (ISPs)

- TOPNET: **http://www.topnet.tn**
- GlobalNet: **www.gnet.tn**
- HEXABYTE: **www.hexabyte.tn**
- TUNET: **www.tunet.tn**
- OOREDOO: **www.ooredoo.tn**
- ORANGE Tunisia: **www.orange.tn**
- TUNISIE TELECOM: **www.tunisietelecom.tn**
  Lycamobile Tunisia: www.lycamobile.tn

USEFUL WEBSITES

- Official Journal of the Republic of Tunisia
  www.iort.gov.tn
- National Institute of Statistics
  www.ins.nat.tn
- Tunisian Union of Industry, Trade and Crafts
  www.utica.org.tn
- El Ghazala TECHNOPARK
  www.elgazalcom.nat.tn

TRADE FAIRS AND EXHIBITIONS

Events	Dates	Organisers
SITIC AFRICA 2018	10-12	Société Foire Internationale de Tunis (SFIT)

For additional analytical, business and investment opportunities information, please contact Global Investment & Business Center, USA at (703) 370-8082. Fax: (703) 370-8083. E-mail: ibpusa3@gmail.com
Global Business and Investment Info Databank - www.ibpus.com

International Exhibition of Information and Communication Technologies in Africa contact@siticafrica.com	April 2018 Tunis	www.fkram.com.tn
SIB IT International Exhibition of Computer Science, Office Automation and Information and Communication Technologies www.sib-exponet	November 2019 Tunis	SOGEFOIRES www.sogefoires.com
SIEL Expo International Exhibition of Electrical and Electronic Industries www.sielexpo.net	March 2019 Tunis	SOGEFOIRES www.sogefoires.com

USEFUK GOVERNMETN SITES

Tunisian Government: **www.ministeres.tn**

Tunisian Customs: **www.douane.gov.tn**

Central Bank of Tunisia: **www.bct.gov.tn**

Exports Promotion Center: **www.cepex.nat.tn**

Tunis Stock Exchange: **www.bvmt.com.tn**

Tunisian industry: **www.tunisieindustrie.nat.tn**

Invest in Tunisia: **www.investintunisia.tn**

Tunisia TradeNet: **www.tradenet.tn**

Webmanagercenter: **www.webmanagercenter.com**

Tunisia Web: **www.tunisie-web.org**

IMPORTANT LAWS AND REGULATIONS AFFECTING ICT SECTOR

DIGITAL ECONOMY LAW

Law n ° 2007-13 of February 19, 2007, relating to the establishment of the digital economy.

In the name of the people,

In the name of the people,

The Chamber of Deputies and the Chamber of Councilors having adopted,

The President of the Republic promulgates the law of orientation whose content follows:

Article 1. - The digital economy is one of the national priorities given its contribution to strengthening the competitiveness of the national economy and its positive impact on the various activities. For the purpose of this law, the term "digital economy" refers to the economy consisting of high value-added activities based on information and communication technologies.

The list of activities related to the digital economy is fixed by decree.

Article 2. - The State and the local authorities take care to promote this sector and to reinforce its place in the national economy notably by the contribution to:

the establishment of the necessary infrastructure,

the supply of training opportunities,

the promotion of scientific research,

the supervision of companies operating in the field of the digital economy to strengthen their place, promote their products and services and ensure the consolidation of the partnership between Tunisian companies to attract more foreign investment in this area.

Article 3. - The State, local authorities, institutions and public enterprises may, in the field of the digital economy, entrust one or more economic enterprises with the fulfillment of all or part of their activities or participation in the realization of economically important projects.

Article 4. - In the context of the public-private partnership in the digital economy, the agreements are concluded by negotiation with competition on the basis of the principles of equal treatment of participants and the transparency of procedures.

The state, local authorities, institutions and public enterprises can conclude partnership agreements through direct negotiation.

The rules and procedures for the conclusion of partnership agreements by negotiation with call for competition or by direct negotiation are laid down by decree.

Partnership agreements concluded through direct negotiation are approved by decree.

Article 5. - The use of direct negotiation to conclude partnership agreements is possible in the following cases:

projects that can only be carried out or operated by a specific service provider,

major national projects.

Article 6. - The conclusion of partnership agreements through competitive negotiation must follow clear and detailed procedures laid down in a specific regulation for each project.

Article 7. - The partnership agreement must provide in particular for:

the risk sharing arrangements between the different parties,

the obligations of the contractors;

the resources allocated by all parties to the project,

the deadlines for carrying out the project,

the terms and conditions of operation of the project,

the procedures for monitoring and monitoring by the public part of the execution of the agreement and in particular the achievement of the quality objectives,

conditions ensuring continuity of service in the event of termination upon the expiry of the period of validity of the agreement.

Article 8. - Partnership agreements may only be concluded with natural or legal persons capable of binding themselves and presenting the guarantees and references necessary for the proper performance of their obligations.

Article 9. - The State, the local authorities, the establishments and the public enterprises are obliged, before the conclusion of the partnership agreements, to proceed to the evaluation of the project object of the convention and to compare the various possible solutions for the realization the project and the financial and legal schemes that are appropriate for it.

Article 10. - The State, local authorities, institutions and public enterprises may participate in the financing of partnership projects related to the establishment of the digital economy in accordance with the legislation in force.

The agreements provided for in article 4 of this law set the conditions for this participation and the obligations of the intervening parties.

Article 11. - For projects carried out by small and medium-sized enterprises in the field of the digital economy during the first five years of their creation, the State may assume part of the wages paid, in respect of new recruits permanent staff of Tunisian nationality holding a higher education diploma issued at the end of schooling at least two years after the baccalaureate or an equivalent diploma, without this part exceeding 25% of the salary paid each recruit and within the limit of 250 dinars monthly for a period not exceeding 3 years.

Article 12. - The current procedures for industrial upgrading are applied to companies operating in the digital economy in order to adopt the methods and standards in force at the international level.

This law of orientation will be published in the Official Gazette of the Republic of Tunisia and executed as law of the State.

ELECTRONIC COMMERCE LAW

Law No. 2000-00083 of 9 August 2000 on Electronic Commerce and Commerce

width = "14" Chapter I: General Provisions

Official Gazette of the Republic of Tunisia No. 64 of August 11, 2000, pages 1887 to 1892

Tunisian law in free access

Article One . - This law lays down the general rules governing electronic commerce and commerce.

Electronic commerce and commerce shall be governed by the laws and regulations in force insofar as this Law does not derogate therefrom.

The written contract system applies to electronic contracts as to the expression of the will, their legal effect, their validity and their performance insofar as it is not derogated from by this Act.

Article 2 . - For the purposes of this Law:

Electronic exchanges: exchanges that take place using electronic documents.

Electronic commerce: the commercial operations that take place through electronic exchanges.

The electronic certificate : the electronic document secured by the electronic signature of the person who issued it and who certifies after verifying the veracity of its content.

The electronic certification service provider : any natural or legal person who issues, issues, manages certificates and provides other services associated with the electronic signature.

Encryption : the use of non-standard codes or signals allowing the conversion of information to be transmitted into incomprehensible signals to third parties or the use of codes and signals essential for the reading of information.

Signature creation device : a unique set of personal encryption elements or a set of equipment specifically configured for the creation of the electronic signature.

Signature verification device : a set of public encryption elements or a set of equipment enabling verification of the electronic signature.

Electronic means of payment : the means by which the holder can carry out remote direct payment transactions through public telecommunications networks.

Product : any natural, agricultural, artisanal or industrial service or product, material or immaterial.

Article 3 - The use of encryption in electronic commerce and commerce through public telecommunications networks is governed by the regulations in force in the field of telecommunications value-added services.

Chapter II: Electronic Document and Electronic Signature

Tunisian law in free access

Article 4 . - The preservation of the electronic document is equally authentic as the preservation of the written document.

The issuer undertakes to keep the electronic document in the form of the program. The recipient agrees to keep this document in the form of the receipt.

The electronic document is kept on an electronic medium allowing:

The consultation of its contents throughout the duration of its validity,

Its preservation in its final form so as to ensure the integrity of its contents,

Retention of information relating to its origin and destination and the date and place of its transmission or reception.

Article 5. - Each person wishing to affix his electronic signature on a document can create this signature by a reliable device whose technical characteristics will be fixed by order of the Minister of Telecommunications.

Article 6 . - Each person using an electronic signature device must:

Take the minimum precautions that will be set by the decree provided for in article 5 of this law, in order to avoid any illegitimate use of encryption elements or personal equipment related to his signature.

Inform the provider of electronic certification services of any improper use of his signature.

Ensure the veracity of all data that they have reported to the electronic certification service provider and to any person to whom they have asked to rely on their signature.

Article 7 . - In case of breach of the commitments provided for in article 6 of this law, the holder of the signature is responsible for the damage caused to others.

Chapter III: From the National Electronic Certification Agency

Tunisian law in free access

Article 8. - A non-administrative public enterprise is created with legal personality and financial autonomy, called national electronic certification agency and submitted in its relations with third parties to the commercial legislation. Its seat is fixed in Tunis.

Article 9 . - This company is in charge of the following missions:

The granting of the authorization to exercise the activity of electronic certification service provider throughout the territory of the Republic of Tunisia.

The compliance check by the electronic certification service provider of the provisions of this application and its application texts.

Setting the characteristics of the device for creating and verifying the signature.

The conclusion of mutual recognition agreements with foreign parties.

The issue, issue and retention of electronic certificates relating to public officials authorized to carry out electronic exchanges. These operations can be performed directly or through public electronic certification service providers.

Participation in research, training and study activities related to electronic commerce and commerce.

And in a general way, any other activity entrusted to it by the supervisory authority in relation to the field of its intervention.

The agency is subject to the supervision of the ministry in charge of the sector.

Article 10. - It may be allocated to the national electronic certification agency, by assignment, movable or immovable property of the State necessary for its operation. In the event of the dissolution of the enterprise, its assets return to the State which executes the obligations and the commitments contracted, in accordance with the legislation in force.

Chapter IV: Electronic Certification Services

Tunisian law in free access

Article 11. - Any natural or legal person wishing to perform the activities of electronic certification service provider must obtain prior authorization from the Tunisian Electronic Certification Agency.

The natural person or the legal representative of the legal person wishing to obtain authorization to carry on the activity of an electronic certification service provider must fulfill the following conditions:

to be of Tunisian nationality for at least five years,

to be domiciled in Tunisian territory,

Enjoy your civil and political rights and have no judicial record,

Have at least a master's degree or equivalent

Do not practice another professional activity.

Article 12. - The electronic certification service provider is responsible for issuing, issuing and retaining certificates in accordance with specifications that will be approved by decree and, where appropriate, its suspension or cancellation in accordance with the provisions of this Act.

These specifications include:

Costs of study and follow-up of certificate application files,

Deadlines for studying the files,

The material, financial and human resources that must be provided for the exercise of the activity,

Conditions ensuring interoperability of certification schemes and the interconnection of certificate registers,

The rules relating to the information pertaining to its services and the certificates issued and to be kept by the electronic certification service provider.

Article 13. - The electronic certification service provider shall use reliable means for issuing, issuing and retaining certificates and the means necessary to protect them from counterfeiting and forgery in accordance with the relevant specifications. by article 12 of this law.

Article 14 . - The electronic certification service provider shall keep an electronic register of certificates available to users, which is permanently accessible for electronic consultation of the information contained therein.

The certificate register contains, where applicable, the date of suspension or cancellation of the certificate.

The certificate register must be protected against unauthorized modification.

Article 15. - Electronic certification service providers and their agents must keep secret the information entrusted to them in carrying out their activities except those whose publication or communication has been authorized in writing or electronically by the holder of the certificate or in the cases provided for by the legislation in force.

Article 16. - In the case of a certificate application, the electronic certification service provider shall collect the personal information directly from the data subject or, with his written or electronic agreement, from third parties.

The electronic certification service provider is prohibited from collecting information not necessary for the issuance of the certificate.

The electronic certification service provider is prohibited from using, outside the framework of the certification activities, the information that he has collected to issue the certificate without having obtained the written or electronic agreement of the person concerned.

Article 17. - The electronic certification service provider issues certificates that comply with security and reliability requirements. The technical data relating to the certificate and its reliability will be fixed by order of the Ministry of Telecommunications.

This certificate includes:

The identity of the certificate holder,

The identity of the person who issued it and its electronic signature,

Verification elements of the signature of the certificate holder,

The period of validity of the certificate,

The fields of use of the certificate.

Article 18 . - The electronic certification service provider guarantees:

The accuracy of the certified information contained in the certificate at the date of issue,

The link between the certificate holder and his signature verification device,

The exclusive possession by the holder of the certificate of a signature creation device complying with the provisions of the order provided for in article 5 of this law and complementary to the verification device of the signature identified in the certificate on the date of his deliverance.

When the certificate is issued to a legal person the electronic certification service provider is required to verify in advance the identity and representational power of the natural person who appears.

Article 19. - The electronic certification service provider suspends the certificate immediately upon the request of the holder or when it appears that:

The certificate was issued on the basis of incorrect or falsified information,

The signature creation device has been violated,

The certificate has been fraudulently used,

The information in the certificate has changed.

The electronic certification service provider shall immediately inform the certificate holder of the suspension and its reason.

The suspension is lifted immediately when it is demonstrated the accuracy of the information contained in the certificate and its legitimate use.

The decision suspending the service provider 's certificate is enforceable against the certificate holder and the third parties from the date of its publication in the electronic register provided for in article 14 of this law.

Article 20. - The electronic certification service provider immediately cancels the certificate in the following cases:

At the request of the certificate holder,

When informed of the death of the natural person or the dissolution of the legal person holding the certificate,

Following the suspension, if in-depth examinations prove that the information is incorrect or falsified or not in conformity with reality or that the signature creation device has been infringed or the certificate has been used fraudulently.

The decision to cancel the certificate by the service provider shall be binding on the certificate holder and on third parties from the date of its publication in the electronic register provided for in Article 14 of this Law.

Article 21. - The certificate holder is solely responsible for the confidentiality and integrity of the signature creation device he uses and any use of this device is deemed to be his or her doing.

The certificate holder is required to notify the electronic certification service provider of any changes to the information contained in the certificate.

The holder of the suspended or canceled certificate can no longer use the personal encryption elements of the signature covered by this certificate and can not have these elements re-certified by another electronic certification service provider.

Article 22. The electronic certification service provider is liable for any prejudice suffered by any person who, in good faith, relies on the guarantees provided for in article 18 of this law.

The electronic certification service provider is liable for any loss suffered by any person as a result of the non-suspension or non-cancellation of a certificate in accordance with sections 19 and 20 of this Act.

The electronic certification service provider is not liable for damages resulting from non-compliance with the conditions of use of the certificate or the conditions for the creation of the electronic signature by the certificate holder.

Article 23. Certificates issued by an electronic certification service provider established in a foreign country have the same value as those issued by an electronic certification service provider established in Tunisia, if that organization is recognized under an agreement Mutual Recognition Agreement concluded by the National Electronic Certification Agency.

Article 24. - The electronic certification service provider wishing to terminate its activity is required to inform the national electronic certification agency, at least 3 months before the date of termination.

The electronic certification service provider may transfer to any other supplier all or part of its activities under the following conditions:

Inform holders of valid certificates of their willingness to transfer the certificates to another supplier at least one month before the proposed transfer,

Specify the identity of the electronic certification service provider to whom the certificates will be transferred,

Inform the holders of the certificates of the possibility of refusing the proposed transfer as well as the deadlines and methods of refusal. Certificates are canceled if, at the end of this period, their holders express in writing or by electronic means their refusal.

In the event of the death, bankruptcy, dissolution or liquidation of the electronic certification service provider, the heirs, guardian or liquidator are subject to the provisions of the second paragraph of this article within a period not exceeding three months.

In all cases of cessation of activity, the personal data remaining at the supplier must be destroyed, in the presence of a representative of the national electronic certification agency.

Chapter V: Electronic Business Transactions

Tunisian law in free access

Article 25. - Before the conclusion of the contract, the seller is required during electronic business transactions to provide the consumer with clear and understandable information as follows:

The identity, address and telephone of the seller or service provider,

A complete description of the various stages of execution of the transaction,

The nature, characteristics and price of the product,

The cost of delivery, the product insurance rates and taxes required,

The duration of the offer of the product at fixed prices,

The conditions of commercial guarantees and after-sales service,

The terms and procedures for payment and, if applicable, the proposed credit conditions,

The terms and delivery times, the performance of the contract and the results of the non-fulfillment of the commitments.

The possibility of withdrawal and its delay,

The confirmation mode of the order,

The method of return of the product, exchange or refund,

The cost of using telecommunications facilities when they are calculated on a basis other than the rates in force,

Conditions of termination of the contract when it is concluded for an indefinite period or for a duration of more than one year,

The minimum duration of the contract, for contracts for the long-term or periodic supply of a product or service.

This information must be provided electronically and made available to the consumer for consultation at all stages of the transaction.

Article 26 . - The seller is prohibited from delivering a product not ordered by the consumer when it is accompanied by a request for payment.

In case of delivery of a product not ordered by the consumer, it can not be solicited for the payment of its price or the cost of its delivery.

Article 27 . - Before the conclusion of the contract, the seller must allow the consumer to definitively summarize all his choices, to confirm the order or to modify it according to his will and to consult the electronic certificate relating to his signature.

Article 28. - Unless otherwise agreed by the parties, the contract is concluded at the address of the seller and at the date of acceptance of the order by the latter by an electronic document signed and sent to the consumer.

Article 29 . - The seller must provide the consumer, at his request, and within 10 days of the conclusion of the contract, a written or electronic document containing all the data relating to the sales transaction.

Article 30. - Subject to the provisions of article 25 of this law, the consumer can retract within 10 working days, common:

from the date of receipt by the consumer, for the goods,

from the date of conclusion of the contract, for services.

The notification of the retraction is made by any means previously provided in the contract.

In this case, the seller is obliged to refund the amount paid to the consumer within 10 working days from the date of return of the goods or the renunciation of the service.

The consumer bears the cost of returning the goods.

Article 31. - Notwithstanding the repair of the damage for the benefit of the consumer, the latter can return the product in the state if it is not in conformity with the order or if the seller has not respected the delivery time and this, in a period of 10 working days from the date of delivery.

In this case, the seller must refund the amount paid and the related expenses to the consumer within 10 working days from the date of return of the product.

Article 32. - Subject to the provisions of article 30 of this law and except for apparent or hidden defects, the consumer can not retract in the following cases:

When the consumer requests delivery of the service before the expiry of the withdrawal period and the seller provides it to him,

If the consumer receives products made up with personalized characteristics or products that can not be re-dispatched or are likely to be damaged or expired due to the expiry of the validity period,

When the consumer loosens audio or video recordings or computer software delivered or downloaded,

The purchase of newspapers and magazines.

Article 33. - When the purchase transaction is fully or partially covered by a credit granted to the consumer by the seller or by a third party on the basis of a contract concluded between the seller and the third party, the withdrawal of the consumer results in the termination , without penalty, of the credit agreement.

Article 34 . - With the exception of cases of misuse, the seller shall bear, in cases of test sale, the risks to which the product is exposed until the product's trial period has been completed. Any exemption from liability contrary to the provisions of this article shall be considered null and void.

Article 35. - In the event of unavailability of the product or service ordered, the seller must inform the consumer within a maximum of 24 hours before the delivery date stipulated in the contract and refund the full amount paid to the holder.

Except in case of force majeure, the contract is terminated if the seller violates its commitments and the consumer recovers the sums paid without prejudice to damages.

Article 36. - The seller must prove the existence of prior information, confirmation of information, compliance with deadlines and the consent of the consumer. Any agreement to the contrary is considered null and void.

Article 37. - Payment transactions relating to exchanges and electronic commerce are subject to the laws and regulations in force.

The holder of the electronic means of payment has the obligation to notify the issuer of the loss or theft of this means or of the instruments that allow its use, as well as any fraudulent use relating thereto.

The issuer of an electronic means of payment must fix the appropriate means for this notification in the contract concluded with its holder.

Notwithstanding cases of fraud, the holder of the electronic means of payment:

assumes, until notification to the issuer, the consequences of the loss or theft of the means of payment or its fraudulent use by a third party,

is released from any liability for the use of the electronic means of payment after notification to the issuer.

The use of the electronic means of payment, without presentation of the means and identification by electronic means, does not engage its holder.

Chapter VI: Protection of personal data

Tunisian law in free access

Note Article 38. - The certification service provider may process personal data only after agreement with the certificate holder concerned.

Electronic consent may be retained if the provider guarantees that:

The user has been informed of his right to withdraw his consent at any time,

The parties who use the personal data may be identified,

Proof of consent is retained and can not be changed.

Article 39. - Except with the consent of the certificate holder, the electronic certification service provider or one of its agents may collect information relating to the certificate holder only to the extent that such information * is necessary for the conclusion of the contract, the setting of its content, its execution and the preparation and issuance of invoices.

The data collected in accordance with the first paragraph of this Article may be used by the supplier or a third party for purposes other than those mentioned above, only to the extent that the certificate holder has been informed and not not opposed.

Article 40. - Users of personal data collected in accordance with Article 39 of this Law shall not send electronic documents to the holder of a certificate who expressly refuses to receive them.

The holder of a certificate must notify his opposition to the national electronic certification agency by registered letter with acknowledgment of receipt.

This notification is considered a legal presumption of the knowledge of this opposition by all suppliers and third parties.

Note Article 41.- Before any processing of personal data, the electronic certification service provider must inform the certificate holder, by a special notification, of the procedures it applies in the field of protection of personal data. These procedures must enable the certificate holder to obtain automatic and simplified information about the content of the data.

These procedures must determine the identity of the controller on the processing, the nature of the data, the purposes of the processing, the categories and locations of processing and, where appropriate, any information necessary to ensure secure data processing.

Note Article 42.- The holder of the certificate may, at any time, by request, signed in writing or electronically access the personal information concerning him and modify them. The right of access and modification extends to all personal data relating to the certificate holder.

The supplier must make available to the holder of the certificate the necessary technical means enabling him to send his signed request for the modification of the information or its deletion by electronic means.

For additional analytical, business and investment opportunities information,
please contact Global Investment & Business Center, USA
at (703) 370-8082. Fax: (703) 370-8083. E-mail: ibpusa3@gmail.com
Global Business and Investment Info Databank - www.ibpus.com

COMPUTER SECURITY LAW

CHAPTER ONE - FROM THE NATIONAL AGENCY FOR COMPUTER SECURITY

First article. - The purpose of this Act is to organize the field of computer security and to establish the general rules for the protection of computer systems and networks.

Article 2. - A non-administrative public enterprise with legal personality and financial autonomy called "National Agency of Information Security" is created. It is subject in its relations with third parties to the commercial legislation and its head office is fixed in Tunis.

The agency is subject to the supervision of the ministry in charge of communication technologies.

The administrative and financial organization and the operating procedures of the agency are laid down by decree.

Article 3. - The national computer security agency carries out a general control of computer systems and networks belonging to various public and private bodies and is responsible for the following tasks:

ensure the implementation of national guidelines and the general strategy for the security of computer systems and networks,

monitor the implementation of computer security plans and programs in the public sector, with the exception of specific applications for defense and national security, and ensure coordination among stakeholders in this area,

ensure the technological watch in the field of computer security,

to establish specific standards for computer security and to prepare technical guides in the subject and to publish them,

work to encourage the development of national solutions in the field of information security and to promote them in accordance with the priorities and programs to be set by the Agency,

participate in the consolidation of training and retraining in the field of computer security,

ensure the implementation of regulations relating to the obligation of the periodic audit of the security of computer systems and networks.

The supervisory authority may entrust the agency with any other activity related to the field of its intervention.

Article 4. - In the event of the dissolution of the agency, its property will return to the State which executes its obligations and commitments in accordance with the legislation in force.

CHAPTER II - MANDATORY AUDIT

Article 5. - Computer systems and networks belonging to various public bodies are subject to a system of mandatory and periodic computer security audit, except for computer systems and networks belonging to the Ministries of National Defense and the Ministry of Defense. and local development.

Also subject to the periodic mandatory audit of computer security, the computer systems and networks of organizations that will be fixed by decree.

The criteria relating to the nature of the audit, its frequency and the procedures for monitoring the application of the recommendations contained in the audit report are set by decree.

Article 6. - In the event that the bodies provided for in Article 5 of this Law do not carry out the periodic mandatory audit, the National Agency for Computer Security shall notify the organization concerned, which shall carry out the audit in a period not exceeding one month from the date of this warning.

At the end of this period without result, the agency is required to appoint, at the expense of the offending body, an expert who will be responsible for the aforementioned audit.

Article 7. - Subject to the exceptions provided for in articles 3 and 5 of this law, public and private bodies must allow the national computer security agency and the experts who will be in charge of the audit operation to consult all documents and records related to computer security in order to fulfill their missions.

CHAPTER III - AUDITORS

Article 8. - The audit operation is carried out by experts, natural or legal persons, previously certified by the national computer security agency.

The conditions and the procedures for certification of these experts are laid down by decree.

Article 9. - It is forbidden for the agents of the national computer security agency and the experts in charge of the audit operations to divulge any information of which they became aware during the exercise of their missions.

Any person who discloses, participates or incites to the disclosure of this information is liable to the penalties provided for in Article 254 of the Penal Code .

CHAPTER IV - VARIOUS PROVISIONS

Article 10. - Any operator of a computer system or network, whether public or private, shall immediately inform the national computer security agency of any attacks, intrusions or other disturbances that may hinder the operation of a computer. other computer system or network, to enable it to take the necessary measures to deal with it.

The operator is required to comply with the measures adopted by the national computer

For additional analytical, business and investment opportunities information,
please contact Global Investment & Business Center, USA
at (703) 370-8082. Fax: (703) 370-8083. E-mail: ibpusa3@gmail.com
Global Business and Investment Info Databank - www.ibpus.com

security agency to put an end to these disturbances.

Article 11. - In the cases provided for in the previous article and in order to protect computer systems and networks, the national computer security agency may propose the isolation of the computer system or the network concerned until these disturbances cease. The isolation is pronounced by decision of the minister in charge of the technologies of the communication.

With regard to the exceptions provided for in Article 3 of this Law, adequate procedures shall be agreed upon in coordination with the Ministers of National Defense and the Interior and Local Development.

This law will be published in the Official Gazette of the Republic of Tunisia and executed as the law of the State.

CODE OF TELECOMMUNICATIONS

CHAPTER I - GENERAL PROVISIONS

SECTION ONE. - TERMINOLOGY

Article One -

The purpose of this Code is to organize the telecommunications sector.

This organization includes:

the installation and operation of telecommunications networks,

the supply of Note Basic services Universal services telecommunications,

the provision of telecommunications services,

the provision of television broadcasting services,

management of rare telecommunications resources.

Article 2:

For the purposes of this Code, the term

Telecommunications means any method of transmitting, broadcasting or receiving signals by means of metallic, optical or radio medium;

Radio Frequencies : the frequencies of electromagnetic waves used in telecommunications in accordance with the international rules in force;

Rare resources : radio frequencies, numbering and addressing;

Telecommunication network : all equipment and systems providing telecommunications;

Public telecommunications network: the telecommunications network open to the public;

Private telecommunications network: a telecommunications network reserved for private use or use by a closed group of users for particular purposes in the common interest;

Telecommunications network operator : any legal entity holding a Note concession Licence for the operation of a public telecommunications network;

Concession Licence: lien on a corporation under an agreement for the installation and operation of a public telecommunications network;

Interconnection : connection of two or more public telecommunications networks;

Telecommunications Service : any service providing telecommunications between two or more users;

Note Basic services Universal servicestelecommunications : minimum telecommunications services to be provided to the public on the basis of technological developments in the field;

Television broadcasting services: telecommunications services providing transmission and broadcasting of radio and television programs by means of radio frequencies;

Telecommunication value-added services: services offered to the public through public telecommunications networks by means of computer systems that allow access to data relating to specific areas for the purpose of consulting, consulting and exchanging them;

Telecommunications service provider : any natural or legal person who meets the legal and regulatory requirements and provides the telecommunications services;

Encryption : the use of non-standard codes or signals that allow the conversion of information that is to be transmitted into unintelligible signals by third parties, or the use of codes and signals without which information can not be read;

Telecommunications terminal equipment : any equipment that can be connected to the termination of a telecommunications network for the purpose of providing telecommunications services to the public;

Radio equipment : any telecommunications equipment using radio frequencies;

Homologation : all expert and verification operations carried out by an accredited body to certify that the prototype of telecommunications equipment and systems complies with the regulations and technical specifications in force.

Note Independent private network : private network borrowing the public domain or a third private property.

Internal Private Network : A private network that does not borrow from the public domain or third private property.

Switching equipment: Equipment that receives the traffic and routes it to the recipient.

Local Loop : The segment of the wired or wireless network connecting the terminal equipment to the switching equipment to which the subscribers are connected.

Access Network: A segment of the public telecommunications network composed of the local loop and the switching equipment to which the subscribers are connected.

Access network operator : Any legal entity holding a license within the meaning of Article 31a of this Code for the installation and operation of an access network.

Unbundling Local Loop : A service provided by a public telecommunications network operator to another operator to allow access to all elements of the local loop of the first operator to provide the service directly to subscribers of the local loop. second operator.

Physical co-location : Service provided by a public telecommunications network operator that consists of making its buildings and spaces available to other operators for the purpose of installing and operating their equipment.

Common use of the infrastructure : A service provided by a public telecommunications network operator which consists in responding to the requests of other operators for the operation of the channels, pylons, cells and high points at its disposal.

SECTION 2. - RIGHT TO TELECOMMUNICATIONS

Article 3 :

Everyone has the right to benefit from telecommunications services. This right consists of:

access to Note Basic services Universal services telecommunications throughout the territory of the Republic of Tunisia;

the benefit of other telecommunications services according to the coverage area of each service;

freedom of choice of the provider of telecommunications services, depending on the coverage area of each service;

equal access to telecommunications services;

access to basic information on the conditions for the provision of telecommunications services and their pricing

Article 4 :

Any person benefiting from telecommunications services is required to comply with the regulations in force relating to the connection to public telecommunications networks.

CHAPTER 2 - TELECOMMUNICATIONS SERVICES

SECTION ONE. - PROVISION OF TELECOMMUNICATIONS SERVICES

Article 5 -

The provision of telecommunications services is subject to the prior authorization of the Minister of Telecommunications. The terms and conditions for the granting of this

For additional analytical, business and investment opportunities information,
please contact Global Investment & Business Center, USA
at (703) 370-8082. Fax: (703) 370-8083. E-mail: ibpusa3@gmail.com
Global Business and Investment Info Databank - www.ibpus.com

authorization are laid down in a decree that sets out, in particular, the conditions for submitting the authorization application and the deadline for response from the Ministry of Telecommunications, as well as the reasons for the refusal decision.

Articthe 6 (new) Note -

The telecommunications services are provided in accordance with specifications, approved by order of the Minister in charge of telecommunications, and obligatorily stipulating the general conditions of exploitation.

The provisions of Article 5 of this Code and paragraph 1 of this Article shall not apply to basic telecommunications services, television broadcasting services and telecommunications value-added services, and any other telecommunications service to be fixed by decree.

The provision of these services is governed by the provisions of Articles 10 ,12 and 91 of this Code.

The provisions of Article 5 of this Code do not apply to universal telecommunications services, television broadcasting services and any other telecommunications service to be fixed by decree. The provision of these services is governed by the provisions of Articles 10 , 12 and 91 of this Code.

Article 7 -

The authorization is granted to the provider of telecommunications services on a personal basis and can only be transferred to third parties after obtaining the agreement of the Minister of Telecommunications.

Article 8 -

Subject to the provisions of Article 5 of this Code, the provider of telecommunications services shall fulfill the following conditions:

for the natural person, to be of Tunisian nationality;

for the legal person, to be constituted in accordance with the Tunisian legislation.

Article 9 -

The conditions and procedures for the use of encryption facilities or services through public telecommunications networks and the exercise of related activities shall be established by decree.

Article 10 (new) Note -

The provision of value-added services in telecommunications and other telecommunications services, as determined by the decree provided for in Article 6 of this Code, shall be subject to a prior declaration to be filed with the Ministry of Telecommunications before the opening of the service.

This declaration must provide the following particulars:

the type of service offered, the terms and conditions of access to the service;

the rates that will be applied to the services;

The list of telecommunication value-added services as well as the conditions for exercising the activity of provider of these services will be set in accordance with specifications, approved by order of the Minister of Telecommunications.

The provision of the services fixed by the decree provided for in Article 6 of this code, is subject to specifications, approved by order of the minister in charge of telecommunications

SECTION 2. - PROVISION OF SERVICESNOTE BASIC SERVICES UNIVERSAL SERVICES TELECOMMUNICATIONS

Article 11 -

Subject to the provisions of Article 3 of this Code, the supply ofBasic services Universal services telecommunications is subject to the following conditions:

provide contact points open on a regular basis throughout the territory of the Republic of Tunisia;

guarantee equal access of all users to these services;

promote these services in terms of technical, economic and social development and the needs of users;

The list of these services is fixed by order of the Minister in charge of Telecommunications, after opinion of the National Instance of Telecommunications.

This list must include minimum telephone services, the routing of emergency calls, the provision of intelligence services and the directory of subscribers in printed or electronic form.

Article 12 -

Any operator of a telecommunications network may be responsible for ensuring theBasic services Universal servicestelecommunications. The conditions for the provision of services are laid down in the agreement provided for in Article 19 of this Code.

Article 13 -

Any operator of a telecommunications network responsible for providing theBasic services Universal services telecommunications is required to provide free emergency calls.

Article 14 -

Any operator of a telecommunications network responsible for providing theUniversal services Telecommunications is required to make available to the public a directory in printed or electronic form, allowing access to:

information relating to the names, telephone numbers and addresses of subscribers to Basic services Universal services telecommunications offered by public telecommunications networks, with the exception of subscribers who expressly refuse the publication of such information;

numbers and useful addresses relating to services of general interest.

Article 15 -

The operators entrusted with the basic telecommunications services shall be obliged to exchange the lists of their subscribers with these services, with the exception of the lists of subscribers who expressly refuse the publication of information concerning them.

Article 16 -

Any telecommunications network operator shall provide a subscription to telecommunications services to any person who requests it. The owner of a building or his agent can not oppose the installation of the telecommunications lines in accordance with the request of the tenant.

Article 17 -

The maximum rates applied to basic telecommunications services are subject to approval, by order of the Minister of Telecommunications.

In return, the State may award compensation to the operators concerned.

CHAPTER 3 - TELECOMMUNICATIONS NETWORKS

SECTION ONE. - INSTALLATION AND OPERATION OF NETWORKS

Article 18 -

The State may award Notes concessions licensing for the installation and operation of public telecommunications networks to public or private companies selected in accordance with the provisions of Article 20 of this Code.

Article 19 -

Any Note concession Licenceis granted by agreement concluded between the State, as licensor on the one hand represented by the Minister in charge of telecommunications, and the operator of the telecommunications network on the other, as a concessionaire, and, after consulting the competent bodies.

The concession Licence concession is approved by decree.

Article 20 -

The candidate is selected after competitive bidding by open or restricted invitation to tender, preceded by a pre-selection stage.

Article 21 -

The installer and operator of telecommunications networks must be a legal entity incorporated in accordance with Tunisian legislation.

Article 22 -

The concession Licenceis awarded for a period not exceeding fifteen (15) years, with the possibility of extension. This period is fixed in the agreement provided for in Article 19 of this Code.

Article 23 -

The concession Licenceis granted in a personal capacity and does not confer on the holder any exclusive right. It can only be transferred to a third party after the approval of the Minister of Telecommunications, after consultation with the competent bodies.

The concession Licence is transferred under an agreement approved by decree.

Article 24 -

The attribution of the concession Licence is subject to the payment of a fee, in accordance with the conditions set out in the concession agreement.

Article 25 -

The Convention concession Licence specifies in particular:

the installation conditions of the network;

the conditions for providing network-related services;

the general conditions of interconnection;

the human and material resources, as well as the financial guarantees to be presented by the candidates;

the amount and terms of payment of the fee provided for in Article 24 of this Code;

the amount and terms of payment of the fee for the exploitation of scarce resources allocated;

the methods for determining the rates applicable to customers, as well as the modalities for adjusting and revising these rates;

the procedures for controlling the accounting specific to the concession Licence ;

the conditions and methods of awarding the indemnity provided for in Article 29 of this Code;

the conditions and arrangements guaranteeing the continuity of the supply of services, in the event of non-compliance by the concessionaire with his obligations, or in the event of the end of the concession Licence ;

the conditions for access to high points in the public domain, if applicable;

For additional analytical, business and investment opportunities information,
please contact Global Investment & Business Center, USA
at (703) 370-8082. Fax: (703) 370-8083. E-mail: ibpusa3@gmail.com
Global Business and Investment Info Databank - www.ibpus.com

Note the geographical area which will be covered by the service as well as the planning necessary for its realization.

Article 26 -

The holder of the concession Licence is obliged to:

Note make available to the Ministry of Telecommunications information on the technical, operational, financial and accounting aspects of each network and service; Make available to the Ministry of Telecommunications and the National Telecommunications Authority information on the technical, operational, financial and accounting aspects of each network and service in accordance with the methods established by the Mechanism;

submit to the National Telecommunications Authority for approval, a model of the service contract to be concluded with the customers as well as all the agreements that will be concluded with the suppliers of telecommunications services;

undertake to comply with the conditions of secrecy and neutrality with regard to the signals carried;

respect the conventions and international treaties approved by the Tunisian State;

to commit to the application of technical standards for networks and the provision of telecommunications services;

participate in training and scientific research programs related to the telecommunications sector;

meet the requirements of national defense and public safety;

send free emergency calls.

Jurisite Article 26 bis- Note

Operators of public telecommunications networks and access networks undertake to maintain an analytical accounting system making it possible to distinguish between each network and each service and to refrain from any anti-competitive practice including cross-subsidy operations.

The general conditions of operation of public telecommunications networks and access networks are set by decree.

Article 27 -

The concessionaire is exempted from the authorization provided for in Article 5 of this Code when offering the telecommunications services linked to the network and defined in theconcession Licence.

Article 28 -

During the installation of the network, the concessionaire may use the infrastructure belonging to any telecommunication network operator or to a public service.

The concession Licence does not relieve the concessionaire of the respect of the necessary procedures for the installation of the elements of the network and in particular those relating to the crossing of the network through the public way, as well as to the realization of the constructions and their modification.

Article 28 bis Note -

The National Office of Broadcasting may lease to operators of public telecommunications networks the excess capacity available to it on its network after having exploited the resources needed for his needs.

Article 29 -

The Ministry of Telecommunications may revise certain provisions of the concession Licenceduring its period of validity, if this amendment is necessary to safeguard the general interest and the requirements of national defense and public security.

If it results from the revision of the concession Licencea reduction in the rights granted, the concessionaire will receive compensation proportional to the loss suffered.

The concession defines the conditions and the modalities of attribution of this indemnity.

Article 30 -

Every public telecommunications network operator shall provide its customers with a directory in printed or electronic form, enabling them to offer:

information relating to the names, telephone numbers and addresses of network subscribers with the exception

of subscribers who expressly refuse the publication of this information;

telephone numbers and useful addresses relating to services of general interest.

Article 31 -

The installation and operation of private networks Note telecommunications independentare subject to prior authorization by the Minister of Telecommunications, after consulting the Ministers of National Defense and the Interior and the National Telecommunications Authority.

This authorization does not relieve the holder of the respect of the necessary procedures for the installation of the elements of the network and in particular those relating to the passage of the network through the public road and to the realization of the constructions and to their modification.

This authorization is subject to payment of a fee set by order of the Minister of Telecommunications, after consulting the National Telecommunications Authority.

The general conditions of installation and operation of private telecommunications networks are set by decree.

Note The installation and operation of internal private networks are not subject to authorization.

Jurisite Article 31 bis - Note

The installation and operation of access networks are subject to a license issued by order of the Minister of Telecommunications after appeal to competition.

The rules and the tendering procedures are laid down by decree.

The granting of the license is subject to the payment of a fee in accordance with the conditions defined in the license.

Article 32 -

Are subject to prior approval, telecommunications terminal equipment imported or manufactured in Tunisia and intended for marketing or public use, and radio terminal equipment, whether or not intended to be connected to the public telecommunications network.

The terms and conditions of this approval are set by decree.

Article 33 -

Radio equipment consisting of devices of low power and limited range are not subject to the authorization provided for in Article 31 of this Code.

The maximum power and the limit of the range of these devices are fixed by decree of the Minister in charge of telecommunications after opinion of the National Frequency Agency envisaged in Article 47 of this code.

Article 34 -

Are exempted from the application of the provisions of this chapter, the telecommunications networks belonging to the State and installed for the needs of the national defense and the public safety.

SECTION 2. - INTERCONNECTION

Article 35 -

Any operator of public telecommunications networks must respond to requests for interconnection expressed by the holders of the Note concessions licensingissued in accordance with the provisions of Article 19 of this Code. The operator can not refuse any request for interconnection, as long as it is technically feasible considering the needs of the applicant on the one hand and the possibilities of the operator to satisfy them on the other hand. If this is not possible, the applicant must propose alternative solutions, after consulting the National Telecommunications Authority.

Article 36 -

The interconnection is the subject of an agreement between the two contracting parties. This agreement defines the technical and financial conditions of the interconnection.

Article 37 -

The terms and conditions of interconnection and the method of determining rates are set by decree.

Article 38 -

The operator of a public telecommunications network is required to publish the technical interconnection offer and its tariffs, after consulting the National Telecommunications Authority.

Jurisite Article 38 bis - Note

Operators of public telecommunications networks are required to allow other operators of public networks and access operators to exploit components and resources of their networks related to local loop unbundling, physical collocation and common use of the infrastructure.

The convention provided for in Article 36of this code sets the technical and financial conditions for the exploitation of the components and resources of these networks, failing which, the National Telecommunication Authority, at the request of one of the parties, makes a final decision concerning the aspects relating to the technical and financial conditions for the operation of the components and resources of these networks.

The technical and tariff offer for the interconnection provided for in Article 38 of this Code must include the technical and financial conditions for access to the components and resources of the network.

The general conditions of access to resources and network components are set by the decree provided for by

SECTION 3 - NUMBERING AND ADDRESSING

Article 39 -

The ministry in charge of telecommunications elaborates the national plan of numbering and addressing. This plan defines the conditions for assigning, distributing and assigning numbering and addressing.

The national numbering and addressing plan is approved by order of the Minister in charge of telecommunications after opinion of the National Instance of Telecommunications.

Article 40 -

The National Telecommunication Authority manages the national numbering and addressing plan, so as to cover the needs of network operators and service providers, as well as the easy and fair access of users to different telecommunications networks and services.

Article 41 -

The allocation of numbers and addresses is subject to a fee set by order of the Minister of Telecommunications, after consultation with the National Telecommunications Authority.

Article 41 bis Note -

Article 42 -

In case of availability of the technical means, the network operators must allow their subscribers, if they request it, to keep their numbers and addresses, in case of change of operator.

Note National Instance of Telecommunications fixes the conditions and the methods of activation of the conservation of the numbers.

SECTION 4. - EASEMENTS

Item Parte 43 -

In case of necessity, operators of public telecommunications networks benefit from easements' instituted after the declaration of the public nature of the works decided in accordance with the legislation in force, and this, for:

the installation, operation and maintenance of connection lines and equipment of public telecommunications networks in the public domain of the State and in the public road domain of the State;

the installation, operation and maintenance of connection lines and equipment of public telecommunications networks in the private domain;

the installation, operation, maintenance and protection of radio equipment against obstacles, electromagnetic disturbances and other forms of interference.

The methods of application of the provisions of this Article are fixed by decree.

Article 44 -

Where the easements referred to in Article 43 of this Code entail the removal or modification of buildings, and failing an amicable agreement with their owners or with one of them, the said buildings may be expropriated in accordance with the legislation in force.

After bringing these buildings into compliance with the requirements of this code and the texts adopted for its application, the network operator may proceed with the resale of the expropriated buildings, at the expense of the purchasers to respect the modifications made and to keep the easements encumbering the building.

The former owners of the expropriated buildings have the right to exercise a priority right to the purchase within a period of three (3) months, as from the date of notification by notary bailiff of the intention of the network operator to sell these buildings, for former owners to comply with the modifications introduced on these buildings and to retain the easements provided for in Article 43 of this Code.

Article 45 -

Where the easements referred to in Article 43 of this Code result in damage to the owners of the property or works, they shall be entitled to compensation from their dependents.

The claim for compensation must, under pain of forfeiture, be notified to the operator of the network concerned and to the Minister in charge of telecommunications by registered letter or by reliable electronic document with acknowledgment of receipt, within a period of six months from the date of occurrence of the damage.

In the event of disagreement between the two parties, the dispute relating to compensation is brought before the competent court.

CHAPTER 4 - RADIOCOMMUNICATIONS AND RADIO FREQUENCIES

Article 46 -

The radio frequencies belong to the public domain of the State, and their use is subjected to the authorization of the National Agency of the Frequencies, envisaged in Article 47 of the present code, in accordance with a national plan of the frequencies radio.

The national radio frequency plan is approved by order of the Minister of Telecommunications.

Item Parte 47 -

A non-administrative public enterprise is established with legal personality and financial autonomy called the National Agency of Frequencies. It is subject, in its relations with third parties, to the commercial legislation and its head office is fixed in Tunis.

Article 48 -

The National Agency of Frequencies ensures the following missions:

development of the national radio frequency plan, in coordination with the relevant bodies;

radio frequency management in coordination with the relevant bodies;

the control of the technical conditions of radio equipment and the protection of the use of radio frequencies;

the control of the use of frequencies in accordance with the authorizations granted and the records of the frequency register;

to ensure the application of international conventions and treaties in the field of radiocommunications;

registration of radio frequencies with the competent international bodies;

ensure the protection of national interests in the field of use of registered radio frequencies and orbital positions reserved for Tunisia;

the contribution to research, training and studies related to radiocommunications, and in general any other activity for which it may be charged by the supervisory authority, in relation to the field of its intervention.

It is subject to the supervision of the Ministry of Telecommunications.

Article 49 -

The National Agency of Frequencies may be allocated, by assignment, public movable or immovable property necessary for the execution of its missions. In the event of the dissolution of the agency, its assets return to the State which executes the obligations and the commitments contracted by it, in accordance with the legislation in force.

Article 50 -

The radio frequencies are allocated by the National Frequencies Agency, in accordance with the national plan of the radio frequencies, after opinion of the Ministers in charge of the national defense and the interior.

However, the Ministers responsible for national defense and the interior, may establish and use radio equipment in accordance with the national radio frequency plan, subject to notify, as soon as possible, the National Agency of Frequencies, and this , to ensure frequency coordination.

Article 51 -

The allocation of radio frequencies is subject to the payment of a fee fixed by order of the Minister of Telecommunications.

Article 52 -

Notwithstanding the radio equipment intended to be connected to the public telecommunications networks and the equipment envisaged in Article 33 of the present code, are subjected to the approval of the National Frequencies Agency, after opinion of the Ministers in charge of the defense and the interior, the manufacture, import, installation and operation of telecommunications and broadcasting equipment using radio frequencies. This approval sets the frequencies used, the power of the equipment and the extent of their coverage.

Are subject to the same procedures, any transfer of such equipment from one place to another, any modification to any of their elements and any destruction of such equipment.

Article 53 -

In order to ensure a better propagation of radio waves, it may be made, where appropriate, to delimit, in the urban development plans of a specific perimeter forming part of the public or private domain, for the purpose set the height limits for buildings and plantations established within this perimeter and required by the specificities of wave propagation.

Article 54 -

Any owner or user of radio equipment installed at any point in Tunisia and generating or propagating disturbances impeding the operation of the centers of the telecommunications networks shall comply with the provisions which shall be indicated to him by the Minister responsible telecommunications, with a view to curbing the interference. In any case, it must be open to investigation by sworn officials in charge of control.

Article 55 -

The operation of private radio equipment shall not interfere with the operation of other radio equipment. In case of inconvenience, it is the responsibility of the Minister in charge of telecommunications to prescribe all the technical provisions which he will judge useful.

Article 56 -

The operator of private radio equipment shall not be allowed to deal with foreigners, be they State, enterprise or individuals, in the field of telecommunications, except under the control and with the approval of the Minister in charge of telecommunications, after consulting the Ministers in charge of national defense and the interior.

Article 57 -

Radio equipment of any kind may be provisionally seized, without compensation until the lifting of the reasons for the seizure, by decision of the Minister of Telecommunications, on the proposal of the Minister of National Defense of such equipment or the Minister of Telecommunications. the interior, in any case where the use of such equipment would be likely to harm the national defense and public safety, and after hearing the owner of the equipment.

The same measures may be taken in cases where the use of such equipment results from radio disturbances or where such use does not comply with the conditions laid down in the authorization.

The ministries of national defense and of the interior proceed, each in his case, in search of underground stations and the control of the content of their broadcasts.

Article 58 -

In exceptional circumstances, radio equipment of any kind may be requisitioned for

For additional analytical, business and investment opportunities information,
please contact Global Investment & Business Center, USA
at (703) 370-8082. Fax: (703) 370-8083. E-mail: ibpusa3@gmail.com
Global Business and Investment Info Databank - www.ibpus.com

public utility, by decree on the proposal of the Minister concerned, in all cases where their use would be necessary for reasons of national defense and security public.

In any case where the use of such equipment would be such as to impair the requirements of national defense and public security, the requisition shall be without indemnity.

Article 59 -

The cessation of the operation of radio equipment or any of its components must be immediately notified to the Minister in charge of telecommunications who may order the affixing of seals on the equipment or on the element that the operator stopped using.

 Article 60 -

Without prejudice to the restrictions that may be enacted by the texts adopted for the application of this Code concerning the installation and operation of radiocommunication equipment on board aircraft or vessels using the airspace or territorial waters of the Republic of Tunisia, foreign aircraft and vessels are authorized to use their radiocommunication equipment only for the exclusive needs of the navigation or operation of such aircraft or vessels, and only when they have no other possibility of communications with the land. In any case,

Any contravention of the provisions of this Article shall entail, in addition to the penalties provided for in this Code, the closure of equipment and the affixing of seals, until the offending aircraft or vessel has left the airspace or the territorial waters of the Republic of Tunisia.

Article 61 -

Diplomatic and consular representations accredited in Tunisia may, at their request, be exempted from payment of the fee provided for in Article 51 of this Code, subject to reciprocity.

Article 62 -

The provisions of Articles 51 , 52 , 53 , 54 and 59 of this Code do not apply to the equipment of the Ministries of National Defense and the Interior.

CHAPTER 5 - NATIONAL TELECOMMUNICATIONS AUTHORITY

Article 63 -

There is created a specialized body called "National Instance of Telecommunications", having for seat Tunis, and charged with:

to express an opinion on the method of determining the rates of networks and services;

manage national plans for numbering and addressing;

to monitor compliance with the obligations arising from the laws and regulations in the field of telecommunications;

to review disputes relating to the installation, operation and operation of networks;

to give an opinion on any subject falling within the scope of its powers and submitted to it by the Minister of Telecommunications.

Note Determine the method of sharing of the costs between the different services provided by each network operator.

Establish the costing methodologies used in calculating interconnection rates, local loop unbundling, physical collocation, and common use of infrastructure

Article 63 bis Note -

Article 63 ter Note -

Article 64 -

The National Instance of Telecommunications is composed of:

a full-time president

a vice-president, advisor to the court of cassation and practicing full-time;

an advising member of one of the two chambers responsible for auditing public companies at the Court of Auditors, practicing full-time;

four members selected from among the persons competent in the technical, economic or legal field pertaining to telecommunications;

The president, the vice-president and the members of the body are appointed by decree.

Note The mandates of the President of the Instance and the permanent member are fixed at five years renewable once. The mandate of the Vice President of the Mechanism is five years. The mandates of the other members of the National Instance of Telecommunications are fixed at three years renewable once.

Article 65 (new) Note -

The President of the National Telecommunications Authority appoints a rapporteur from among the members of the body.

The chairman of the authority may appoint contract experts chosen in consideration of their experience and competence in the field of telecommunications, to assist in the investigations and investigations they are charged by the President within the scope of its powers.

He is designated at the National Telecommunication Authority a general rapporteur and rapporteurs appointed by decree among magistrates and officials category "A". The general rapporteur coordinates, monitors and supervises the work of the rapporteurs. The president of the body may appoint contractual rapporteurs chosen for their experience and expertise in the field of telecommunications. The rapporteur proceeds with the investigation of the requests entrusted to him by the President of the Mechanism and which fall within the scope of his prerogatives.

Article 66 (new) Note -

The president may call, if necessary, agents of the ministry in charge of telecommunications to carry out specific investigations and expertise.

The members of the body may, upon appointment of the president, carry out all investigations and investigations on site, in accordance with the legal conditions. They may also have all the documents they consider necessary for the investigation of the case.

Installers and operators of telecommunications networks are required to provide the President of the Authority with the documents and information necessary to carry out the investigations and investigations that fall within the scope of his duties.

The rapporteur checks the documents in the file and can ask the natural and legal persons for any additional information needed for the investigation.

He may proceed, under the regulatory conditions, to all inquiries and investigations on the spot. He may also be sent any document he deems necessary for the investigation of the case.

The rapporteur may request that inquiries or expert opinions be carried out by officials of the Ministry of Telecommunications.

During the examination of the cases for which they are responsible, the non-contractual rapporteurs may:

to enter, during normal working hours, into the business premises, to make all the necessary investigations, and to produce, on first requisition and without displacement, documents and evidence whatever their medium and the books necessary for their searches and findings and to obtain certified copies thereof,

convene and hear all persons who may provide information related to their missions.

Article 67 (new) Note -

Are brought, before the National Telecommunications Authority by the Minister in charge of telecommunications or by the installers and the operators of the networks, the requests relating to the litigations relating to:

interconnection and access to networks;

the conditions of common use between the operators of the available infrastructure networks.

Requests are sent directly or through a lawyer to the President of the National Telecommunications Authority, by registered letter or reliable electronic document with acknowledgment of receipt or by filing with the authority against discharge. The motion must contain preliminary evidence and must be in four copies.

The President of the National Telecommunications Authority is responsible for transmitting to the Minister of Telecommunications a copy of all the requests received, with the exception of those introduced by the Minister himself.

Before the National Telecommunications Authority, applications relating to interconnection, unbundling of the local loop, physical co-location, common use of infrastructures and telecommunication services are brought by:

the minister in charge of telecommunications,

installers and network operators,

Internet service providers,

legally established consumer organizations or groups,

professional organizations in the field of telecommunications.

The National Telecommunications Authority may, on the report of the general rapporteur, take judicial action to rule on infringements of the laws and regulations in the field of telecommunications.

The requests are addressed directly or through a lawyer to the president of the National Telecommunications Authority, by registered letter with acknowledgment of receipt or by electronic document preserved in its final form reliably and authenticated by an electronic signature or by filing with the Instance against discharge.

The request must be submitted in four copies and must include the following information:

the name, legal form, registered office of the applicant and, where applicable, the registration number in the commercial register,

the name and registered office of the defendant,

a detailed statement of the subject of the dispute and the claims.

The request must be accompanied by all documents, correspondence and preliminary evidence.

The office of procedures of the National Instance of Telecommunications is in charge of the registration of the request according to its number and its date, in the register of the businesses.

The president of the body is responsible for transmitting to the minister in charge of telecommunications and the defendant a copy of the request and the accompanying documents, by registered letter with acknowledgment of receipt or by electronic document preserved in its definitive form in a reliable way and authenticated by an electronic signature.

The President of the Instance grants the defendant a period of one month, from the date of receipt, to present his answers and failing that, the Instance continues the examination of the request in view of the documents provided. .

All actions brought before the Mechanism going back more than three years from the date of the loss suffered are prescribed.

Article 68 (new)- Note

At the end of the investigation, the rapporteur drafts a report for each dispute in which he presents his observations. This report is sent by the President of the National Telecommunications Authority to the parties concerned by registered letter or by reliable electronic document with acknowledgment of receipt. The parties concerned are required to respond to this report within 15 days of receipt of the notice of notification, either directly or through a lawyer, by means of a memorandum the defenses they deem useful.

Subject to the provisions of the second paragraph of of this Code, the parties are entitled to take note of the attachments to the file.

The rapporteur may, after receiving the defendant's reply, if he deems it useful or at the request of one of the two parties, and before commencing the investigations and investigations, make an attempt at conciliation in order to find an amicable solution to the dispute. It may also take such measures as it deems useful for this purpose and in particular to be assisted, where appropriate, by experts.

The rapporteur is required to close the conciliation phase within one month from the date of receipt of the respondent's reply.

If the dispute is resolved amicably in whole or in part, the rapporteur writes a report which he transmits accompanied by the conciliation agreement and the file to the president of the National Instance of Telecommunications which will be in charge of summoning the members of the Body to a hearing to rule on the subject.

In case of failure of the conciliation attempt, the rapporteur writes a report which he transmits to the President of the Instance and continues the investigations and investigations necessary to decide the dispute.

Article 68 bis Note -

The President of the National Telecommunications Authority may request the parties information and documents necessary to decide the dispute.

The chairman of the body may also, if necessary, appoint external experts and determine the tasks assigned to them. Expert fees are advanced by the applicant. Experts may be challenged in accordance with the provisions of the Code of Civil and Commercial Procedures.

The rapporteur may request, during each stage of the case, the parties all the documents necessary for the resolution of the dispute.

The rapporteur shall conclude his investigations and draw up a report in which he shall submit his observations within two months from the date of receipt of the respondent's reply or from the date of the drafting of the report provided for in paragraph four of the section 68 of this code. The President of the Mechanism may, if necessary, extend this period at the request of the rapporteur.

In the event of failure of the conciliation attempt, the President of the Instance shall transmit the instruction report to the parties to the dispute by registered letter with acknowledgment of receipt or by electronic document kept in final form reliably and authenticated by an electronic signature. Parties are required to respond to this report within one month of the date of notification, either directly or through a lawyer. and by means of a brief containing the elements of defense which they consider useful.

Article 69 (new) Note -

The sessions of the National Telecommunications Authority are not public. The reports are presented to the authority according to the rotation decided by its president.

The Body hears the parties to the dispute who have the right to be represented by a lawyer and to be assisted by an expert, and to the hearing of the parties concerned who have been convened regularly to present themselves before the court. The body also hears any person who appears to him likely to contribute to the resolution of the dispute.

The body rules by majority vote and in the presence of the parties. Each member of the body has one vote, in case of a tie vote, the president has the casting vote.

The presiding judge may request the replacement of any member who is absent three times without cause at the meetings of the proceeding.

The President of the Mechanism sets the date of the hearing of the members of the Mechanism within 30 days from the date of receipt of the parties' response to the case report.

The sessions of the National Instance of Telecommunications are not public. The reports are submitted to the Forum following the rotation of the meeting decided by its president.

The Body hears the parties or their lawyers and anyone who appears likely to contribute to the resolution of the dispute. It may also, if necessary, be assisted by an expert.

The proceedings of the body are recorded in minutes of meetings signed by the president of the National Telecommunications Authority.

After the close of the debate, the case is put in deliberate. The deliberations are secret.

The Forum can validly deliberate only if at least five of its members, including the president or, where applicable, the vice president are present.

The President of the Mechanism may request the replacement of any member who is absent three times without cause at meetings of the Mechanism. Replacement is by order.

Article 70 -

The function of member of the National Instance of Telecommunications is incompatible with the direct or indirect possession of interests in any company that operates in the field of telecommunications.

Any party concerned may challenge any member of the proceeding by written request signed by its author or by electronic application accompanied by the signature of its author. The request is submitted to the president of the body who decides the matter within five days after hearing both parties.

The vice-president replaces the president of the body, in case of recusation of the latter.

Article 71 (new) - Note

The body can validly deliberate only if at least two-thirds of its members, including the president and the vice-president, are present.

No member of the Board may take part in the deliberations in a case in which he has a direct or indirect interest or if in this case he represents or has represented one of the parties concerned.

The body rules by majority vote and in the presence of the parties.

Each member has one vote and in the event of a tie, the chairman has the casting vote.

The decision of the body must be motivated and must include a solution to the dispute and the following indications:

the names, the registered offices of the parties and, where appropriate, the names of their lawyers and their legal representatives,

a detailed statement of the respective requests of the parties and their means,

the date of the decision and the place where it is rendered,

the names of the members who took part in the decision.

Article 72 -

The members of the body and its agents are bound by the obligation of professional secrecy concerning the works and information of which they were informed during the exercise of their functions.

Note The presiding judge may refuse to disclose any documents implicating business secrets, except in the case where the communication or consultation of these documents is necessary for the procedure or the exercise of their rights by the parties. The President of the Mechanism may refuse to disclose documents questioning the secrecy of business and which are not necessary for the procedure or the exercise of the parties' rights. Both parties are obliged to respect the confidentiality of information exchanged between them. They are also strictly prohibited from exploiting this information for purposes other than those of the dispute or to disclose it to their services, partners or subsidiaries.

Article 73 (new) Note -

When deciding on the fund, the decisions rendered by the National Telecommunications Authority must include a solution to the dispute.

One of the parties to the dispute may request the President of the Authority to order the cessation of the provision of the service or to put an end to the infringements before deciding on the merits.

The request is addressed to the President of the Mechanism and must contain the statement of facts and the evidence.

The president of the National Instance of Telecommunications decides on the request within one week as from the date of its deposit and orders the taking of the provisional measures envisaged by the first paragraph of this Article if it judges that the request is founded and aims to avoid irreparable harm.

The decision of the President of the Mechanism ordering the taking of provisional measures may be revised following the request of the party against whom they were taken and this within one week, from the date of submission of the application.

Article 74 (new) Note -

The National Telecommunications Authority may take one or more of the following measures:

issue orders to the parties concerned to put an end to infringements of the provisions of this Code and its implementing regulations, within a specified period, or to impose on them specific conditions in the exercise of their activity;

decide to stop the exercise of the activity concerned by these offenses for a period not exceeding three months, the resumption of the activity can only occur once the parties have terminated the offenses subject to the dispute .

forward the file to the territorially competent public prosecutor with a view to instituting criminal proceedings where appropriate.

The National Telecommunications Authority, within the scope of its powers, imposes penalties on operators of telecommunications networks and suppliers of infringing telecommunications services, including non-compliance with laws and regulations in the field of telecommunications or telecommunications decisions. National Instance of Telecommunications has been proved according to the following procedures:

A formal notice is sent to the offender by the President of the National Instance of Telecommunications to put an end to the infringements within a period not exceeding one month.

If the offender fails to comply with the notice sent to him within the prescribed time, the National Telecommunications Authority may issue an injunction to him to immediately put an end to the infringements or to impose special conditions in the exercise of his activity.

If the offender does not comply with the injunction indicated above, the National Telecommunications Authority imposes a fine not exceeding 1% of its turnover in the previous year excluding taxes.

If investigations and investigations show that the offense constitutes a danger to the normal functioning of the telecommunications sector, the National Telecommunications Authority decides to stop the exercise of the activity concerned by this offense for a period of no not exceeding three months. The resumption of the activity can only occur once the parties have terminated the offense concerned.

If the investigations have proved the existence of an offense or an offense punishable by a criminal penalty, the National Telecommunications Authority transmits the file to the prosecutor of the Republic with territorial jurisdiction to initiate the prosecution if necessary criminal.

Article 75 -

The decisions of the Mechanism must be motivated and are filled with the executory form by its president, and if necessary by its vice president.

These decisions are notified to the interested parties by notary bailiff.

The decisions of this body are subject to appeal to the Tunis Court of Appeal.

Article 76 -

The National Telecommunications Authority may establish technical commissions to carry out technical studies in the field of telecommunications. They are chaired by one of the members of the National Telecommunication Authority and composed by experts and technicians in the field of telecommunications and information technology.

These commissions may be assisted by Tunisian or foreign experts, selected in view of their competence in the field, and this by virtue of conventions submitted to the Minister for Telecommunications for approval.

Article 77 -

The National Telecommunications Authority transmits to the Chamber of Deputies and the Ministry of Telecommunications an annual report on its activity.

CHAPTER 6 - OFFENSES AND SANCTIONS

SECTION ONE. OFFENSES

Article 78 -

Infringements of the provisions of this Code and the texts adopted for its application are recorded in minutes drawn up by two of the agents mentioned in Article 79 of this Code, in accordance with the legislation in force.

Article 79 -

Infringements of the provisions of this code are noted by:

the judicial police officers referred to in Nos. 3 and 4 of Article 10 of the Code of Criminal Procedure ;

sworn agents of the Ministry of Telecommunications;

sworn agents of the Ministry of the Interior;

officers of the national coastal surveillance service and officers and commanders of units of the navy.

Article 80 -

Subject to the provisions of Article 89 of this Code, the minutes shall be transmitted to the Minister in charge of Telecommunications who shall forward them, for prosecution, to the territorially competent public prosecutor.

SECTION 2. - CRIMINAL SANCTIONS

Article 81 -

Is punished with a fine of one thousand (1000) to five thousand (5000) dinars who unintentionally destroys or deteriorates, in any way whatsoever, the lines or the equipments of the telecommunications.

Article 82 -

is punished with imprisonment of six (6) months to five (5) years and a fine of one thousand (1000) to twenty thousand (20000) dinars or only one of these two sentences:

Anyone who installs or operates a public network Note telecommunications independent, without having obtained the concession Licence provided for in Article 19 of this Code;

Any person who provides telecommunications services to the public has obtained the authorization provided for in Article 5 of this Code or maintains the offer of such services after withdrawal of the authorization;

Anyone who uses radio frequencies without having obtained the agreement of the National Frequency Agency;

Any person who installs or operates a private telecommunications network without having obtained the authorization provided for in Article 31 of this Code or maintains its operation after the withdrawal of the authorization;

Any person who voluntarily causes the interruption of telecommunications by the breaking of lines or the deterioration or destruction of equipment by any means whatsoever.

Article 83 -

Is punished with imprisonment of one (1) month to six (6) months and a fine of one thousand (1000) to ten thousand (10,000) dinars or one of these two penalties, whoever manufactures for the domestic market, imports, holds for sale or for distribution free of charge or for sale or sells or sells terminal equipment or radio equipment provided for in Article 32 of this Code and the one which connects them to a public telecommunications network without obtaining certification.

Is punished with the same penalty anyone who advertises the sale of equipment n '

Article 84 -

Is punished in accordance with the provisions of Article 264 of the Penal Code whoever:

hijacks telecommunications lines or voluntarily uses diverted telecommunication lines;

knowingly uses a call sign of the international series assigned to a station within a telecommunications network.

Article 85 -

Notwithstanding the cases provided for by law, any person who discloses, incites or participates in the disclosure of the content of communications and exchanges transmitted through the telecommunications networks shall be punished in accordance with the provisions of Article 253 of the Penal Code.

Article 86 -

Is punished by imprisonment of one (1) year to two (2) years and a fine of one hundred (100) to one thousand (1000) dinars who knowingly harms third parties or disturbs their tranquility through the networks public telecommunications.

Article 87 -

is punishable by imprisonment from six (6) months to five (5) years and a fine of one thousand (1000) to five thousand (5000) dinars or one of these two penalties anyone who uses, manufactures, imports, exports, holds for sale or distribution for free or for a fee or sells or sells the means or services of cryptology and their modification or destruction in violation of the provisions of the decree provided for in Article 9 of this Code.

SECTION 3. - ADMINISTRATIVE PENALTIES

Article 88 -

Without prejudice to the penal sanctions envisaged by the present code, the Minister in charge of the telecommunications can inflict to the violators with the provisions of this code and its texts of application one of the following administrative sanctions, after hearing the offender:

the provisional or definitive restriction of the authorization and the conditions of its exploitation;

the temporary suspension of the authorization;

the definitive withdrawal of the authorization with affixing of seals.

Article 89 -

Without prejudice to the rights of victims, the Minister in charge of telecommunications may carry out transactions concerning the offenses provided for in Article 81 of this Code and which are established and prosecuted in accordance with the provisions of this law.

The payment of the sum fixed by the deed of transaction extinguishes the public action and the prosecution of the administration.

CHAPTER 7 - VARIOUS PROVISIONS

Article 90 -

Is assigned by right aconcession Licencefor the operation of telecommunications networks and services for the benefit of the Note National Office National Societyof Telecommunications for which it is responsible at the date of publication of this Code.

This Note concession Licence includes the provision of basic telecommunications services.

Article 91 -

Is assigned by right a concession Licencefor the operation of telecommunication networks and services for the benefit of the National Broadcasting Office for which it is responsible on the date of publication of this code.

This concession Licence includes the provision of television broadcasting services throughout the Republic.

Article 92 -

Subject to the provisions of Articles 90 and 91 of this Code, the installation and operation of telecommunications networks and the provision of new telecommunications services and the scarce resources necessary for the operation of the networks by theNational Office National Society Telecommunications and the National Office of Broadcasting are governed by the provisions of this Code.

INTERNET SERVICE PROVIDERS REGULATIONS

Decree No. 2014-4773 of 26 December 2014, setting the conditions and procedures for granting authorization for the activity of Internet service provider.

CHAPTER I GENERAL PROVISIONS

Article 1 - This Decree lays down the conditions and procedures for granting the authorization to carry on the activity of internet service provider, in accordance with the provisions of indent 29, 30, 31 of Article 2 and the Article 31 (quater) of the Telecommunication Code, as well as the obligations of service providers and the penalties to which they are subject in the event of infringement of the provisions of this decree.

The ISP activity may include the provision of Internet services or Internet access services or both.

Article 2 - The activity of Internet Service Provider is subject to the prior authorization of the Minister of Telecommunications, after consultation with the Minister of the Interior and the National Telecommunications Authority.

The authorization provided for in the first paragraph of this article sets out the service provider's field of activity and its rights and obligations according to the nature of its activity in accordance with the provisions of this decree.

CHAPTER 2 CONDITIONS FOR GRANTING AUTHORIZATION

Article 3 - Anyone wishing to obtain an authorization from an internet service provider, must fulfill the following conditions:

- for the natural person: to be of Tunisian nationality and holder of a diploma of higher education or an equivalent diploma or an equivalent certified training diploma at the aforementioned level in the fields of computer or telecommunications or multimedia,

- for the legal person: to be incorporated in accordance with Tunisian law, having a registered capital of one million (1) dinars minimum, held by name and in Tunisian majority,

- the natural person legal representative of the legal person must not have a criminal record and must not be in a situation that is not in conformity with the conditions of practice of a profession of a commercial nature in accordance with the legislation in force.

Article 4 - The granting of the authorization of Internet service provider is subject to the payment of a fee of one hundred and fifty (150) thousand dinars payable at the date of obtaining the authorization.

CHAPTER 3 PROCEDURES FOR GRANTING AUTHORIZATION

Article 5 - Applications for authorization for the activity of Internet service provider activity are sent to the Ministry of Telecommunications by registered letter with acknowledgment of receipt or reliable electronic document, or by direct deposit with the Ministry against receipt of a receipt.

These requests must include the following documents:

- a copy of the national identity card of the natural person or the legal representative of the legal person,

- bulletin no. 3 of the natural person or the legal representative of the legal person,

- a copy of the scientific diploma provided for in article 3 of this decree of the natural person,

- a copy of the statutes of the legal person,

- an undertaking on the honor to incorporate within a period of three months from the date of obtaining the agreement in principle for natural persons,

- a certificate of non-bankruptcy or a declaration on the honor,

- a technical study of the services and the technical characteristics of equipment and systems adopted to provide services specifying the location of connectable equipment to public telecommunications networks and connection mode to be adopted,

- the documents justifying the means human, material and technical requirements for the provision of Internet services in accordance with national and international standards in force,

- a detailed statement of the services and the conditions of their supply and the proposed tariffs,

- if necessary, the necessary authorizations for the exploitation of the data or the exercise of the activities in relation.

Article 6 - The Ministry in charge of telecommunications must respond to the holder of the request within a maximum period of one (1) month as from the date of reception of the documents envisaged with the article 5 of this decree, or from the date the presentation of the requested information, either to signify the granting of the authorization or the refusal that must be justified, and in case of refusal, the file is returned to its holder.

The minister in charge of telecommunications can grant an agreement in principle which empowers its holder to carry out the steps relating to the formation of the legal entity as well as the installation of the equipments and all other procedures necessary for the supply of the service object of the request obtaining authorization.

The agreement in principle remains valid for a period of three (3) months non-renewable from the date of its obtaining.

Article 7 - The authorization is granted for a period of five (5) years from the date of its obtaining, in a personal capacity and may be assigned or transferred to third parties only by authorization of the Minister in charge of telecommunications after opinion of the commission provided for in Article 8 of this decree.

The authorization is granted against a receipt attesting the deposit of the total amount of the royalty referred to in article 4 of this decree for the benefit of the general treasury of the Republic of Tunisia.

The authorization shall be renewed for the same duration and under the same conditions and procedures of its granting on the basis of an application submitted by the ISP at least two (2) months before the expiry of the authorization.

Article 8 - An advisory commission is set up with the Minister for Telecommunications, responsible in particular for:

- studying and issuing its opinion on applications for granting or renewing authorizations of internet service providers,

- issuing its opinion on the files on offenses and penalties,

- expressing its opinion on applications for transfer or transfer of authorizations,

- expressing its opinion on all questions submitted to it by the Minister for Telecommunications and falling within the scope of his powers.

This commission is chaired by the minister in charge of telecommunications or his representative, it is composed of the following members:

- a representative of the Ministry of National Defense,

- a representative of the Ministry of the Interior,

- a representative of the Ministry of Telecommunications,

- a representative of the Ministry of Commerce,

- a representative of the National Telecommunications Authority,

- a representative of the Tunisian Union of Industry, Trade and Handicrafts.

The members of the commission are appointed by decision of the Minister of Telecommunications on the proposal of the ministries and bodies concerned.

The commission meets at the invitation of its chairman on the basis of an agenda communicated to the members at least two (2) weeks before the meeting. The commission can only meet in the presence of a majority of its members at least, in case this quorum is not reached, the committee will hold a second meeting after ten (10) days regardless of the number of members present . In all cases, the commission delivers its opinions by a majority of the votes of the members present, and in the event of a tie, the chairman has the casting vote.

The chairman of the commission may invite, in an advisory capacity, any person whose contribution is deemed useful without the right to vote.

The work of the commission is recorded in a report communicated to all its members within ten (10) days of the date of the committee meeting.

The services of the Directorate-General for Digital Economy, Investment and Statistics under the Ministry of Telecommunications are responsible for the secretariat of the Commission.

CHAPTER 4 RIGHTS AND OBLIGATIONS OF THE SERVICE PROVIDER

SECTION 1 - SERVICE PROVIDER RIGHTS

Article 9 - The internet service provider may, according to the authorized area of activity, benefit from the following services and resources in accordance with the laws and regulations in force:

- the IP protocol numbering resources in accordance with the legislation and regulations in force,

- addressing resources in accordance with the laws and regulations in force,

- wholesale telecommunications services provided by the operators of the public telecommunications networks in the context of offers approved by the national telecommunications authority related to the nature of the activity the service provider,

- physical co-location services, the common use of infrastructure, the leasing of interconnection links provided by the operators of public telecommunications networks in the context of interconnection offers approved by the national telecommunications authority,

- Internet connection network capacity rental services and international telecommunication link rental services.

Article 10 - The internet service provider can provide all the services related to the nature of its activity. For this purpose, it is entitled to make any investments or transactions required for the provision of its services, such as the establishment of telecommunications infrastructure or the leasing of the excess capacity of telecommunications resources available on the public service networks in accordance with to the provisions of the telecommunications code.

These provisions do not waive the requirement to obtain licenses or authorizations in the case of an activity that requires a license or authorization in accordance with the legislation and regulations in force.

SECTION 2 - THE OBLIGATIONS OF THE SERVICE PROVIDER VIS-À-VIS THE STATE

Article 11 - The ISP is obliged to:

- place at the disposal of the Ministry of Telecommunications and the National Telecommunications Authority all information relating to technical, operational, financial and accounting matters in accordance with the terms and conditions set forth in the authority,

- submit for approval to the National Telecommunication Authority the model of the service contract to be concluded with customers,

- be able to meet the needs of national defense and public safety and security in accordance with the legislation and regulations in force,

- provide the competent authorities with the means necessary for the performance of their duties, and in this context, the internet service provider must obey the instructions of the judicial, military and national security authorities,

- respect the conventions and ratified international treaties by Tunisia.

Article 12 - Subject to the following provisions, the rates of the services provided by the internet service provider are freely determined.

The rates of the services provided for in the first paragraph of this article are fixed while respecting the principle of equal treatment of users. Internet service providers are required to render their services in the best economic conditions. They are also required to inform the public of their general conditions of offers and services and to publish the supply rates for each category of service.

Internet service providers are required prior to the marketing of the service, to present a notice advertising tariffs under the following conditions:

- a copy of the notice is sent to the national telecommunications authority at least fifteen (15) days prior to the marketing of any proposed new offer,

- the national telecommunications authority may require the internet service provider to make changes the rates of their services or conditions of sale, if it appears that such offers do not comply with the rules of fair competition and the principle of fixing the tariffs as provided for in this Article,

- a copy of the final definitive advertising notice searchable is made available to the public electronically and in all areas of the services concerned.

SECTION 3 - THE SERVICE PROVIDER'S OBLIGATIONS TO CUSTOMERS

Article 13 - The internet service provider is committed to customers to:

- provide access to Internet services to all applicants using the most effective technical solutions,

- provide subscribers with clear information about the object and methods of accessing the service and supporting them when requested,

- providing a service for answering questions and requests from subscribers and their follow-up through a permanent focal point.

Article 14 - The service provider is obliged to take the necessary measures to ensure the quality of the services he provides to subscribers and to respect their rights resulting from the service contract concluded with them, for this purpose he is obliged to:

- take the necessary measures necessary to ensure the neutrality of its services, the confidentiality and completeness of the data transmitted in the context of the services provided in accordance with the laws and regulations in force,

- take the necessary measures to ensure the protection, security and confidentiality of personal data that they keep or process or record at the subscriber identification unit in accordance with the laws and regulations in force,

- the non-disclosure to third parties of data transmitted or held, relating to subscribers and in particular the nominative subscribers, without the agreement of the subscriber concerned, subject to the requirements of national defense and public security and the prerogatives of the judicial authority and by the legislation in force,

- guarantee the right of any subscriber not to be included in any nominative database of the provider with the exception of those relating to billing,

- guarantee the right to any subscriber to oppose the use of the billing data relating to him for commercial prospecting purposes,

- guarantee the right of any subscriber to rectify personal data concerning him or to supplement or clarify them or to update them, or to delete them,

- to respect his obligations relating to the conditions of confidentiality and neutrality in the framework of its contractual relations with service marketing companies,

- provide a support and information service on the nature of the services to be offered to its subscribers by ensuring the protection of their personal data through the network of Internet,

- adopt the solutions and mechanisms that ensure a secure child browsing service on the Internet,

- Define the service of the secure navigation of children on the Internet and provide for it in service contracts as a service of choice that depends on the wishes of the customer.

- give subscribers the opportunity to change their choice about the service of the secure navigation of children on the Internet and this through simple and instant mechanisms.

Article 15 - The ISP commits itself according to the nature of the contracts to be concluded with its subscribers, to assure the continuity of the services and to guarantee the permanence of functioning of the equipment and the computer programs exploited and to take the necessary measures to maintain the level of Internet service quality indicators provided by national and international standards.

The National Telecommunications Authority sets standards and standards for Internet service quality at the national level and monitors and assesses compliance by Internet Service Providers.

Chapter 5

Dispute Resolution

Article 16 - The national telecommunication authority is responsible in accordance with the provisions of Article 67 of the Telecommunications Code to settle disputes that may arise between Internet service providers between them and disputes that may arise with operators of public telecommunications networks contracted with which they have concluded agreements.

It is also responsible for disputes arising from the execution of service contracts concluded between Internet service providers and their clients brought before the authority by legally established consumer organizations.

Chapter 6

Offenses and Administrative Penalties

Article 17 - Without prejudice to the penal sanctions provided for in the legislation relating to telecommunications, the legislation relating to the press and the literary and artistic property and the legislation relating to competition and the prices and to the protection of the consumer, the infringements with the provisions of the this decree gives rise to the administrative penalties provided for in the telecommunications code.

Offenses are recorded by minutes drawn up by authorized agents in accordance with the provisions of the telecommunications code.

Article 18 - The minister in charge of telecommunications sends a reminder to the respect of the regulations to the Internet service provider concerned by registered letter or by a reliable electronic document with acknowledgment of receipt within a period not exceeding one month as from the date of the observation of the infringements .

The internet service provider must remedy the infringements found and submit observations by registered letter or a reliable electronic document with acknowledgment of receipt to the commission referred to in Article 8 of this decree within a period not exceeding fifteen (15) days from the date of the point of order.

At the end of this period and in the event of persistent infringements, the committee's secretariat prepares a reasoned report which it sends to the commission which may propose one of the administrative sanctions provided for in Article 88 of the telecommunications code.

The chairman of the commission must convene the internet service provider to submit his observations on the offenses with which he is accused before the commission, by registered letter or by a reliable electronic document with acknowledgment of receipt at least ten (10) days before the meeting of the commission.

Article 19 - The sanction decision must be notified to the internet service provider within a period not exceeding fifteen (15) days from the date of the decision by registered letter or a reliable electronic document with acknowledgment of receipt .

Article 20 - In case of serious failure or flagrant breach of the provisions of this decree, the Minister in charge of telecommunications, on the basis of a report established by the national telecommunication authority, can pronounce the immediate suspension of the activity and convene the internet service provider to submit its observations on the facts before the commission which draws up a reasoned report concerning the settlement of the operator's situation within a period not exceeding one month from the date of the suspension.

Article 21 - The authorization is withdrawn automatically to the ISP in the dissolution or bankruptcy of the legal person.

Chapter 7

Transitional provisions

Article 22 - Is granted under this decree and within the limit of the authorized activity, An authorization to Internet service providers holding an authorization on the date of its entry into force.

The Internet Service Providers provided for in the first paragraph of this Article shall have a period of six (6) years from the date of entry into force of this Decree to fulfill the conditions provided for by its provisions.

Article 23 - Is granted by virtue of this decree, an authorization of Internet service provider to the public intervenor in the field of the Internet provided for by article 5 of the decree n ° 97-501 of March 14, 1997, relative to the value-added telecommunications services.

This intervenor has a period of six (6) months from the date of coming into force of this decree to fulfill the conditions provided for by its provisions.

Article 24 - Operators of public telecommunications networks holding a license for the establishment and operation of a public telecommunications network in accordance with the laws and regulations in force shall not be subject to the provisions of this Chapter.

Article 25 - Are repealed, the provisions of the decree n ° 97-501 of March 14, 1997, on the services with added value of telecommunications.

Article 26 - The Minister of Higher Education, Scientific Research, Information Technology and Communication is responsible for the implementation of this decree which will be published in the Official Gazette of the Republic of Tunis

DECREE ON THE ORGANIZATION OF THE MINISTRY OF INFORMATION AND COMMUNICATION TECHNOLOGIES[1]

The head of government,

On the proposal of the Minister of Information and Communication Technologies,

Having regard to the Constitutive Act 2011-6 of 16 December 2011 on the provisional organization of public authorities,

Considering the law n ° 83-112 of December 12th, 1983, on the general statute of the personnel of the State, the local public authorities and the public institutions with administrative character, all the texts which modified or completed it and in particular the decree- Law No 2011-89 of 23 September 2011,

Considering the law n ° 98-38 of June 2nd, 1998, relating to the code of the post, as it was modified and completed by the law n ° 2007-40 of June 25th, 2007,

Having regard to Law No. 2001-1 of January 15, 2001, promulgating the Telecommunications Code, as amended and supplemented by Law No. 2002-46 of May 7, 2002 and Law No. 2008-1 of January 8, 2008,

Considering the decree n ° 80-526 of May 8th, 1980, fixing the regime applicable to the persons in charge of mission with the ministerial cabinets, as modified by the decree n ° 2000-1182 of May 22nd, 2000,

Considering the decree n ° 88-1981 of December 13th, 1988, fixing the conditions and the procedures of the management of the current archives and intermediary archives, the sorting and elimination of the archives, the payment of the archives and the communication of the public archives, as it was amended by Decree No. 982548 of 28 December 1998,

Considering the decree n ° 93-1549 of July 26th, 1993, creating the offices of the relations with the citizen, all the texts which modified or completed it and in particular the decree n ° 98-1152 of May 25th, 1998,

Considering the decree n ° 96-49 of January 16th, 1996, fixing the contents of the plans of leveling of the administration and the modalities of their elaboration, realization and follow-up,

Considering the decree n ° 96-1047 of June 3rd, 1996, fixing the attributions of the Secretary of State to the Prime Minister in charge of the Informatics,

Considering Decree No. 97-1320 of July 7, 1997, on the organization of services under the Secretary of State to the Prime Minister in charge of Informatics,

Having regard to Decree No 99-2843 of 27 December 1999 on the organization of the Ministry of Communications,

Having regard to Decree No 2006-1245 of 24 April 2006 laying down the system of allocation and withdrawal of functional central administration posts,

Having regard to Decree No. 2011-4796 of 29 December 2011, appointing members of the Government,

Considering the decree n ° 2012-1997 of September 11th, 2012, fixing the attributions of the ministry of the technologies of the information and the communication,

Having regard to the opinion of the Minister of Finance,

Having regard to the opinion of the Administrative Court,

Given the deliberation of the Council of Ministers and after information of the President of the Republic.

Decrees:

---

[1] No. 2012-1998 of 11 September 2012,

CHAPTER I GENERAL PROVISIONS

Article 1 - The Ministry of Information and Communication Technology includes, in addition to the higher committee of the Ministry, the conference of directors and the permanent secretariat of the departmental commission of the markets:
1. the cabinet,
1. the General Inspectorate of Information and Communication Technologies,
2. 3. the common services,
2. the specific services. Art. 2 - The Higher Committee of the Ministry of Information and Communication Technologies is an advisory body that assists the Minister in
the study of any question that it deems useful to submit to it, in particular as regards:
-developing plans,
- coordination of the different action programs of the department,
- Training and Development Policy for Executives and Ministry Agents,
-organization and use of material and personal means.
The Higher Committee of the Ministry of Information and Communication Technology meets at the request of the Minister and under his chairmanship.
He understands :
-the chief of the cabinet,
-Inspector General Director of Information and Communication Technologies,
- the director of the Higher School of Communications of Tunis
-
the director of the Higher Institute of Communication Technology Studies of Tunis,
- the persons in charge of the common and specific services and any other person whose participation is considered useful by the minister.
Anyone with expertise in the technical, economic or legal field related to information and communication technologies may be invited to attend the meetings of the Committee.
Art. 3 - The conference of directors constitutes a body of reflection and information on the general activity of the department and matters of general interest.
The management conference meets at least four (4) times a year at the invitation of the Minister, it periodically reviews the progress of the work of the department and the main files submitted to it.
The conference of directors is chaired by the minister or his representative and includes the first heads of the department from among the directors general, directors and any other person whose participation would be considered useful by the minister for the subjects on the agenda.
Art. 4 - The permanent secretariat of the departmental commission of the markets is in charge notably:
-the receipt and examination of public procurement files sent by the various public purchasers under the Ministry,
- the organization of the meetings of the departmental markets commission, the proposal of the agenda and the drafting of the minutes as well as the notification of the opinions of the commission to the various public purchasers concerned,
-the monitoring of the execution of public contracts and the preparation of the annual activity report,
-provide consultations in the field of public procurement to the different public purchasers,
- to coordinate with the various stakeholders in public procurement,
- to issue opinions on legal issues relating to public procurement.

The permanent secretariat of the Departmental Contracts Commission is headed by a Deputy Head of Central Administration assisted by a Head of the Central Administration Service.

CHAPTER II THE CABINET

Art. 5. The Cabinet is responsible for the execution of all the tasks entrusted to it by the Minister.

Its mission is to:

- keep the Minister informed of the general activity of the Department, transmit its instructions and ensure their execution,
- assure liaison and coordination between the different organs of the Ministry,
- maintain relations with official bodies, national organizations and the press,
- supervise, control and monitor the activities of the structures directly attached to it.
- the monitoring of government programs falling within the scope of the Ministry's missions.

The firm is headed by a chief of staff assisted by project managers or cabinet attachés.

Art. 6 - Are attached to the cabinet, the following structures:

1- the Office of General Affairs, Security and Tenure,

2- the central order office,

3-the office of information and communication,

4- the office of the relations with the citizen,

5- the office of relations with associations and organizations,

6- The Office for International Cooperation and External Relations,

7- the office of administrative reform and good governance,

8- Cabinet decisions follow-up office, restricted ministerial councils and interdepartmental councils,

9- the office of information systems,

10- the office of supervision of strategic projects.

Art. 7 - The General Affairs Office of the security and permanence is responsible in particular:

- to ensure the material preparation of the various meetings within the Ministry,
- the follow-up of conferences and seminars organized under the supervision of the Ministry,
- to carry out all the monitoring and coordination missions relating to the guarantee of the normal operation of the various services,
- to collect and analyze the events recorded at the central and regional levels indicated by the daily information bulletin,
- organize the official travel of the Minister and members of the Cabinet,
-

to follow permanently the reported technical disturbances,

-

to process urgent claims brought to the attention of the Minister,

- the coordination between the different operational emergency communications cells,
- to manage the department's internal security affairs,
- to organize and ensure the continuity of services during closing hours.

The General Security and Tenure Office is headed by a Director of National Headquarters, assisted by a Deputy Headquarters and a Head of National Headquarters.

Art. 8 - The central registry office is responsible for:

For additional analytical, business and investment opportunities information, please contact Global Investment & Business Center, USA at (703) 370-8082. Fax: (703) 370-8083. E-mail: ibpusa3@gmail.com Global Business and Investment Info Databank - www.ibpus.com

- the receipt, dispatch and registration of mail,
- the ventilation and follow-up of the mail,
the coordination between the different sub-offices. The Central Registry is headed by a Head of Central Administration.

Art. 9 - The office of information and communication is responsible in particular for:
- to establish and organize relations with the media,
- to collect, analyze and distribute media data relating to the activities of the Ministry,
-prepare internal information periodicals,
- update the Ministry's Website,
-develop communicative media,
-to document departmental activities. The information and communication office is headed by a cabinet attaché.

Art. 10 - The office of the relations with the citizen is in charge in particular:
- to welcome citizens, to receive their requests and to instruct them in collaboration with the services concerned, with a view to finding the appropriate solutions,
-to respond to citizens directly or by post or email,
- to inform the citizens about the procedures and administrative formalities concerning the granting of the various services,
- to centralize and study the files emanating from the administrative mediator as well as the coordination with the different parties concerned,
-to analyze suggestions from citizens to improve administrative services, in coordination with the services concerned.
The head of the office of the relations with the citizen is named in accordance with the provisions of article 5 of the decree n ° 93-1549 of July 26th, 1993 referred to above.

Art. 11 - The office of the relations with the associations and the organizations is in charge in particular:
- to follow up on files relating to organizations and associations and to draw up periodic reports on their activities,
- to represent the department at union meetings,
- monitoring of sectoral social negotiations and the various professional associations of the sector,
- to ensure the link with the associative organizations,
- to participate in events organized by components of civil society.
The office responsible for relations with associations and organizations is headed by a director of central administration.

Art. 12 -The Office of International Cooperation and External Relations is responsible for:
-centralize and monitor issues relating to international cooperation and external relations of interest to the department and the sub-trust bodies,
- coordinate with other departments and international and regional bodies on matters within the remit of the Ministry,
- represent the department in all bilateral, regional and multilateral negotiations in the field of information and communication technologies,
- represent the department on bilateral joint commissions and multilateral sessions and conferences,
-promote relations with international and regional bodies dealing with matters falling within the attributions of the Ministry and the sub-trustees.
The Office of International Cooperation and External Relations is headed by a senior official assisted by a director of central administration and two deputy heads of central administration.

Art. 13 - The Office of Administrative Reform and Good Governance is responsible in particular for:
-the follow-up of the administrative reform plans in coordination with the parties concerned and the specific services,
-to establish the procedures and trades manuals and the loader employment plans of agents as well as their follow-up and updating,
- put in place perceptions and proposals to improve the quality of services and the development of skills,
- to receive reports from the Institution of Citizen Supervisor, and to ensure the implementation of the suggestions contained therein,
- to make available to the competent bodies and following their request any statements, data, documents or information, with a view to achieving the objectives of good governance,
- put in place guidelines and programs that promote transparency and the application of the principles of good governance and the eradication of corruption causes,
- to allow citizens to access any information, data, decision, expense, program and other annual reports concerning the activity of the office whether directly or through the electronic site and this in accordance with the legislation and regulations in force .
The Office of Administrative Reform and Good Governance is headed by a chargé de mission.
Art. 14 -The Office of the Cabinet Ministers' Decisions Follow-up, Restricted Ministerial Councils and Interdepartmental Councils is responsible for:
- to ensure the preparation of departmental council files, limited ministerial councils and interdepartmental councils,
- monitor the implementation of decisions made at ministerial councils, limited ministerial councils and interdepartmental councils relating to the activities of the department and sub-trust organizations,
- to prepare periodic reports on the application of these decisions, the Office of the Follow-up of the Decisions of the Councils of Ministers, the Restricted Ministerial Councils and the
interdepartmental boards are headed by a director of central administration assisted by a deputy director of central administration and a department head central administration.
Art. 15 - The Office of Information Systems is responsible for:
- to prepare an action plan aimed at developing information and communication systems in the short and long term, in coordination with the parties concerned,
-to ensure the development of the use of computer tools and data exchange within the Ministry, taking into account the national objectives in this area,
-to approve the strategic master plan for the information system of all the services of the Ministry and the institutions concerned, as well as the annual operational master plan of the Ministry,
-to set the Ministry's policy on the acquisition of computer hardware and software as well as recruitment programs for information and communication technology staff,
- set up project management and monitoring mechanisms as well as the measurement of the level achieved with regard to the pre-defined objectives,
-provide website development services, guaranteeing participation and open access to administrative data, as well as its administration, updating and accessibility through search engines,
-Manage and maintain hardware and software.

The Information Systems Office is headed by a Director of Central Administration assisted by a Deputy Head of Central Administration and two Heads of Headquarters.

Art. 16 - The strategic projects supervision office is responsible for:

-propose strategies, projects and programs of action,

-to set up the legislative orientations that guarantee the realization of the strategies, projects and other programs of actions,

-to monitor the technologies related to the sector and to propose their use and their adaptation for an efficient exploitation within the framework of the choices of the plans of economic and social development,

-develop the dashboards for monitoring the progress of implementation of departmental or national strategic projects,

- promote new services and advise on matters referred to it by the Minister,

-evaluate the achievements of the development plans related to the communication and information technologies sector.

The Strategic Projects Supervision Office is headed by a Project Manager, assisted by a Deputy Director of Central Administration.

CHAPTER III

The General Inspectorate of Information and Communication Technologies

Art. 17 - The Inspectorate General of Information and Communication Technologies is responsible, under the authority of the Minister, for the control of the administrative, financial and technical management of all departments under the Ministry, enterprises and institutions under supervision.

It is responsible in particular:

- to carry out any administrative, financial or technical inspection and investigation aimed in particular at evaluating the operating methods of the services and ensuring the legality and sound management of resources,

- to note the offenses committed against the provisions of the post and telecommunications codes and all the legislative or regulatory texts governing the field of information and communication technologies,

- to undertake any missions or investigations entrusted to it by the Minister,

-to prepare reports of the results of these missions and investigations at the end of each inspection and submit them to the Minister,

-to follow up and implement the recommendations made in the aforementioned reports.

Art. 18 - The members of the general inspectorate of information and communication technologies act under a mission order issued to them by the minister in charge of information and communication technologies.

For the accomplishment of their missions, the members of the general inspectorate are given the most extensive investigative power and they have, for this purpose, the right to communicate any document.

The departments of the Ministry, the establishments and enterprises under supervision in which the inspection missions provided for in the previous article are carried out may not oppose professional secrecy to the members of the General Inspectorate.

Art. 19 - The members of the General Inspectorate of Information and Communication Technologies may call on any person competent to examine specific questions.

Art. 20 - The body of the Inspectorate General of Information and Communication Technologies includes the following functional positions:

-an inspector general director of information and communication technologies with rank and benefits of director general of central administration:

-four chief inspectors of information and communication technologies with rank and benefits of director of central administration: 4,
- eight Deputy Inspectors of Information and Communication Technology with rank and benefits of Deputy Head of Central Administration: 8,
- eight inspectors of information and communication technologies with rank and benefits of head of central administration service: 8
Art. 21 - In addition to the inspection body referred to in Article 20 above, the Inspectorate General of Information and Communication Technologies includes a reporting unit responsible for the study and monitoring of reports. audit and investigation reports.
The reporting unit is headed by a Head of Headquarters.

CHAPTER IV THE COMMON SERVICES BRANCH

Art. 22 - The General Directorate of Common Services is in charge of:
- departmental human resources management,
-the preparation of the training plan,
- the elaboration and the control of the law of the frames,
- the development and implementation of social policy,
- the preparation and monitoring of the implementation of the budget,
- the management of logistics issues,
- to assist the structures of the Ministry in legal matters,
-develop and format draft legislative and regulatory texts in association with the specific services concerned,
-to educate and follow the litigation of the ministry,
-
manage and execute public contracts,
- manage documents and archives.
Art. 23 - The General Directorate of Common Services includes:
- the Directorate of Administrative and Financial Affairs,
-the direction of equipment and means,
- the Directorate of Legal Affairs and Litigation,
- the Document and Documentation Management Branch. It also includes a monitoring and coordination unit.
Art. 24 - The Directorate of Administrative and Financial Affairs is responsible for:
-to manage the career of ministry staff,
-to prepare training plans and ensure their execution,
- to promote social, cultural and sports activities for the benefit of Ministry staff and institutions under guardianship,
- coordinate the activities of the mutual and the medical center,
-prepare, discuss and execute the operating and investment budget,
- prepare and schedule the salaries, bonuses and allowances of Ministry staff,
- to follow the administrative and financial management of public administrative establishments under the supervision of the Ministry.
Art. 25 - The administrative and financial affairs department comprises three (3) sub-divisions: The sub-directorate of administrative affairs with three (3) departments:
the personnel management service,
the service of training and competitions,
the service of follow-up of the administrative management.
- the Financial Affairs Sub-Department with three (3) departments:

the budget service,

the scheduling service,

3. the financial management monitoring service.

- the Social Affairs Sub-Directorate with two

(2) services:

the service of social action,

the service of cultural and sports action.

Art. 26 - The Directorate of Equipment and Resources is responsible for:

-manage the supply of services,

- manage and maintain ministry lands and buildings,

- manage and maintain the department's fleet of rolling stock,

-monitor the switchboard and the administrative telephone functions,

- organize and supervise the telecommunication networks of various central services of the Ministry,

- maintain the means of the services,

-Study and monitor the execution of the different markets, purchases and public projects,

- follow the projects of creation of the technological poles, and this, in coordination with the concerned parties.

Art. 27 - The direction of the equipment and the means comprises two (2) sub-directions:

-The Markets Branch with two (2) services:

1. the public purchasing department,

2. the service of the follow-up of the stages of execution of the public markets.

-The sub-direction means with three (3) services:

1. the supply department,

the service of buildings and technological centers,

the maintenance and transport equipment department.

Art. 28 -The Directorate of Legal Affairs and Litigation is responsible for:

-to study the legal files submitted to it by the Minister,

-to establish legal consultations on the questions submitted to it by the various departments of the Ministry,

-develop the draft legal texts relating to the sector in coordination with the specialized services of the Ministry,

- study and follow the Ministry's litigation and coordinate with the specialized services of the Ministry for the execution of judgments.

Art. 29 -The Legal Affairs and Litigation Department comprises two (2) sub-divisions:

-The Legal Studies Branch with two

(2) services:

1. the service of regulations and conventions,

2. the consultation service.

-The Litigation Branch with two (2) services:

the service of the follow-up of the litigation,

the service of the follow-up of the execution of the judgments. Art. 30 - The Subdivision Management Branch

documents and documentation is loaded including:

-developing and implementing the program of management of the current documents produced or received by the services of the department in the exercise of their activity, and this, in collaboration with the national archives,

-to establish systems of classification of the current documents of the services of the ministry and to ensure their good application,

For additional analytical, business and investment opportunities information,
please contact Global Investment & Business Center, USA
at (703) 370-8082. Fax: (703) 370-8083. E-mail: ibpusa3@gmail.com
Global Business and Investment Info Databank - www.ibpus.com

-develop a schedule for the retention of departmental records and ensure compliance with its requirements,

-to collect, organize and maintain the intermediate archives of the Ministry in appropriate premises,

- to organize the communication and the exploitation of the intermediate archives of the ministry and to deposit the definitive archives with the national archives,

-to acquire and collect documents and information regardless of their origin and their support and which concern the areas falling within the remit of the Ministry,

-

to perform for these documents and information, all operations relating to their material and intellectual treatment, their preservation and their communication to users,

- to contribute to the national plan for the establishment of electronic archives.

Art. 31 - The Records and Documentation Management sub-directorate includes three (3) departments:

1. the service of the management of the administrative documents,

the documentation service,

the library service. Art. 32 - The Monitoring and Coordination Unit at the Directorate-General for Common Services is responsible for:

-the follow-up of the reports of the services belonging to the inspection and the supervisory bodies and the jurisdictional bodies,

-the study of requests falling within the remit of the Directorate General of Common Services,

-

to contribute to the implementation of programs aimed at improving the quality of administrative services and monitoring their implementation,

- to ensure coordination between the different departments within the Common Services Directorate-General,

-to ensure coordination between the General Directorate of Common Services and the various structures of the Ministry,

-to supervise the work of the secondary order office of the general services branch.

The Common Services Monitoring Unit is headed by a Deputy Director of Central Administration.

CHAPTER V SPECIFIC SERVICES

Art. 33 - The specific services of the Ministry of Information and Communication Technologies include:

the general direction of information technologies,

- the Directorate-General for Communication Technologies,

- the general direction of the digital economy, investment and statistics,

-the general management of companies and public establishments.

Art. 34 - The Directorate General of Information Technologies is responsible for:

- coordinating between the various stakeholders to promote the development and use of information technologies in the public and private sectors,

give an opinion on national, sectoral and innovative projects related to information technologies with a view to ensuring their coherence and avoiding any form of duplication in terms of planning or investment,

-Develop studies and analyzes relating to the promotion of the uses of information technologies and propose the programs and mechanisms likely to guarantee the right of access to users.

Art. 35 - The Information Technology Branch includes:
the Strategic Studies and Planning Directorate,
2. project and program management,
the director of software and information systems promotion.
Art. 36 - The Directorate of Strategic Studies and Planning is responsible for:
- drawing up national plans of action for the development of information technologies and promoting their use in the public and private sectors and monitoring their implementation,
-monitoring action plans related to the development of information systems in public bodies,
- develop prospective studies in the fields of information technology and ensure technological intelligence in this area,
- to elaborate the studies related to the definition of the standards, standards and technological reference points likely to be adopted in the domains of the development of information systems and to follow up their realization,
- monitoring of indicators relating to the development of information and communication systems and their uses.
Art. 37 - The Directorate of Strategic Studies and Planning has two (2) sub-divisions:
-The department of studies and prospecting with two (2) services:
1. the department of studies in the field of information technologies,
2. the technology watch service.
-The Planning Branch with two
(2) services:
the service of elaboration of the national plan of the development of the technologies of the information,
the service of elaboration of the sectoral plans of the development of information systems in the public sector.
Art. 38 -The Projects and Programs Department is responsible for:
- to propose major national and sectoral public projects in relation to the promotion of the uses of information technologies and to ensure their proper execution by the public bodies concerned,
-assuring at the request of the public organizations, the expertise and assistance for the relationship with the realization of the projects of development of the uses of the technologies of the information and the communication,
-provide technical advice in any area related to government procurement related to information technology,
- to elaborate the methodological guides in relation with the planning, the programming and the realization of the development of the uses of the technologies of the information and the communication.
Art. 39 -Project and program management includes two (2) sub-divisions:
-The Public Sector Assistance and Support Branch with two (2) services:
1. the help desk and support service,
2. the public procurement monitoring service in relation to information technologies.
-The project and program monitoring sub-directorate with one (1) service:
1. The service of major sectoral and national projects.
Art. 40 - The Software and Computer Systems Promotion Department is responsible for:
-propose programs and provisions that promote the production of software and computer systems and monitor their implementation,

For additional analytical, business and investment opportunities information,
please contact Global Investment & Business Center, USA
at (703) 370-8082. Fax: (703) 370-8083. E-mail: ibpusa3@gmail.com
Global Business and Investment Info Databank - www.ibpus.com

- propose the programs relating to the dissemination of digital culture and the development of the uses of information technologies to the general public and ensure their implementation in coordination with the stakeholders concerned,

-work for the establishment of a national observatory of software and computer systems in Tunisia.

Art. 41 - The Software and Computer Systems Promotion Department includes:

-The sub-department for the promotion of the uses of information technologies with two (2) services:

1. the service of the diffusion of the digital culture to the general public,

2. the service of the promotion of the uses of the technologies of the information with the private companies.

Art. 42 - The Directorate-General for Communication Technologies ensures, in particular:

- coordination between the structures responsible for the postal, telecommunications and communication technology strategy,

-the development of strategic objectives ensuring access to television broadcasting networks and services,

-determine the standards and technical specifications.

Art. 43 - The Directorate General of Communication Technologies includes:

1. the Directorate of Telecommunications Technology,

the direction of the postal techniques,

the department of promotion of services.

Art. 44 -The Telecommunications Technology Department is responsible for:

-develop the profitability studies and the procedures for setting telecommunications tariffs,

- to coordinate with the structures concerned in order to set standards and specifications specific to the sector,

-to ensure the application of specifications and technical standards.

Art. 45 -Technology Telecommunications Department includes two (2) subdirections:
-

The Telecommunications Studies Sub-Department with (2) two services:

the studies department,

development service.

- The Sub-Directorate of Telecommunications Programs and Projects with two (2) services:

the service of the technical regulation,

the service of monitoring and quality.

Art. 46 - The direction of the postal techniques is charged in particular:

-develop the profitability studies and the methods for setting postal rates,

- to lay down the procedures and conditions for carrying out activities in the postal sector,

- to coordinate with the structures concerned in order to set standards and specifications specific to the sector,

-to ensure the application of specifications and technical standards in postal matters.

Art. 47 - The Department of Postal Techniques has two (2) sub-divisions:

-The Postal Studies and Standards Branch with two (2) services:

1. the postal studies department,

2. the postal standards and regulations service.

-the sub-directorate of postal activities.

Art. 48 - The department for the promotion of services charged in particular with:
- set the conditions and modalities for the establishment and operation of telecommunications services in coordination with the relevant departments of the Ministry,
- to ensure the application of technical specifications and standards in the field of communication technologies.
Art. 49 - The department of promotion of services includes two (2) sub-divisions:
-the Telecommunications Services Branch and access with two (02) services:
Internet service,
the telecommunications service.
-The broadband promotion sub-branch with two (2) services:
service provision to the public sector,
the benefit service to the general public. Art. 50 - The Directorate-General for the Digital Economy, investment and statistics is responsible in particular for:
- carrying out economic studies and choosing national guidelines and programs in the field of the digital economy,
- the contribution to strengthening investment in the digital economy, supporting institutions and improving their competitiveness,
- the development and support of skills and talents and their adaptation to the needs of the public and private sectors,
- the launching of collaborative research, development and innovation programs in coordination with the structures and institutions concerned,
-the collection and analysis of data, the exploitation and dissemination of statistics, the development of indicators related to information and communication technologies and the monitoring of the evaluation of the sector,
- monitoring the implementation of public-private partnership projects in the digital economy,
-the submission of proposals to further promote partnership projects between the public and private sectors,
-the monitoring of the implementation of the decisions and recommendations relating to the promotion of the digital economy,
- the realization of all the missions coming within the framework of the development of the digital economy.
Art. 51 - The Directorate-General for the Digital Economy, Investment and Statistics includes:
the direction of the investment,
the Department of the digital economy,
the Statistics and Indicators Department.
Art. 52 - The investment department is responsible for:
-develop the business climate and propose incentives for investment,
-provide technological spaces for accommodation and their layout,
-Marketing investment in the field of the digital economy and activate the incentive mechanisms,
-develop and support skills and expertise and ensure they are adapted to the needs of the public and private sectors,
- to supervise investors and intervene on their behalf with the companies concerned with a view to helping them obtain services in the sector under the best conditions,
-complementation of the activities of the stakeholders in the fields of post and information technologies and telecommunications,

- follow-up of the work of the approval committees in the provision of telecommunications services.

Art. 53 -The investment department comprises two (2) sub-divisions:

-the business climate and skills development sub-department with two (2) services:

the service of skills development programs,

the marketing and incentive service and incentive mechanisms,

-the sub-director of organization of activities related to information and communication technologies with two (2) services:

the guidance and monitoring service,

the service of the specifications and approvals.

Art. 54 - The direction of the digital economy is responsible in particular for:

-state orientations and choices to national programs in the field of the digital economy,

-to study the technical, economic, legal and social aspects relating to the realization of projects of the digital economy,

-coordinate between the various structures and institutions in relation to the realization of projects of the digital economy,

- monitor the implementation of public-private partnership projects in the digital economy,

-submit proposals to further promote partnership projects between the public and private sectors,

- launch collaborative programs of research, development and innovation in coordination with the structures and institutions concerned,

-complete the implementation of the decisions and recommendations relating to the promotion of the digital economy.

Art. 55 - The direction of the digital economy comprises two (2) sub-divisions:

-The innovation and private public partnerships sub-department with two (2) services:

1. the monitoring service for partnership projects and innovation,

2. the partnership promotion service.

-The economic studies sub-directorate with two (2) services:

1. the economic studies department,

2. the project monitoring service of the digital economy.

Art. 56 - The Statistics and Indicators Directorate is responsible for:

-the collection, analysis and dissemination of statistics relating to the activities of the Ministry,

-the elaboration, monitoring and evaluation of sectoral indicators,

Art. 57 - The Statistics and Indicators Directorate has one (1) sub-directorate:

- The sub-directorate of statistical data and indicators with two (2) services:

the service for the exploitation and dissemination of statistical data and indicators,

the service of collection and analysis of statistical data and indicators.

Art. 58 - The Directorate General for Enterprises and Public Institutions is responsible for exercising the supervision of public enterprises and establishments under the Ministry of Information and Communication Technologies by:

-

the approval of program contracts, objective contracts and the monitoring of their execution,

- the approval of the estimated budgets and the follow-up of their execution,

-the elaboration of the programs of use of the receipts of the funds of treasure and the follow-up of their execution,

-the approval of the financial statements of public enterprises that do not have general meetings and public institutions that are not administrative in nature,

-examination of files relating to the restructuring of public enterprises and establishments under the Ministry,

-the follow-up of the human resources management of the companies and establishments under guardianship,

-approval of the resolutions of the management and deliberation bodies of companies and public institutions,

- participation in the procedure for approving compensation schemes and salary increases granted to employees of companies with public participation,

- the approval of arbitration agreements and arbitration clauses and dispute settlement transactions, in accordance with applicable laws and regulations.

Art. 59 - The Directorate-General for Enterprises and Public Institutions includes: management of the management of companies and public institutions,

the monitoring department of the organization of public enterprises and institutions,

the unit for monitoring social negotiations and improving working conditions.

Art. 60 - The management of the management of companies and public institutions is in charge of:

-the study and approval of the provisional budgets,

- the approval of the financial statements and the follow-up of the reports of the internal and external audit bodies as well as the preparation of reconciliation statements with the provisional budgets, -the approval and monitoring of the execution of the contractsprograms, contracts-objectives and action plans,

-the elaboration of the programs of use of the receipts of the funds of treasure and the follow-up of their execution,

-the preparation of the operating and equipment budgets of the sub-trustees' public enterprises and institutions and the monitoring of their execution,

- the examination of the productivity files and the study of the performances.

Art. 61 - The management of the management of enterprises and public institutions comprises three

(3) sub-directions:

-The Management Control Sub-Department with two (2) departments:

1. the service of the follow-up of the reports of control and audit,

2. the financial analysis service.

- The Treasure Funds Management Sub-Directorate with two (2) services:

the service of monitoring of the programs of jobs of the recipes, the service of follow-up of realization of the financial operations.

-The management of the forecast management with two (2) services:

1. The contract-program and contract-objective service,

2. the service of budgets.

Art. 62 - The monitoring department of the organization of public enterprises and establishments is responsible for:

- review of specific statuses and job classification tables,

- review of compensation plans as well as salary increases,

- review of organizational charts, executive laws and conditions of appointment to functional positions, follow-up of the regulation on companies and public establishments,

- the proposal to appoint members of the management and deliberation bodies of companies and public establishments,

-examination of the remuneration of the heads of companies and public establishments,

- follow-up of the litigation and the requests,
- follow-up of restructuring programs.
Art. 63 - The directorate of the follow-up of the organization of enterprises and public establishments includes two
(2) under directions:
- The Organization and Regulatory Branch with two (2) departments:
the service of organizational texts,
the restructuring service.
- The management monitoring sub-branch with two departments:
the service followed by the management bodies, the human resources department. Art. 64 - Social Negotiations Monitoring Unit and the improvement of working conditions is responsible in particular for:
1. follow-up of social negotiations and petitions,
2. participation in the settlement of collective labor disputes.
The unit for monitoring social negotiations and improving working conditions is headed by a head of the central administration service.

CHAPTER VI TRANSITIONAL PROVISIONS

Art. 65 - Employees with functional employment provided for in Decree No 97-1320 of 7 July 1997 and Decree No 99-2843 of 27 December 1999 referred to above shall continue, on the date of entry into force of this Decree, to benefit from the bonuses and benefits to their jobs until they are assigned to other duties for a maximum of one year.
CHAPTER VII
Final provisions
Art. 66 - Are repealed, all previous provisions contrary to this decree and in particular the decree n ° 96-1047 of June 3rd, 1996, the decree n ° 971320 of July 7th, 1997 and the decree n ° 99-2843 of December 27th, 1999 referred to above.
Art. 67 -The Minister of Information and Communication Technologies and the Minister of Finance are responsible, each in his respective respects, for the implementation of this decree, which will be published in the Official Gazette of the Republic of Tunisia.
Tunis, September 11, 2012.

For additional analytical, business and investment opportunities information,
please contact Global Investment & Business Center, USA
at (703) 370-8082. Fax: (703) 370-8083. E-mail: ibpusa3@gmail.com
Global Business and Investment Info Databank - www.ibpus.com

STRATEGIC AND LEGAL INFORMATION FOR INVESTING IN TUNISIA

TUNISIA LEGAL SYSTEM AND BUSINESS LAWS

JUDICIAL CAPACITY

Courts in Tunisia suffer from a severe deficit in material and human resources. Many judges lack sufficient judicial training and opportunities to specialise. The process of allocating cases to judges is not sufficiently transparent nor is it efficient, and court decisions lack predictability. Recent reforms have led to the creation of commercial court departments that specialise in commercial dispute resolution, and there is a trend towards an increased use of alternative dispute resolution, including mediation. However, both litigation and enforcement procedures remain lengthy and uncertain.

The judicial system in Tunisia is structured with District Courts being at the base, followed by the Courts of First Instance, then the Courts of Appeal. A Court of First Instance is located in each governorate. The Supreme Court of Cassation serves as the final court of appeals and ensures the proper implementation of the law. It is located in Tunis. The past two decades have seen a trend towards supporting the specialisation of judges in family affairs, social security and the implementation of sanctions. Specialised departments were created in the Courts of First Instance, which now include over 10 employment and commercial departments. There is no separate *Shari'a* or 'personal status' courts in Tunisia. Rather, these types of cases are regulated by codified law and handled by specialised sections in the civil courts.

As is the case in a number of jurisdictions in the region, there is a sharp distinction between public and private law. The separation between administrative courts and courts with general civil jurisdiction stems from that distinction. Administrative law proceedings are heard in the State Council (*Conseil d'Etat*), which operates on two levels. Both the Supreme Council of the Administrative Tribunal and the Supreme Council of the Chamber of Accounts supervise administrative judges.

On the other hand ordinary courts have general jurisdiction to handle civil and criminal litigation as well as commercial disputes. Under the 1959 Constitution[44] the Supreme Judicial Council (SJC) supervises the courts and oversees judge affairs. The SJC is composed of members from both the judicial and executive branches. The Ministry of Justice and Human Rights generally controls court budget and administration, as well as appoints judges.

Following the December 2010 political uprising, reform of the legal framework for the judiciary is more than ever in focus. Previously, there have always been concerns that the executive authority systematically sought to interfere with the independence of the judiciary. Commonly cited evidence of that is the fact that judges are made subject to the authority of the Ministry of Justice, and ultimately, the president who had control over the careers of judges in terms of assignment and discipline. The president also directly and indirectly appointed the majority of SJC members, the real powers of whom have always been contested.

Accordingly, key priorities for reform include strengthening the principles of independence and impartiality of magistrates, in particular by clearly providing for the tenure of magistrates in the constitution, which is currently being redrafted.

In addition, the judicial system requires a greater budget to cover its needs in terms of material resources. Reform should also be directed at investing in capable human resources, particularly by ensuring that both magistrates and court staff receive good quality training. A regular system for ongoing training is required, as well as improved mechanisms for judges to specialise in specific areas of law, not least in commercial law.

SPECIALISED COURTS

Recent reforms have led to the creation of specialised courts in Tunisia. Chapter 40 of the Commercial Code establishes departments within the courts that are specialised in commercial disputes[45]. These departments are comprised of a judge (or three, depending on the type of the dispute), and two 'merchants'[46] from the sector involved in the dispute.

Although this arrangement is perceived by many as a positive step, it also emphasises a lack of commercial expertise among judges leading to the formation of these departments, which rely in large measure on their lay appointees for specialisation. This highlights a need for a greater understanding of commercial practice by judges so that they are able to play a more meaningful role in resolving commercial disputes.

LEGISLATIVE AND PROCEDURAL FRAMEWORK

In a legal system that contributes to an environment conducive to economic development, the judiciary should operate in an optimum legislative and procedural framework. Legislation, regulations and court rules should facilitate the practical administration of justice. Court procedures are generally regulated under the 1959 Civil and Commercial Procedures Law. In addition specific procedures for certain areas of commercial law are regulated under separate legislative texts, such as the 1995 reorganisation law[47], and the bankruptcy code[48].

The assessment highlighted some drawbacks with respect to the procedural regulations for court proceedings. For instance in relation to the procedural rules relating to handling companies in economic distress, the assessment emphasized a need to simplify, revise and update certain litigation procedures. The current system does not provide an efficient mechanism for the law to achieve its objectives in reorganising companies under financial distress when those can be rescued. As a result, instead of benefiting from the advantages of reorganisation, most companies facing financial difficulties are generally sold or end up going bankrupt. Judges of the court of first instance are required in some cases to approve or disapprove the amicable settlement or recovery plan without being able to provide serious input with respect to its content. The rules should therefore be reviewed in order to reinforce the role of the chairman of the Court of First Instance during reorganisation proceedings by giving him more discretion, or the ability to suggest changes to cure potential defects in amicable settlements, so that judges are able to improve the functioning of the reorganisation mechanism. At the same time, specific training would be needed in order to enable judges to play such a role effectively.

In order to reduce lengthy procedural steps, certain types of less important/administrative matters would better be dealt with if channelled to bodies other than the courts. Examples are disputes related to the registration and the deposit of documents in the commercial registry. Procedural difficulties also arise in attempting to obtain any kind of excerpts containing information on pending or closed cases, or in relation to the content of judicial decisions.

The assessment also highlighted a need to simplify and clarify the rules for tax proceedings, especially with respect to procedures relating to the temporary suspension of the execution of tax court decisions. In handling these cases, judges attempt to fill the procedural gaps by clarifying the rules where possible.

In an ideal situation both the legislature and the courts would consider how legal issues could be channelled to the most appropriate forum for resolution. In particular, the court system could benefit from a greater use of alternative dispute resolution in commercial cases given the significant volume of lawsuits that are filed before the courts and the lack of sufficient resources to enable judges to render high quality decisions within a reasonable timeframe.

Quality of judicial decisions

Judicial decisions should be clear, relevant and well reasoned. Court judgments should engender public confidence in the administration of justice and courts should set and enforce policies on the quality of decisions. Of the major problems that were identified in relation to the quality of judicial decisions in Tunisia are the poor structuring and drafting of legal decisions in some instances, which results in the decisions being unclear. These problems are reportedly linked to the fact that judges are overloaded with cases and suffer from a general lack of training and resources.

Another problem with judicial decision-making is a general lack of harmonisation between court decisions. Setting out policies to encourage uniformity in judicial decisions making, as well as on the quality of decisions, and enforcing these policies, is likely to result in better quality decisions.

In addition, judges could be assisted by competent clerks or court assistants who are able to work on cases and to draft initial legal opinions, while the judge determines the case, its reasoning, and renders the final decision. These court assistants could be appointed following a competitive process and upon undergoing training with the High Institute of Magistrates.

Encouraging a more transparent process of allocation of cases and assignment of roles to judges, which takes into consideration each judge's relevant experience, is likely to improve the quality of judicial decisions. Currently, the annual assignment of magistrates does not take into account considerations of specialisation or the level of compatibility between the judge's new assignment and his past experience. As a result, it is not uncommon to find that judges with significant experience in criminal law matters are assigned to commercial divisions.

Finally, improving the initial and on-going training of magistrates, and increasing the number of trained judges is likely to enhance the quality of judicial decisions to a great extent. Current judicial training arrangements are described further below.

For additional analytical, business and investment opportunities information, please contact Global Investment & Business Center, USA at (703) 370-8082. Fax: (703) 370-8083. E-mail: ibpusa3@gmail.com Global Business and Investment Info Databank - www.ibpus.com

Speed of justice

Justice should be rendered within a reasonable timeframe, which takes into account subject matter and complexity. The time between filing and hearing, and between hearing and judgment, should be practical. Benchmark clearance rates should be set for key categories of proceedings, which should be monitored by courts or ministries.

Litigation proceedings are generally lengthy in Tunisia. The large number of cases filed annually before courts and the lack of material and human resources to handle the case load impact both case processing times and the quality of decisions rendered.

In addition, the constant referral of disputes to external experts for opinion results in the unnecessary prolongation of an already lengthy court proceeding. Rationalising and determining reasonable timeframes for those referrals would greatly contribute to reducing the processing time for cases. This should be coupled with enhanced training for judges on fundamentals so that they would have less need for expert advice.

Delays in case processing times are also often due to the untimely transfer of files between different courts or districts. Cases decided by lower courts in different regions are all appealed before the Court of Cassation located in Tunis. Establishing a modern computerised system through which files can be transferred promptly and efficiently between courts would thus greatly reduce the amount of time required for the final settlement of the case.

Because commercial cases are particularly important to the investment climate, allowing special recourse to expedited proceedings in commercial matters might be a good way to overcome lengthy litigation proceedings.

Furthermore, channeling uncontested matters and small claims to be resolved through truncated/ non-judicial procedures could help in mitigating the problem by allowing for the speedy resolve of simple matters, which do not really require judicial attention. An example of issues that could be removed from court jurisdiction is claims concerning trade registry filings and small personal status claims such as corrections to birth or marriage certificates.

Courts would also benefit from a more effective case management system where benchmarks for clearance rates are established and monitored, and relevant data collated for analysis.

Applying a computerised court system throughout the country and providing access to court clerks will also eventually enable each court to establish its own statistics on the types of cases it handles and will provide the judiciary system with proper data on timing. The maintaining of such data should be both transparent and thorough, and thus should be published. Encouraging litigants and their lawyers to append soft copies of their reports and documents that are filed with the registry of the court would also enhance the speed of dealing with the computerised system.

Impartiality and transparency

The independence of the judiciary must be guaranteed so that the operation of courts remains free from government influence. The judiciary must be impartial and must function as a cohesive institution. In an optimal environment, decisions will be based on fact and law, without favour to any party.

Courts should also establish codes of conduct on impartiality for judges and court staff, and monitor compliance. Allegations of bias and corruption should be investigated, and new cases allocated objectively and transparently.

The independence of the judiciary is currently a heated topic in Tunisia. Judges and civil society alike are calling for deep reforms to guarantee the independence and impartiality of the judiciary. A significant demand is to expressly ensure judicial independence in Tunisia's new constitution, which is currently being drafted.

In addition, judges have been stressing that the principle of security with respect to the tenure of judges must be clearly stipulated, with any exceptions clearly defined. The aim is to strengthen confidence in the judicial system and allow the delivery of justice without fear from the executive power or the Ministry of Justice and Human Rights.

Under the former regime, the law regulating the High Council of the Judiciary[49], granted the Minister of Justice the right to decide on the transfer of judges for service needs. This right is claimed to have been used in the past to intimidate judges. A priority therefore is to ensure the financial, institutional and operational independence of the High Council of the Judiciary. Further, the right granted to the Ministry of Justice and Human Rights to transfer judges and prosecutors against their will should be abolished. Similarly of concern is that the law provides that the President of the Republic assumes the position of Chairman of the High Council of the Judiciary, and the Minister of Justice the position of Vice-Chairman, which affects the autonomy of the Council and its independence.

Decisions relating to judge nomination would be better handled by the High Council of the Judiciary upon its reform, or a similar independent body. These decisions should be transparent, and based on objective and pre-set criteria. The appointment of court chairmen and presidents could be better made through elections by magistrates who serve in the same jurisdiction.

In addition, interviewed experts noted that the composition of the High Council of the Judiciary should be reconsidered so that the council solely consists of elected judges. The seat of representative members from the executive power or the Ministry of Justice and Human Rights should be eliminated.

Ensuring the independence and impartiality of judges also requires that judges are sufficiently remunerated. According to local advisors, Tunisian judges receive a salary that is neither consistent with their status and workload nor sufficient to ensure a certain level of independence and impartiality.

An appropriate mechanism should also be put in place in order to detect and avoid situations of conflict of interest, which sometimes arise due the existence of family ties or nepotism between judges, prosecutors and lawyers. The assignment of cases should be based on clear and objective criteria, as under the current regime it is sometimes difficult to detect problems relating to conflict of interest.[50]

The assessment also identified a need for a more transparent and effective disciplinary system for judicial misconduct. Both judges and court staff should be subject to a compulsory code of conduct. Once a code of conduct is put in place, it must be efficiently monitored and enforced. There should also be more active investigation of alleged bias or cases of irregular payments within the court system.[51]

Finally, with respect to case assignment, a system of random allocation within a pool of adequately trained and experienced judges should be encouraged to ensure that the process is transparent.

Judicial education

Judges in a well functioning, well-trusted system should receive comprehensive initial training. In addition, proper on-going training should also be strongly encouraged, mandatory in appropriate cases, and a factor in judicial promotion. Training curricula should be shaped by higher courts or independent supervisory bodies. They should cover all relevant substantive areas and vocational subjects such as decision-writing and ethics. Court management staff should receive managerial and financial training. Better training would assist in granting courts greater rule-making powers to improve trial procedures especially where the governing legal texts are not sufficiently clear.

In Tunisia, the High Institute of Magistrates (*Institut Superieur de la Magistrature*) is in charge of judicial training. The Institute operates under the supervision of the Ministry of Justice. Although the current system for *initial* judicial training is generally perceived by local practitioners to be sufficient, there remains a need for an enhanced system of *on-going* judicial training.[52]

In addition to the Higher Institute of Magistrates, a research body, the Center for Legal and Judicial Studies, was established in the Ministry of Justice in 1992. The Centre is required to opine on different legal and judicial matters including all subjects relevant to the development of judicial functions. It also has authority to carry out practical research and comparative law studies in order to develop the country's legislation and improve the means of their enforcement. Judges serving in the Centre are amongst the most qualified and skilled in Tunisia.

Nevertheless, the professional training available at present is optional and insufficient. Among other things judicial training in Tunisia should specifically target practical commercial knowledge and financial literacy of judges, and encourage specialisation in areas such as banking, capital markets, corporate, and international trade law.

It is also important that continuous training for magistrates is made compulsory and that it involves all magistrates regardless of their level of experience. It is also crucial that training is extended to different regions in the country, as the fact that training is exclusively offered in the capital discourages judges exercising in areas outside of Tunis from attending, given the need to travel and the costs involved.

Enforcement

In an effective economic system, court decisions must be implemented and enforced within a reasonable timeframe and in an efficient manner. Courts must promptly notify parties of decisions, and effective enforcement mechanisms must be in place.

Implementation of decisions should be monitored. High incidence of non-compliance in particular areas should be investigated and remedied by government action.

Globally, Tunisia stands at number 76 in the ranking of 183 economies on the ease of enforcing contracts.[53] The enforcement of judicial decisions, especially against private parties faces considerable obstacles. In certain circumstances, the legal framework allows individuals to use the executive power to have themselves declared a 'needy social case' against whom the court may not enforce. In other cases, enforcing authorities face technical challenges such as in the case where it is difficult to identify property that would cover a claimed debt.

To increase the efficiency of the enforcement of judgments, certain reforms should be made. Of foremost importance is limiting the ability of the executive power to hinder the enforcement process. The involvement of police officers and bailiffs in the enforcement process should be strictly monitored and supervised to avoid any chances of corruption, which could lead to more delays in enforcement. Procedures for seeking the police force's assistance in the enforcement of court decisions against private parties should be clearly defined, as these are not currently delineated in any specific text.

In addition, the establishment of a reliable database of commercial registration for companies, containing up-to-date information, would greatly facilitate swift enforcement against commercial entities. This is also true with respect to enhancing Credit Bureau databases with comprehensive and reliable information.

The enforcement of judgments against State and public institutions, and government authorities is even more difficult. In this respect, a major legislative obstacle lies in Article 37 of the Public Accountancy Code which provides that State and public institutions "are exempt from seizure, even pursuant to duly enforceable deeds, for money, taxes and other receivables, securities, stocks, movable or immovable property, and generally, all goods without exception belonging either to the State, public institutions or local communities."[54] A suggestion for reform that has been cited in this respect is to abrogate Article 37 of the Public Accounting Code and to impose sanctions against private and public persons or entities that refuse to execute a court decision.

Predictability/access to decisions

An efficient judiciary should ensure maximum predictability in its processes and judgments, and produce a coherent body of case law. There should be a court policy to promote certainty, and procedures for court oversight of jurisprudence.

Due to the lack of clarity of certain legislation in Tunisia, court decisions are in many cases inconsistent, and thus unpredictable. A clarification of texts defining the procedures would ensure a greater predictability of decisions. So would the regular scanning and publication of court decisions so as to make them more accessible to the public.

Contributing to the low levels of predictability is the fact that lower court decisions are neither automatically nor promptly published. In order to ensure maximum predictability in its processes and judgments, courts should attempt to harmonise a coherent body of case law.

Finally, predictability also refers to the amount of time it takes for a dispute to be resolved. Thus it would be useful if indicative timelines were set for the determination of cases which vary according to the complexity of the subject, and the value of the claim.

Resources

To function effectively, the judicial system requires adequate material and human resources, including appropriate court premises and equipment, court leadership and management, and court staff. At present, courts in Tunisia generally suffer from low resources. Reportedly, the deficiency that existed before the 2010 uprising in both material and human resources has been made worse when certain courts and other judicial institutions were vandalised and destroyed during the events of the Tunisian revolution.

The assessment has identified, as a high priority matter, the courts' requirement for greater access to material resources including premises[55], equipment, technology, and means of transport. Court premises were reported to be inadequate. Shortage in equipment includes computers, printers, scanners, shredders etc... Providing scanners would help in retaining soft-copies of the various documents contained in the records, and in turn facilitate the creation of a virtual database for computerised archives. In addition, a sufficient number of printers should be made available to court staff in order to facilitate the prompt provision of services.

Laying out a computerised system to replace the current physical archiving system throughout the country, and establishing a network that links regional courts with courts in Tunis is likely to reduce case processing times and increase efficiency. Similarly, making available remote access to records which allows litigants to consult the content of court records and case files from a distance is likely to release the excessive pressure on court staff. Access should also be given to court clerks in order to enable them to efficiently process and manage data that is relevant to case files.

Courts do not have vehicles that allow them to carry out the various tasks inherent to their activities. When judges or prosecutors need to travel to locations outside the court, they are forced to share hired vehicles with litigants, use police vehicles, or their personal cars. Any of those situations is likely to create uneasiness for the judge and might negatively affect his reputation for impartiality.

Given the large number of cases filed before Tunisian courts[56], greater human resources are also required. This includes judges, administrators and court clerks. According to information received in the course of our assessment, magistrates are overworked[57] and higher judicial salaries are required to attract and retain sufficiently qualified judges.

Court registries are understaffed. Not only are court staff overworked, but they also lack proper training and qualification. Cases are often delayed or remain pending, which could be due – among other things - to the clerk's unfamiliarity with certain registration procedures, or because a clerk has to leave his/her post in order to assist another colleague.[58]

Another issue that was identified in the assessment is the lack of any system to effectively monitor the conduct of court employees. As a result, irregular payments to court clerks are not uncommon. This is also the case because despite efforts to maintain reasonable judicial and court personnel salaries, the government has not been able to accomplish this objective, specifically with regards to support personnel. Increasing the budget that is allocated to the judiciary is likely to improve working conditions for judges and court employees and therefore ultimately improve the quality of court decisions and services.[59]

Alternative dispute resolution

An Arbitration Code was passed by law No. 93-42 in 26 April 1993, and a Tunisian Centre for Reconciliation and Arbitration established in 1996. The code draws extensively on the UNCITRAL model law. It provides dispute settlement guarantees in favour of investors, and flexible procedures aimed at ensuring effective settlement. A Decree dated 10 December 1992 provided for administrative mediation. However, the use of alternative dispute resolution mechanisms remains in need for further encouragement, and enhanced training.

THE EXECUTIVE POWER

The executive power is exercised by the President of the Republic assisted by the Government presided by the Prime Minister. The draft constitution grants more powers to the government and states that 'executive power is exercised by the President of the Republic and the Government'.

The President of the Tunisian Republic

One of the many reasons for the Revolution in Tunisia was the abuse of power by the executive, namely, former President Ben Ali. Therefore, although the new Constitution has not been voted yet and it is therefore not possible to fully examine the future functioning of the executive, one can assume that the Constitution will attempt to hold the president accountable to the people. The draft states that the President cannot hold office for more than two terms and limits his executive powers. Despite these attempts to amend the flaws in the old Constitution regarding abuses of the executive powers many NGOs such as Amnesty International are raising their concerns persistent discrimination that continues in the draft of the new Constitution such as "specifying that only a Muslim can become a president".

The following paragraph on the working of the executive power is based on the former Constitution as Tunisia has only an interim President.

The president of Tunisia is the elected head of state. He is elected for 5 years based on the majority of votes gained according to a universal, free, direct and secret suffrage within the last thirty days of the term of office. He is the guarantor of national independence, the integrity of the Tunisian territories, respect for the Constitution and the applicable laws, law enforcement, ratification and execution of treaties, as well as governing according to a decree during the expiration of the term of the legislative power. He watches over the regular functioning of the constitutional public powers and assures the continuity of the State.

Designation

The president of the Republic of Tunisia appoints and dismisses the Ministers as well as the prime minister. He leads and coordinates the work of the Government and promulgates the laws. The president also represents the republic in international affairs, and he formally appoints and dismisses the civil servants, soldiers, and judges of the state. He may temporarily delegate his powers to the Prime Minister except the right to dissolve the Chamber of Deputies.

A candidate for the Presidency must be a Tunisian who does not carry another nationality, who is of Muslim religion and whose father, mother, and paternal and maternal grandfather have been of Tunisian nationality without interruption. Also, the candidate must be at least forty years and at most seventy five years of age on the day of submitting his candidacy, and enjoy all his civil and political rights.

The declaration of candidacy must be recorded in a special register before the constitutional council. The council rules on the validity of the candidacy, announces the results of the ballot and settles the challenges received accordingly.

Functions

The President is the Supreme Commander of the Armed Forces. He accredits diplomatic representatives to foreign powers.

The President may submit to a referendum any bill relating to the organization of the public powers or seeking to ratify a treaty which, without being contrary to the Constitution, may affect the functioning of the institutions.

Also, the President ratifies the treaties, declares war and concludes peace with the approval of the Parliament exercises the right of pardon and directs the general policy of the Nation, defines its fundamental options, and informs the National Parliament accordingly. He communicates with the Parliament either directly or by message.

He promulgates constitutional, organic, or ordinary laws and ensures their publication in the Official Journal of the Tunisian Republic within a maximum period of fifteen days counting from the transmission by the President of the National Parliament. During this period, the President of the Republic may return the bill to the National Parliament for a second reading. If the bill is adopted by the National Parliament with a majority of two-thirds of its members, the law is promulgated and published within a second period of fifteen days.

He watches over the execution of the laws. He exercises the general regulatory power and may delegate all or part of it to the Prime Minister.

The President nominates the highest civil and military officers on the recommendation of the Government.

Term of Presidential functions

In case the Presidency of the Republic becomes vacant on account of death, resignation, or total incapacity, the constitutional council immediately convenes and confirms the vacancy of the office with the majority of its members. The council consequently notifies the President of the Chamber of Advisors and the President of the Chamber of deputies who immediately assumes the office for a minimum period of 45 days and a maximum of 60 days. In case such a vacancy occurs during the end of the term of the Chamber of deputies, the President of the Chamber of advisors shall assume the office for a similar period. The acting President of Republic shall take the constitutional oath before the Chambers of deputies and advisors.

The acting President of the Republic may not be a candidate for the Presidency of the Republic even in the case of resignation.

The interim President of the Republic discharges the functions of the President of the Republic, however, without resorting to referendum, dismissing the Government, or dissolving the National Parliament. During this period, a motion of censure against the Government cannot be presented.

During the same period, presidential elections are organized to elect a new President of the Republic for a term of five years.

The new President of the Republic may dissolve the National Parliament and organize early legislative elections.

THE PRIME MINISTRY

The President nominates the Prime Minister, and on his suggestion, the other members of the Government. The President presides over the Council of Ministers. In the draft, the head of Government calls in and presides over the Council of Ministers, except on Foreign affairs, Defense and National Security issues where the President is presiding.

The Prime Minister directs and co-ordinates the work of the government. He substitutes, as necessary, for the President in presiding over the Council of Ministers or any other Council.

The President dismisses the Government or one of its members on his own initiative or on the recommendation of the Prime Minister.

Bills are deliberated on in the Council of Ministers. Decrees of a regulatory character are countersigned by the Prime Minister and the interested member of the Government.

The members of the Government have the right of access to the Parliament as well as to its committees. Any deputy may address written or oral questions to the Government.

The Parliament may, by a vote on a motion of censure, oppose the continuation of the responsibilities of the government, if it finds that the government is not following the general policy and the fundamental options. The motion is not receivable unless it is motivated and signed by at least the third of the Parliament's members. The vote may not take place until 48 hours have elapsed after the motion of censure. When a motion of censure is adopted by a majority of two-thirds of the deputies, the President accepts the resignation of the government presented by the Prime Minister.

MINISTERS

The Government (the Ministers) puts into effect the general policy of the nation, in conformity with the orientations and options defined by the President of the Republic. The Government is responsible to the President for its conduct.

For additional analytical, business and investment opportunities information, please contact Global Investment & Business Center, USA at (703) 370-8082. Fax: (703) 370-8083. E-mail: ibpusa3@gmail.com Global Business and Investment Info Databank - www.ibpus.com

In the draft, the Government is responsible to the Assembly of People's Representatives. This new wording probably reflects intent to create a better balance between the executive and the legislative to avoid abuses by the executive.

Ministries

- Ministry of Interior
- Ministry of Foreign Affairs
- Ministry of National Defense
- Ministry of Industry
- Ministry of Information and Communication Technologies
- Ministry of Tourism
- Ministry of Education
- Ministry of Higher Education, Scientific research and Technology
- Ministry of Public Health
- Ministry of Social Affairs
- Ministry of Youth and Sports
- Ministry of Transportation
- Ministry of Agriculture, Hydraulic Resources and Fisheries
- Ministry of Finance
- Ministry of Trade and Handicrafts
- Ministry of Culture and Preservation of Legacy
- Ministry of equipment, housing and land planning
- Ministry of the State Property and Land Affairs
- Ministry of Environment and Sustainable Development
- Ministry of Justice
- Ministry of Vocational Training and Employment

THE LEGISLATIVE POWER: PARLIAMENT

By the decree law of March 23, 2011, the lower house, "the Chamber of Deputies" and the upper house, "the Chamber of Advisors" were dissolved. In the future Constitution the wording the "Assembly of the People's Representatives" will replace the "Chamber of Advisors" and "Chamber of Deputies". Its representatives shall be elected for five years by a universal, free, direct, secret, sincere and transparent ballot according to the modalities and conditions determined by the Electoral Law. The draft added the terms "sincere and transparent" as an attempt to break with former regime. To recall "Under the former regime of Zine el-Abidine Ben Ali, the cabinet, much of the legislature, and many regional officials had been appointed directly by the president. Elections were tightly controlled, and term limits were extended to allow Ben Ali to remain in power."

Furthermore, the draft stresses the importance of the opposition and enshrines its rights within the Assembly. The former regime in "the parliament passed a law that criminalized opposition activities deemed to be fomented by 'agents of a foreign power.'"

With the resignation of Ben Ali, "in the 2011 elections, all 217 members of the Constituent Assembly were directly elected through party-list voting in 33 multimember constituencies, and voters were able to choose from political parties representing a wide range of ideologies and political philosophies, including Islamist and secularist groups. Many of the parties that competed were excluded from political participation under Ben Ali." With the former election system while the members of the Chamber of Deputies were "elected by universal, free, direct and secret vote" the Chamber of Advisors was tied to the executive. Indeed "The members of the Chamber of Advisors are elected as follows: One or two members from each governorate, according to population's number, are elected at the regional level from among the members of elected local authorities.

One-third of the members shall be elected at the national level from among employers, farmers and workers whose candidacies shall be proposed by the respective professional syndicates from a list comprising at least twice the number of seats allocated for each category. Seats are distributed equally among the concerned sectors. [...]

The remaining members of the Chamber of Advisors are appointed by the President of the Republic from prominent and qualified figures at the national level."

Regarding the adoption of organic and ordinary law, the Assembly of People's Representative will probably maintain a similar organization, meaning, "Chambers of Deputies and Advisors ratify organic laws by the absolute majority of the members. Both Chambers also ratify ordinary laws by the majority of the members present in the session, considering that such majority reaches at least one third of the concerned Chamber."

Lastly, it should be noted that while the Constitution of 1959 stated "During the recess of the Chamber of Deputies and the Chamber of Advisors, the President of the Republic may issue decree-laws which will be submitted, as the case may be, for ratification by the Chamber of Deputies or by the two chambers during the ordinary session following the recess" the draft mentions the Head of the Government and not the president as the authority that may issue decree-laws.

THE CONSTITUTIONAL COUNCIL

The role of a Constitutional Court or Council is to control the constitutionality of draft laws and proposals. Its independence is essential for a proper implementation of the Constitution. In a desire to avoid abuses such as the ones perpetrated by former regime, the draft will enforce several changes. First, while the Constitutional Council was composed of nine members, the Constitutional Court will be composed of twelve members. Furthermore, the President of the Republic will have less saying in their appointments. To recall, the President used to appoint four of the members and the President of the Chamber of Deputies two. The draft states that the President of the Republic will only propose candidates.

The Amendment of the Constitution

Despite the fact that most of the draft is in line with the former constitution there are several safeguards proposed that prevent altering and abusing Presidential executive powers. For instance, no amendment can be made to the term of the presidential mandates if it is with the intent to extend the term. To recall, in 1988 an amendment to the Constitution permitted the President to serve for three five-year terms and again, in 2002 an amendment abolished the term limits.

Independent Constitutional Authorities

The draft shall also introduce several independent constitutional Authorities. They will deal with elections, information, Human Rights, Corruption.

A new authority, an institution of sustainable development and right for future generations will probably take over the Economic and Social Council. To recall, the Economic and Social Council is a consultative assembly in economic and social matters. Its composition and relations with the National Parliament are determined by law.

ADMINISTRATIVE SETUP

The municipal and regional councils conduct the local affairs under the conditions determined by law. For administrative purposes, Tunisia is divided into 23 governorates, each headed by a governor who is appointed by the president.

OTHER (SEMI) GOVERNMENTAL INSTITUTIONS

- Central Bank of Tunisia
- Export Promotion Center
- National Institute of Statistics
- Tunisian National Tourism Office

LAW FACULTIES

- Free University of Tunis
- University of Sfax: Faculty of Law

  Route de Sidi Mansour, km 10
  B.P. 704
  3061 Sfax, Tunisia
  Phone: (216 4) 27.2441; 27.2331

Fax: (216 4) 27.2245

- Faculté des sciences juridiques, politiques et sociales de Tunis
  14, Rue Hédi Karray
  2080 Ariana, Tunisia
  Phone: (216 1) 23.0235; 75.3892; 76.6919
  Fax: (216 1) 71.7255

- Faculty of Law, Politics and Economics Science of Tunis
  Campus Universitaire
  1060, Tunis, Tunisia
  Phone: (216 1) 51.0323; 51.0627; 51.0500
  Fax: (216 1) 51.0139

- Faculty of Human and Social Sciences of Tunis
  94 A. 9 Avril 1938
  1007, Tunis, Tunisia
  Phone: (216 1) 56.4713; 26.4797
  Fax: (216 1) 56.7551

- University of Zaituna: Faculty of Law
  29, rue Asdrubal
  1002, Tunis, Tunisia

TUNISIA BUSINESS LAW

LEGAL SYSTEM

Tunisia applies a mixed legal system that is mainly based on the French civil law system, with some influence from Islamic law in the areas of personal status and property. Two of the first legislative texts to be codified were the Code of Obligations and Contracts (1906), and the Civil Procedure Code (1913), both of which remain to this day, but not without significant modifications.

Until 15 January 2011, the governing Constitution was that drafted in 1959 following Tunisia's independence from France. Under the original Tunisian constitution, Tunisia was a presidential republic with the president enjoying a myriad of powers, including heading a number of strategic institutions such as the Supreme Judicial Council. The president also directed general state policy and promulgated laws.[1]

The legislative system is bicameral with two houses of Parliament. The upper house is the Chamber of Councilors (Majlis Al Mustashareen), and the lower house is the Chamber of Deputies (Majlis Al Nuwab). A Constitutional Council examines drafts of laws that are proposed by the President to ensure their conformity with the Constitution. The Council also has the power to resolve disputes that arise between the legislative and executive branches on the interpretation of legal texts. Treaties and questions of institutional organisation must be submitted to the Constitutional Council for review, and the views of the Council are binding.

The court system in Tunisia is divided into four levels with the District Courts at the base of the structure, followed by the Courts of First Instance, then the Courts of Appeal, and the Court of Cassation. A Court of First Instance is located in each governorate, whereas the Court of Cassation is located in Tunis. It serves as the final court of appeals and ensures the proper implementation of the law. In addition, there is a High Court that is competent to deal with cases of high treason by a member of government, and real estate courts that decide on disputes involving the demarcation of property. The past two decades have seen a trend towards supporting the specialisation of judges and special employment and business departments were created in the Courts of First Instance. There is no separate *Shari'a* or personal status courts in Tunisia. Rather, these types of cases are regulated under codified law and handled by specialised sections in the civil courts.

Similar to a number of other jurisdictions in the region, Tunisia has a separate administrative court system that is applied through a State Council (*Conseil d'Etat*). This system provides two levels of litigation that are the Administrative Tribunal and the Department of Accounts. Furthermore, a special judicial body is responsible for ensuring conformity with state budget and the efficient allocation of public funds.

As part of economic development and liberalisation policies in the country, the past decade has witnessed the establishment of special bodies with judicial powers such as the Competition Council, the National Telecommunications Commission, the General Authority for Insurance, and the Financial Market Council.[2]

Following the 2010 uprising, a Constituent Assembly was elected on October 2011 in order to draft a new Constitution for Tunisia. The Assembly is to act as an interim legislative body until general elections take place.

COMMERCIAL LEGISLATION

Tunisia's commercial law traditions have been strongly influenced by the French legal system. Commercial legislation is mainly to be found in the Code of Commerce of 1959 and the Code of Obligations and Contracts. Although Tunisia applies a civil law system, emphasis is nevertheless placed on court precedent. Tunisian law comprises formal sources such as legislation, decrees, regulations and customs, and interpretive sources such as case law.

In 2012 the EBRD conducted an assessment of Tunisia's commercial laws, with a focus on key areas relevant to "Infrastructure and energy" (concessions/PPPs, energy regulation, telecommunications and public procurement) and to "Private sector development" (corporate governance, insolvency, judicial capacity and secured transactions). In a number of these areas, the Bank's assessment combines two approaches in order to evaluate the state of legal reform in the provided key sectors. The tools assess both the quality of the laws formally adopted (extensiveness) and the actual level of implementation of these laws as well as the framework they underpin (effectiveness). Combining the results of these analytical tools shows not only how advanced the system is compared with international benchmarks, but it also shows how effective the legal system is in a given field in practice, and points to the areas where further reform may be required.

The EBRD's assessment of Tunisian commercial laws shows that in a number of sectors relevant to investments, the legal framework has seen some amendments, but there remain important challenges and there is room for reform in a number of areas. For instance, Tunisia has a history of concession projects and a potentially attractive environment for public-private partnerships. However, the country does not have a single comprehensive act unifying all concession and PPP related provisions.

Recent reforms have led to the creation of commercial court departments that specialise in commercial dispute resolution, including mediation. However, the enforcement of contracts in general remains a lengthy and uncertain process.

In relation to the strengthening of the financial sector and the support of small and medium enterprises (SMEs) via better access to finance, a number of weaknesses in the Tunisian legal regime were identified. The development of SMEs will require better access to finance, which can be accomplished thorough revision of the secured transactions regime. At present the current secured transactions regime still significantly favours the taking of collateral over real estate, which many SMEs do not have to offer. Enforcement of security over any type of property is also a serious issue that will require significant reforms, including of the judiciary. In addition, the high level of non-performing loans in the banking sector will require a revision of the insolvency regime and debt enforcement with the view of allowing for more efficient debt resolution mechanisms as well as a more balanced outcome for both creditors and borrowers.

Corporate governance has also been identified by Tunisian financial sector stakeholders as an area that is in need of strengthening.

TABLE 1 - Snapshot of Tunisia's commercial laws

FOCUS AREA HIGHLIGHTS

the new laws yet.

TELECOMS

Public procurement

The EBRD's assessment of the overall legal and regulatory risks in association with the country's communications sector shows that Tunisia is in the "medium risk category" from the standpoint of investors. The country's legal framework for the sector has provided the formal basis for a competitive market for mobile communications since 2002 and for fixed electronic communications since 2009. Whilst there is competition in the mobile sector, the fixed market remains dominated by the incumbent operator. In practice, the regulator remains under the authority of the ministry and has poor enforcement powers. The state-dominated telecoms company operates all access lines, and does not offer the sharing of its infrastructure. Furthermore, special permissions are required to operate an internet service provider (ISP) business and all ISPs are obliged to use the fixed lines of the state-dominated telecoms company.

While the procedures for obtaining rights of way on public and private property are set out in legislation, they do not seem to have been applied in practice

CORPORATE GOVERNANCE

Secured transactions

The results of EBRD's 2011 assessment of the corporate governance framework in Tunisia showed that national legislation "*on the books*" is in '*high compliance*' with relevant international standards. However, in practice several areas relating to corporate governance, including the institutional framework, are in need for reform. Those areas pertain to transparency and disclosure, the rights of minority shareholders and the possibility of parties to seek and obtain quick and efficient redress.

Source: EBRD legal assessments 2012 (for further details please see the focus analysis in the following sections).

The EBRD has developed and regularly updates a series of assessments of legal transition in its countries of operations, with a focus on selected areas relevant to investment activities. These relate to investment in infrastructure and energy (concessions and PPPs, energy regulation and energy efficiency, public procurement, and telecommunications) as well as to private-sector support (corporate governance, insolvency, judicial capacity and secured transactions).

Detailed results of these assessments are presented below starting with infrastructure and energy and going into private sector development topics.

INFRASTRUCTURE AND ENERGY

CONCESSIONS AND PPPs

In a nutshell...

Results revealed that the law on the books in Tunisia are in "high compliance" with internationally recognised

standards (UNCITRAL Principles), mainly because of modern legislation, which was adopted in 2008 and

supplemented in 2010 to govern PPP projects building on successful PPP experience.

Nevertheless, in measuring the effectiveness of the law in practice, Tunisia was found to be in "low compliance"

with international best practices. This is mainly attributable to a lack of a clear PPP policy, lack of coordination

among public sector participants and no real enforcement experience as no projects have been implemented

under the new laws yet.

PRIVATE SECTOR DEVELOPMENT

CORPORATE GOVERNANCE

In a nutshell...

The results of EBRD's 2011 assessment of the corporate governance framework in Tunisia showed that national

legislation "on the books" is in 'high compliance' with relevant international standards. However, in practice

several areas relating to corporate governance, including the institutional framework, are in need for reform.

Those areas pertain to transparency and disclosure, the rights of minority shareholders and the possibility of

parties to seek and obtain quick and efficient redress.

In 2005, Tunisia issued Law No. 96 of 2005 on the Strengthening of the Security of Financial Relations[25] and amended its Companies Law[26] to make corporate dealings more transparent and set internal controls to help prevent directors from usurping corporate assets. Disclosure and related-party transactions have been the focus of recent regulation in the country, which lead the World Bank to cite Tunisia in its 2011 Doing Business Report, as a leader in the region with respect to investor protection reforms. Tunisian law now requires shareholders' approval for certain dealings and prevents directors with conflicting interests from voting[27].

The 2005 amendments provided a baseline for transparency regarding accessibility of company books to shareholders. It set external checks on the actions of management, and strengthened auditor responsibility, as well as prohibited company loans to directors, managers, and their families. According to the new Tunisian law, a group of shareholders together representing 10% of the capital of the company are entitled to inspect financial statements, annual reports, lists of guarantees, securities, and sureties granted by the company, as well as the minutes of the shareholder meetings over the previous 3 years.[28]

The 2005 amendment was followed by the adoption of the Law on the Stimulation of Economic Initiative in 27 December 2007. This legislation directly addressed prejudicial related party transactions and granted shareholders access to internal documents. The Law also allows minority investors to request a judge to rescind a prejudicial related-party transaction. In 2008, the Arab Institute of Business Managers (IACE) in collaboration with the Center of International Private Enterprise (CIPE), published a guide on corporate governance best practices for Tunisian corporations. The guide encompasses practical recommendations and measures that aim at improving corporate governance in Tunisia.[29]

Efforts such as these resulted in another amendment of the Commercial Companies Law No. 93 of 2000, by Law No. 16 of 2009 in March of the same year.

The law on the Enterprise Accounting System No. 96112 of December 30, 1996, provides for the establishment of the National Accounting Council, which is an advisory body to the Ministry of Finance. The National Accounting Council is responsible for reviewing and opining on draft accounting standards and applications as well as accounting matters set out in other draft laws and regulations. Tunisian Accounting Standards are enacted by Decrees issued by the Minister of Finance. Council membership comprises the Minister of Finance, the Governor of the Central Bank, as well as representatives from other ministries, the Supreme Audit Institution, and the accounting and audit profession.[30] Tunisian accounting requirements pertaining to credit institutions are primarily set out in the Tunisian Accounting Standards which are supplemented by certain regulations issued by the central bank (*Banque Centrale de Tunisie*) "BCT".[31]

For additional analytical, business and investment opportunities information,
please contact Global Investment & Business Center, USA
at (703) 370-8082. Fax: (703) 370-8083. E-mail: ibpusa3@gmail.com
Global Business and Investment Info Databank - www.ibpus.com

LEGISLATIVE FRAMEWORK

The main laws governing corporate governance in Tunisia are law No. 2000-93 of 3 November 2000 enacting the Commercial Companies Code ("The Code"); law No. 2005-96 of 18 October on the Strengthening of the Security of Financial Relations; and law No. 2007-69 of 27 December 2005 on the Stimulation of Economic Initiative.

In addition, there is a series of requirements that apply to companies that are listed on the Tunisian Stock Exchange, namely the Financial Act32, Regulations of the Securities and Exchange Committee (Conseil du Marché Financier)[33], and the Tunis Stock Exchange Code (Réglement Général de la Bourse).

In 2009, Law No. 2009-16 of 16 March 2009 amended the Commercial Companies Code and targeted the approval and disclosure requirements of transactions between interested parties. It required both the board of directors' and shareholders' approval for related party transactions. In addition, interested parties could no longer participate in the approval process and the transaction was to be reviewed by an independent auditor. The law also requires interested directors to disclose their conflict of interest to the board.

Two additional aspects of the 2009 amendments to the Commercial Companies Code are particularly important. These are the introduction of shareholders agreements and the simplifying of the incorporation procedures of companies. The amendments also addressed the relationship between partners, and the obligation to make corporate documents available to shareholders, and to keep records of the list of managers, and records of shares and securities. Shareholders are now able to enter into agreements amongst themselves to regulate aspects of ownership, voting rights, control and management of the company, provided that these arrangements are not contrary to the company's charter. The Law further simplified and reduced company publication formalities.

Recent amendments have also included improvements in relation to stock options companies. These amendments addressed conflict of interest situations, the right of shareholders to submit written questions to the Board,[34] and the possibility for minority shareholders to withdraw from the company.

The Tunisian commercial registry system is regulated by the Law 1995-44 of 2 May 1995. It provides for the establishment of a local commercial registry in each court of First Instance. In addition, the law requires all existing and newly established companies to register in the Central Register, which is maintained by the National Institute of Standards and Industrial Property.[35] A new law enacted in 2010[36] now tackles reformation of the commercial registry. This legislation is aimed at modernising business registration by providing a single registry number for companies, introducing electronic means in the publication procedures and reducing the timeframe for the completion of these procedures.[37]

The results of EBRD's 2012 assessment of the corporate governance framework in Tunisia showed that national legislation is in a 'high level of compliance' with relevant international standards

The quality of legislation on the books appears to be generally sound. Nevertheless, there is room for improvement in a number of key areas such as disclosure and transparency and the responsibilities of the board.

The results of the assessment are further analysed in the following sections:

Ensuring the basis for an effective corporate governance framework

A good corporate governance framework should promote transparent and efficient markets, be consistent with the rule of law and clearly articulate the division of responsibilities among different supervisory, regulatory and enforcement authorities. The framework should be developed with a view to its impact on overall economic performance, market integrity, and the incentives it creates for market participants and promotion of transparent and effective markets.

Our assessment reveals that the corporate governance reform process in Tunisia could benefit from increased transparency and predictability.

International standards require that the legal and regulatory requirements that affect corporate governance practices should be consistent with the rule of law, transparent and enforceable. In Tunisia, the legal and regulatory corporate governance requirements have been reported to be generally clear and well understood by economic participants, as well as sufficiently enforced. Special court sections exist in the judiciary to handle corporate cases, and a sufficient portion of corporate governance law has been tested in court. In addition, the securities market regulator can intervene on behalf of shareholders in corporate disputes.

A dialogue on corporate governance matters between the Government and the private sector has been reported. Workshops and conferences are organized under the responsibility of public bodies to help insure a link between the government and the private sector. Despite those developments, the country has not adopted a voluntary corporate governance code.

In collaboration with different public agencies, the Ministry of Justice is the entity in charge of reviewing and developing corporate governance laws. In addition, other bodies in the public and private sectors (both domestic and foreign) have initiated, supported and been active in promoting corporate governance reform in Tunisia, including a legal and judicial research centre operating under the auspices of the Ministry of Justice that is in charge of legal reforms, an association of certified public accountants and others professional organisations such as the associations of lawyers, auditors, public officers (notaries); the Tunisian Bank Association; and the Tunisian union of industry and trade.

Good corporate governance standards mandate that the division of responsibilities among different authorities in a jurisdiction is clearly articulated and ensures that public interest is served. In this respect, while on one hand, it appears that each economic agency is overseen by a supervisory authority (e.g., the financial market is monitored by the Financial Market Council), on the other hand there does not seem to be an effective system of cooperation in place between the different authorities.

The OECD Principles recommend that supervisory, regulatory, and enforcement authorities should have the authority, integrity and resources to fulfil their duties in a professional and objective manner. Moreover, their ruling should be timely, transparent, and fully explained. Budget of the regulator should be published and its expenses transparently described. In Tunisia the budget of the regulator is not published but is controlled through court auditors. Although the rulings of regulatory agencies are documented and publicly available, access to this information is not easy.

A key drawback remains in the low level of coordination of provisions under different laws, decrees, and regulations, which causes uncertainty. The adoption of a uniform law, consolidating the many company law provisions that are scattered across a wide variety of legislative texts into one uniform code could significantly improve the efficiency of the overall framework and decrease the uncertainty on the scope of application of these different laws and regulations.

SHAREHOLDER RIGHTS

A sound corporate governance framework should ensure that the essential rights of shareholders and key ownership functions are provided. These rights include but are not limited to access to information, voting, and profit sharing. Shareholders should be furnished with sufficient and timely information concerning the date, location and agenda of general meetings, as well as full and timely information regarding the issues to be decided at the meeting. It is not only important that these rights are clearly stated, but also that shareholders – both national and foreign - have easy access to their rights.

In Tunisia, the law grants shareholders with rights such as the right of ownership registration, the right to convey or transfer shares, obtain relevant corporate information, participate and vote in general shareholder meetings, elect members of the board, and share in profits. In line with good international standards, opportunity is provided for shareholders to submit questions to the board (subject to reasonable limitations) and to place items on the agenda at general meetings. However, a good corporate governance framework should also ensure that shareholders are able to obtain information about the company at no costs and without undue delays.

A corporate governance framework should also allow the use of electronic communication and easily accessible and transparent voting in absentia procedures. While on one hand, the law allows shareholders to vote by post, on the other hand, this is an area which Tunisian regulators should consider improving and aligning with best international practices.

The OECD Principles of Corporate Governance mandate that shareholders have the right to participate in, and to be sufficiently informed of decisions concerning fundamental corporate changes such as amendments to the company's statutes, or articles of incorporation; the authorisation of additional shares; and extraordinary transactions, including the transfer of all (or substantially all) of the company's assets, that in effect result in the sale of the company. Most of these rights are provided under Tunisian law.

In Tunisia, shareholders must be informed of and have the exclusive power to vote on amendments to the company charter, issuance of additional shares, merger, take-over, or reorganisation of the company, winding up or voluntary liquidation, waiver of preemptive rights in the event of an increase in capital.

Existing shareholders have pre-emption rights to subscribe for newly issued shares in proportion to their relevant shareholding.

The shareholders' meeting can be requested by an authorised representative appointed by any shareholder or shareholders jointly holding 5 per cent in non-listed joint stock companies or 3 per cent in listed joint stock companies.

A 66 per cent majority is required to pass resolutions in relation to amendments to the company's charter, merger, company's reorganisation, winding up or voluntary liquidation.

The OECD principles recommend that shareholders should have the opportunity to obtain redress for violation of their rights. Effective methods should be in place to ensure redress at a reasonable cost and without excessive delay. In Tunisia, in case of violation of the rules relating to the convening of the shareholders meeting, any shareholder (regardless of his shares' ownership percentage) is entitled to bring action in order to set aside a shareholders' resolution taken in violation of these rules.

The law does not seem to impose restrictions on transactions involving shareholders with a conflict of interest regarding the transaction in order to avoid disadvantageous transaction terms for the company.

THE EQUITABLE TREATMENT OF SHAREHOLDERS

The principle of the equal treatment of shareholders of the same class is a key issue in corporate governance. Within any series of a class, all shares should carry the same rights. All investors should be able to obtain information about the rights attached to all series and classes of shares before their purchase.

Tunisian law recognizes the principle of 'one share one vote' for common shares and shareholders have the right to access information about the voting rights attached to each class of shares before investing.

A good framework should also ensure that minority shareholders are protected from abusive actions by, or in the interest of, controlling shareholders acting either directly or indirectly, and should have effective means of redress. Insider trading and abusive self-dealing should be prohibited. In Tunisia the law requires publicly traded and listed companies to disclose company information which is likely to affect stock-exchange prices without delay.[38] Further, board members, senior management, and controlling shareholders are required to disclose transactions in their company's shares.[39] Directors, officers, or shareholders who have conflicting interests to those of the company's can be legally prevented from voting at meetings where the deal-related conflict of interest issues are to be discussed.

The Commercial Companies Code allows minority shareholders in Tunisia to pool their votes for the election of a certain board candidate (cumulative voting). This particular procedure provides minority shareholders with a better chance to have a say in electing board members and thus allows them the opportunity to share in setting the direction of the company's management.

Although the law contains sanctions for the violation of the rules on notification of shareholder meetings, there are no specific sanctions with respect to the rules allowing shareholders to place items on the agenda for the annual meeting. However a shareholder may instigate a legal action for the violation of their rights.

Members of the board and managers should be required to disclose any material interests in transactions or matters affecting the corporation. In Tunisia the law requires disclosure by the company of loans made to related parties (e.g. parent companies, subsidiaries, directors, employees, their spouses, children or relatives of the company or related companies). All related party transactions must be specifically approved by the board, disclosed to shareholders, and registered in the company financial statements. Transactions made by companies, which are not based on fair market values, may be invalidated and action can be taken against the relevant parties.

THE ROLE OF STAKEHOLDERS

The OECD Principles require a corporate governance framework to ensure that the rights of stakeholders, including company employees and creditors, are both protected by the law and respected in practice. Further, the corporate governance framework should permit performance-enhancing mechanisms for stakeholder participation.

Tunisian law contains provisions on the safety of workers, protection of suppliers as stakeholders, and the protection of creditors as stakeholders. In addition the 1988 Environment Law provides for the protection of the environment. The Tunisian framework also incorporates remedies for the violation of the rights of employees, suppliers, and creditors.

One of the essential rights of stakeholders is to receive regular and reliable information for a sound assessment of the company's management and profitability. A good corporate governance framework should ensure that investors, creditors, employees, the market and all other stakeholders can rely on the information received by the company and act accordingly. The integrity of the market requires information be reliable, timely disclosed, regularly updated and easily accessible. In Tunisia, although corporate information is generally considered to be reliable, stakeholders are not granted special access to such information.

DISCLOSURE AND TRANSPARENCY

According to the OECD Principles, a corporate governance framework should ensure that timely and accurate disclosure is made with respect to all material issues regarding the corporation, including the financial situation, performance, ownership, and governance of the company. In addition disclosure should include, but not be limited to, material information on company objectives, majority shareholder ownership, and remuneration policies for members of the board and key executives, and information about board members, including their qualifications and selection process, other company directorships, and related party transactions.

In Tunisia the rules governing disclosure and transparency could benefit from some improvement (See Chart 10, above), especially with respect to non-financial disclosure such as foreseeable risk factors as investors and market participants should be able to get reliable information on potential risks such as the risks specific to the industry or geographic area, dependence on commodities, risk related to derivatives and off-shore, or environmental liabilities, in order to be able to monitor and protect their investments. The law does not require companies to appoint a body to specifically be in charge of corporate governance issues, although this is common practice in big companies.

With reference to financial disclosure, joint stock companies are required to prepare annual audited financial statements. However, companies are not required to prepare and disclose financial and operating data in accordance with internationally recognised accounting standards. Finally, companies are not required by law to disclose key issues relevant to employees and stakeholders that may materially affect the performance of the company, such as management/employee relationships and relations with creditors, suppliers, and local communities.

RESPONSIBILITIES OF THE BOARD

A sound corporate governance framework should ensure that the board fulfils its role in providing strategic guidance to the company, effectively monitors management, and that the board is accountable to the company and the shareholders. Board members should act on a fully informed basis, in good faith, with due diligence and care, and in the best interest of the company and the shareholders. Further, the board should be able to exercise objective judgement on corporate affairs independent, in particular, from management.

In Tunisia the law does not require that the board includes a sufficient number of non-executive and independent directors. Although publicly traded and listed companies are required to have separate committees for auditing/financial reporting, and for executive and board remuneration the law does not provide a definition for board independence, nor is the board required to have separate committees to deal with board nominations or, corporate governance (to oversee compliance with corporate governance standards). The Tunisian companies' law set out a limitation imposed as to the number of board directorships that a director can hold. Board members cannot be directors in more than 8 Tunisian incorporated companies.

HIGHLIGHTS OF THE CORPORATE GOVERNANCE FRAMEWORK IN PRACTICE

A review of the corporate governance framework is incomplete without an assessment of the effectiveness of corporate governance legislation in practice. Charts 11 and 12 below illustrate the results of an assessment of compliance with corporate governance rules in practice, based on a case-study dealing with related-party transactions.

In Tunisia while the rules for disclosure seem to be relatively developed, the remedies available to minority shareholders in the event of a breach of their rights are in dire need for reform in terms of the enforceability, simplicity, speed, and cost of legal action.

The effectiveness (how the law works in practice) of corporate governance legislation was assessed by the EBRD in 2012, examining a case study dealing with related-party transactions. The case study investigated both the position of a minority shareholder seeking to access corporate information in order to understand if a related-party transaction had been entered into by the company, and how to obtain compensation in

For additional analytical, business and investment opportunities information,
please contact Global Investment & Business Center, USA
at (703) 370-8082. Fax: (703) 370-8083. E-mail: ibpusa3@gmail.com
Global Business and Investment Info Databank - www.ibpus.com

cases where damage was suffered. Effectiveness of legislation was then measured according to four principal variables: complexity, speed, enforceability and institutional environment (See Chart 11 above). The survey revealed a variety of actions available to minority shareholders to obtain disclosure; however, procedures with respect to redress were seen as complex, expensive and time-consuming.

The statutory framework for Tunisian commercial insolvency law comprises:

- law no. 2003 – 79 of 29 December 2003, modifying and completing law no. 95-34 of 17 April 1995 as amended by the law no. 99-63 of 15 July 1999 with respect to the restructuring of businesses in financial difficulty (the ☐eorganisation Law);

- book IV on composition procedures and insolvency (the BBankruptcy Law) of the 1959 Commercial Code (the "CCommercial Code") which, following the introduction of the Reorganisation Law, is intended to apply to businesses that cannot be restructured; and

- the 1959 Code of Civil and Commercial Procedure (the CCivil and Commercial ☐ode).

Rules on distributions upon solvent and insolvent liquidation of companies and priority debts are contained in Title III on liquidation of companies under the Commercial Code and Title VI of the Real Property Code law no. 65-5 of 12 February 1965 (the Real Property Code) respectively.

Tunisia has an old Bankruptcy Law (1959) and a relatively new Reorganisation Law (1995, updated in 1999 and 2003). Both the Bankruptcy Law and the Reorganisation Law follow the French civil law framework.

The approach and style adopted by the Bankruptcy Law and the Reorganisation Law are very different. The Bankruptcy Law contains many provisions of a punitive nature and is, as such, debtor-unfriendly. At the other end of the spectrum, the Reorganisation Law is perceived by some as excessively debtor-friendly. The two pieces of legislation have yet to be harmonised, although a reform project is underway.

An insolvency regime should permit both efficient liquidation/winding-up and reorganisation where possible. As discussed below, the Tunisian regime allows for both liquidation and reorganisation proceedings. However, the regime would benefit from further reform in order to bring it closer to internationally recognised standards and best practice in insolvency.

The following sections provide further information on the main formal proceedings available under the Tunisian insolvency regime:

a. Reorganisation

The Reorganisation Law draws upon a combination of two recent French insolvency procedures: *règlement amiable* and *redressement judiciaire* and, consequently, adopts a more 'modern', debtor-friendly approach. Nevertheless, procedures under the Reorganisation Law have not kept pace with existing French insolvency legislation. Subsequent to the adoption of the Tunisian Reorganisation Law in 1995 and its revision in 2003, *règlement amiable* has been replaced in France in 2005 by conciliation and

For additional analytical, business and investment opportunities information,
please contact Global Investment & Business Center, USA
at (703) 370-8082. Fax: (703) 370-8083. E-mail: ibpusa3@gmail.com
Global Business and Investment Info Databank - www.ibpus.com

redressement judiciaire, has been revised by the law no. 2005-845 of 26 July 2005 (following earlier revisions in 1994 and 1999).

The Reorganisation Law encompasses two procedures aimed at the reorganisation and continuation of a debtor's business: (1) amicable settlement, a court-supervised mediation procedure involving the appointment of a mediator, which is only available for solvent debtors and (2) judicial settlement,. a court-based procedure in which a judge and an insolvency office holder (*administrateur judiciaire*) are appointed, which is only available for insolvent debtors.

The Reorganisation Law sets out strict timeframes in which the debtor is required to act and requires the debtor to file detailed information and

documentation to benefit from the law's application.

However, in practice the time periods prescribed by the Reorganisation Law are not well respected and delays occur. This is due to a number of factors ranging from lack of court resources to failure of the insolvency office holder to deliver his report on time and debtor or creditors to appear before the court when summoned.

(1) Amicable Settlement

Only management of the debtor may apply for amicable settlement under the Reorganisation Law. This is in contrast to the judicial settlement procedure, where both debtors and creditors can petition for entry into the proceedings.

For amicable settlement the debtor must propose an arrangement with its creditors within a period of three months following opening of the procedure. This period is extendable by one month only. There is no automatic moratorium on legal proceedings and security enforcement upon opening of the procedure. Generally a moratorium comes into force upon the requisite majority of creditors agreeing to the amicable settlement arrangement and will last for the duration of such arrangement. A moratorium is only available on an exceptional basis at an earlier stage of the amicable settlement procedure where it is established that payment of a particular creditor would result in deterioration in the condition of the debtor's business and would present an obstacle to its recovery.

Statistics produced by the Commission (*la commission de suivi des entreprises économiques*) on the number of cases under the Reorganisation Law for 2009-2011 indicate that the amicable settlement procedure is rarely used. For example, in 2011, there were only two cases where amicable settlement was used, compared with 61 cases of judicial settlement. This may be due, in part, to the requirement for the debtor not to be insolvent in order to benefit from the amicable settlement procedure. It may also be due to a lack of willingness on the part of creditors to participate in amicable settlement, which is a voluntary procedure. Unlike the concept of *conciliation* in France, amicable settlement proceedings in Tunisia are not confidential. Lack of confidentiality may also discourage the use of amicable settlement.

(2) Judicial Settlement

Judicial settlement constitutes a compulsory point of entry into insolvency proceedings for insolvent debtors. Article 54 of the Reorganisation Law expressly requires any liquidation of the debtor's business to be preceded by judicial settlement. Amicable settlement proceedings will lead to judicial settlement proceedings where it is not possible to reach an agreement with creditors or where the debtor fails to appear before the mediator. Although aimed principally at the development of a recovery plan, in the absence of a viable proposal, the court will assess whether it is possible to effect a sale (*cession*) or a lease (*location*) of the business before ordering the opening of any bankruptcy proceedings. This is because the primary objective of judicial settlement is the saving of the business and employment. If recovery of the business by any of these means is not possible, the court will declare the debtor bankrupt and the debtor will be subject to bankruptcy proceedings under the Bankruptcy Law.

The period for preparation of a recovery plan in judicial settlement proceedings is slightly longer than that in amicable settlement. The initial three month 'observation' period is capable of extension by a further three months by decision of the president of the court. The recovery plan is fundamental since it provides the basis for the opinion of the insolvency judge (*juge commissaire*), appointed by the president of the court to oversee the insolvency case, on the prospects of survival of the debtor's business. Only once the recovery plan is received is the insolvency judge able to order the transfer of the business into bankruptcy or liquidation or, where possible, the sale or lease of the business. A moratorium on legal proceedings and security enforcement arises upon commencement of the observation period and continues for its duration, thus providing debtors with a safe harbour from creditor action.

Following the 2003 reform of the Reorganisation Law, creditor recovery and execution proceedings in respect of personal guarantees (*cautions*) are no longer suspended by the moratorium[41]. Personal guarantees are common in Tunisia and this exception to the general moratorium may undermine the prospect of reorganisation of smaller 'entrepreneur led' businesses. The Reorganisation Law does not give the debtor any responsibility for preparing or assisting the insolvency officeholder with the development of the recovery plan. In addition, the level of qualifications and expertise of insolvency officeholders appear to present an obstacle to the development of an effective recovery plan.[42] Discussions with Tunisian officials during the assessment revealed a general sense of lack of innovation and expertise in recovery plans prepared by insolvency officeholders. The level of training and commercial knowledge of the judges dealing in insolvency matters is also perceived to be an issue. Proper training would likely provide both judges and insolvency officeholders with the skills required to propose and implement more innovative restructuring solutions.

Whilst the Reorganisation Law gives insolvency office holders an initial three months for the preparation of the recovery plan, extendable by a further three months, in practice the plan is never prepared within this maximum six month period. Reasons cited for the delay included the high work burdens of insolvency office holders and the existing pay structure, which favours payment for services on a daily basis and therefore does not encourage the efficient resolution of insolvency cases. There are no consequences for failure of the insolvency office holder to submit the recovery plan within the period required under the Law. Frequent appeals of court decisions made in judicial settlement also lengthen the duration of the proceedings.

The consequences of delay in submission of the recovery plan are severe for debtors. Insolvency proceedings have a negative effect on the debtor's business as they often involve adverse publicity. They also create general uncertainty amongst all parties, from creditors to clients of the business, as to whether the debtor will be able to honour its contractual obligations. In a lengthy insolvency procedure, where there is no agreed plan of action, the debtor's financial position is likely to continue to deteriorate. This hampers the prospect of recovery and, in the event of liquidation, reduces available returns to creditors.

Recovery plans are generally limited to a rescheduling of debt, since the Reorganisation Law stipulates that the consent of each individual creditor is required for any reduction in principal. No possibility exists under the Law for a qualified majority of creditors by value to agree to a reduction in the overall debt of the debtor's business. In practice, the repayment terms of the existing debts have to be rescheduled over a long period in order for the level of debt to be serviceable by the debtor. The Law does not set a maximum time limit for the duration of recovery plans. As a result, many recovery plans typically reschedule debt over a period of 15 to 20 years. The parties are then tied to its implementation over such period.

The requirement to enter into judicial settlement is designed to preserve the business as a going concern. However this may add a layer of judicial process for businesses that are, in fact, destined for liquidation. Businesses that enter into judicial settlement remain in practice within the procedure for a long time, in some cases for many years. This is despite the text of the law, which envisages an efficient and workable timeframe. In practice, the length of the procedure leads to a general sense of inertia by all parties involved.

b. Liquidation/Bankruptcy

The Bankruptcy Law contains the principal mechanisms of an insolvency law: appointment of a judge and official receiver (*syndic*), imposition of a moratorium on legal proceedings, a procedure for realisation of assets, provisions governing consultation with creditors and a limited post-bankruptcy debt compromise procedure for unsecured claims.

Despite the introduction of the 1995 Law more than 15 years ago, the Bankruptcy Law has remained unreformed, although there are proposals to harmonise this with the existing Reorganisation Law. In general, the Bankruptcy Law remains an out-dated piece of legislation. Its primary focus is liquidation of the debtor's business, hence the need for the Reorganisation Law.

The Bankruptcy Law applies to all traders (*commerçants*) for which the judicial settlement procedure is unsuccessful and to any business ineligible for judicial settlement, such as businesses which have ceased trading for more than one year.. Both debtors and creditors can petition for entry into the bankruptcy procedure and it is a criminal offence for a debtor not to file for bankruptcy within one month following suspension of payments. Although the law does not state this expressly, entry by the debtor into judicial settlement will, in practice, suspend the one month filing requirement.

Contrary to modern international insolvency standards, there is an overt emphasis on punitive measures in the Tunisian Bankruptcy Law and frequent cross-reference to the provisions of the Penal Code. For example, under the Bankruptcy Law the court may order the detention of an individual trader in prison or the suspension of trading of a business[43]. Any non-rehabilitated insolvent person is stated to lose his civil rights as a result of being declared insolvent. He may no longer vote, be eligible for appointment to a political or professional assembly or occupy any public role. There is, furthermore, no provision for automatic discharge of the debtor from insolvency. Instead the debtor must apply to court for rehabilitation and will be ineligible for rehabilitation where he has committed certain offences under the Penal Code and has not been rehabilitated thereunder.

The moratorium which arises upon the declaration of bankruptcy in Tunisia does not restrict the enforcement of security by secured creditors in the context of bankruptcy proceedings under the Bankruptcy Law.

Nevertheless, the process of enforcement and sale of secured property under Tunisian law will be overseen at all times by a specialist court. If the secured creditor has a registered title to the asset

(e.g. mortgage over land) then the secured creditor will not need to obtain a court judgment that its claim is due and enforceable. However, the secured creditor will be required to deliver notice to the debtor of its intention to request the court to enforce its security. If the secured creditor does not have registered title to the asset, it will need to apply first to the court for executory title to the asset before requesting the court to commence the sales process. The debtor has the right to challenge the sale of the secured asset, which in practice may lead to further delays in enforcement by the secured creditor. Sale by the court will always be by public auction, with the exception of the right of the debtor under Article 425 of the Tunisian Civil and Commercial Code to proceed with the sale of the secured asset provided that the sale price is enough to repay the secured creditor(s) in full. Sale by the debtor may be by private sale. The option of private sale is not available to secured creditors.

Among the criticisms that were highlighted during our assessment of the Tunisian insolvency regime is a lack of any real harmonisation between the Reorganisation Law and the Bankruptcy Law. Under the Bankruptcy Law, the debtor can theoretically avoid liquidation by reaching a compromise agreement with its creditors; yet this is of limited scope since the compromise agreement cannot bind secured creditors in respect of their secured debts. Also the compromise procedure under the Bankruptcy Law is arguably redundant since the insolvent debtor must first propose a recovery plan to his creditors in judicial settlement proceedings under the Reorganisation Law. It would be more effective if the Bankruptcy Law were to focus instead on liquidation and create insofar as possible a streamlined liquidation procedure.

Rules of Distribution and Priority Debts

The system for determining priority debts under Tunisian law is complex as the rules on priority are contained in a number of different legislative texts, although primarily in the Bankruptcy Law and the Real Property Code.

Title III on the dissolution of companies of the 1959 Tunisian Commercial Code contains rules regarding distributions by liquidators to creditors. Provisions with respect to solvent and insolvent dissolutions of companies are dealt with together, notwithstanding that solvent dissolution aims for the payment of creditors in full, unlike insolvent dissolution which recognises that there may be a shortfall. The rules on distributions in liquidation are not cross-referenced in the Bankruptcy Law.

Article 46 of Title III provides that the liquidator must distribute available assets amongst creditors in accordance with their priority ranking. If assets are insufficient, assets must be distributed *pari passu*

i.e. equally amongst creditors of the same rank in proportion to their debts. Creditors with priority debts are stated to rank ahead of other creditors.

Priority debts described in Title VI of the Tunisian Real Property Code encompass priority debts generally and are not restricted to insolvency situations. The debtor's assets are described as subject to the "common pledge" of his creditors and are thus available for distribution amongst creditors, subject to legitimate preferences. Article 193 of Title VI describes the categories of legitimate preferences as privileges, security and right of retention (*les privileges, le nantissement et le droit de retention*). Title VI provides that privileged creditors i.e. creditors with priority debts rank ahead of all other creditors (including those with mortgages).

Priority debts are classified as either general or special privileges. General privileges apply to all of the debtor's assets (movable and immovable property), whereas special privileges apply only to certain assets. Priority creditors of the same rank are to be treated equally. In a number of jurisdictions taxes no longer have priority status. In Tunisia, however, sums due to the public treasury pursuant to laws in existence are one of the most important priority debts, since they are capped neither as to time nor as to amount. They rank ahead of secured creditors and may significantly reduce returns to secured creditors in a liquidation scenario. Salaries due to employees, workers and other persons in employment, sums for the maintenance and of the debtor and his family, in each case for the last six months also constitute priority debts.

Costs of the actual bankruptcy proceedings are satisfied as and when they fall due in the proceedings pursuant to Article 495 of the Bankruptcy Law. There is no provision regulating unpaid bankruptcy costs and the priority of such costs vis-à-vis other priority debts referred to in the Real Property Code.

STRATEGIC ECONOMIC INFORMATION

Tunisia has a diverse economy, with important agricultural, mining, energy, tourism, and manufacturing sectors. Detailed governmental control of economic affairs has gradually lessened over the past decade with increasing privatization of trade and commerce, simplification of the tax structure, and a cautious approach to debt. Real growth has averaged 4.5% in 1991-96, and inflation has been moderate. Growth in tourism and increased trade have been key elements in this solid record. Agricultural production accounted for a major portion of growth in GDP in 1996, growth having been adversely affected by drought in 1995. Further privatization, the attraction of increased foreign investment, and improvements in government efficiency are among the challenges for the future.

Bordered on the West by Algeria and on the East by Libya (with the Mediterranean to the North), Tunisia has made a concerted effort to develop economic and political stability. This has led to strong efforts by the government to open up the economy and maintain tight control over issues affecting the country's security. World Bank officials have praised Tunisia for its reforms, but would like to see privatization move more rapidly. GDP and exports have risen, due to a recent free trade agreement with the European Union and a healthy agricultural harvest.

POLITICAL STRUCTURE

Tunisia is a constitutional democracy headed by President Zine el-Abidine Ben Ali. Elected in 1987, President Ali has led the country for the last nine years. Under the terms of the Tunisian constitution, the president can be elected for a maximum of three five-year terms. Cabinet members are chosen by the president and are responsible only to him. Tunisia has a 163 member unicameral parliament, whose members are elected to five-year terms. Political parties based on race, religion, region or language are strictly forbidden. The country is divided into 23 governates and has 257 municipalities.

The president's party is the Constitutional Democratic Rally Party (RCD). RCD has a majority hold on the government with 144 seats in parliament and controls all of the country's 257 municipalities. There are six other legal parties: the Movement of Democratic Socialists (MDS); the Party for Popular Unity (PUP); the Socialist Progressive Party (RSP); the Social Liberal Party (PSL); the Union of Democratic Unionist (UDU); and the Communist Party. While these parties are recognized, their small size and lack of any broad-based support do not allow them to play a significant role in the political sphere. The country's legal system is based on French civil law system and Islamic law. There is some judicial review of legislative acts in the supreme court.

ECONOMIC POTENTIAL

Tunisia has a diverse economy, ranging from agriculture, mining, manufacturing, petroleum products and tourism. In 2008 it had a GDP of $41 billion (official exchange rates), or $82 billion (purchasing power parity). It also has one of Africa and the Middle East's highest per-capita GDPs (PPP). The agricultural sector stands for 11.6% of the GDP, industry 25.7%, and services 62.8%. The industrial sector is mainly made up of clothing and footwear manufacturing, production of car parts, and electric machinery.

For additional analytical, business and investment opportunities information,
please contact Global Investment & Business Center, USA
at (703) 370-8082. Fax: (703) 370-8083. E-mail: ibpusa3@gmail.com
Global Business and Investment Info Databank - www.ibpus.com

Although Tunisia managed an average 5% growth over the last decade it continues to suffer from a high unemployment especially among youth.

Tunisia was ranked the most competitive economy in Africa and the 40th in the world by the World Economic Forum. Tunisia has managed to attract many international companies such as Airbus and Hewlett-Packard.

The European Union remains Tunisia's first trading partner, currently accounting for 72.5% of Tunisian imports and 75% of Tunisian exports. Tunisia is a one of the European Union's most established trading partners in the Mediterranean region and ranks as the EU's 30th largest trading partner. Tunisia was the first Mediterranean country to sign an Association Agreement with the European Union, in July 1995, although even before the date of entry into force, Tunisia started dismantling tariffs on bilateral EU trade. Tunisia finalised the tariffs dismantling for industrial products in 2008 and therefore was the 1st Mediterranean country to enter in a free trade area with EU.

Tunisia also attracted large Persian Gulf investments (especially from United Arab Emirates) the largest include:

- Mediterranean gate: a US$ 25 billion project to build a new city in the south of Tunis.

- Tunis Sport City: an entire sports city currently being constructed in Tunis, Tunisia. The city that will consist of apartment buildings as well as several sports facilities will be built by the Bukhatir Group at a cost of $5 Billion.

- Tunis Financial harbour: will deliver North Africa's first offshore financial centre at Tunis Bay in a project with an end development value of US$ 3 billion.

- Tunis Telecom City: A US$ 3 billion project to create an IT hub in Tunis.

REAL ESTATE MARKET

In recent years Tunisia has embarked on a new market. Since the beginning of the 2000's, the real estate market has grown. The market focuses partially on residencies for private persons, but also larger projects aimed at the tourist and sales market. Notable investors reside in the Arab states of the Persian Gulf.

OIL AND GAS EXTRACTION

Oil production of Tunisia is about 97 600 barrels/day. The main field is El bourma.

ENERGY

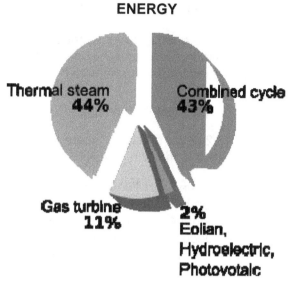

Sources of electricity production

The majority of the electricity used in Tunisia is produced locally, by stateowned company STEG (Société Tunisienne de l'Electricité et du Gaz). In 2008 a total of 13 747 GHW was produced in the country.

OIL AND GAS

Oil production began in 1966 in Tunisia. Currently there are 12 oil fields. Below is a list of the oil fields:

Oil field	Oil field
7 November oil field	El Menzah field
Ashtart field	Belli field
Bouri field	Cercina field
El Biban field	El Borma field
Ezzaouia field	Miskar field
Sidi El Kilani field	Tazarka field

NUCLEAR ENERGY

Tunisia is on the path of installing two nuclear powerplants within a 10 year period. Each one of these is projected at producing 900-1000 MW. In its effort to obtain nuclear energy, France is set to become an important partner. Tunisia and France have inked agreements, where France will deliver training and know-how amongst others.

DESERTEC PROJECT

The Desertec project is a large-scale energy project aimed at installing solarpower panels in, and a grid connecting North Africa and Europe. Tunisia will be a part of this project, but exactly how it may benefit from it remains to be seen.

TRANSPORTATION

- The country maintains 19 232 km of roads, where the A1 Tunis-Sfax, P1 Tunis-Libya and P7 Tunis-Algeria are major highways.

- There are 30 airports in Tunisia, with Tunis Carthage International Airport and Monastir International Airport being the most important ones. A New airport Zine El Abidine Ben Ali International Airport was completed at the end of October 2009, and is due to open December 2009. However, it appears flights are unlikely to start before the Easter season of 2010. The airport is located North of Sousse at Enfidha, and is likely to serve the resorts of Hamammet and Port El Kantoui, together with inland cities such as Kairouan. There are four airlines headquartered in Tunisia: Tunisair, Karthago Airlines, Nouvelair and Sevenair.

- The railway network is operated by SNCFT, and amounts to 2135 km in total. The Tunis area is served by a tram network, named *Metro Leger*.

Tunisia is in the process of economic reform and liberalization after decades of heavy state direction and participation in the economy. Prudent economic and fiscal planning have resulted in moderate but sustained growth for over a decade. Tunisia's economic growth historically has depended on oil, phosphates, agri-food products, car parts manufacturing, and tourism. In the World Economic Forum 2008/2009 Global Competitiveness Report, the country ranks first in Africa and 36th globally for economic competitiveness, well ahead of Portugal (43), Italy (49) and Greece (67).

HISTORICAL TREND

Current GDP per capita soared by 380% in the Seventies. But this proved unsustainable and it collapsed to a paltry 10% in the turbulent Eighties rising to a modest 36% in the Nineties signifying the impact of successful diversification.

This is a chart of trend of gross domestic product of Tunisia (estimated) by the International Monetary Fund with figures in millions of Tunisian Dinars.

Year	Gross Domestic Product (Constant Prices - Billions)	US Dollar Exchange (PPP)	Inflation Index (2000=100)	Per Capita Income (as % of USA)
1980	7.620	0.244 Tunisian Dinars	29	11.16
1985	9.358	0.305 Tunisian Dinars	46	6.59
1990	10.816	0.347 Tunisian Dinars	65	6.50
1995	13.074	0.401 Tunisian	85	7.36

		Dinars		
2000	17.181	0.440 Tunisian Dinars	100	5.85
2005	21.372	0.437 Tunisian Dinars	114	6.89
2007	23.966	0.439 Tunisian Dinars	120	

For purchasing power parity comparisons, the US Dollar is exchanged at 0.44 Tunisian Dinars only. Average wages in 2007 hover around $16-19 per day.

Growing foreign debt and the foreign exchange crisis in the mid-1980s. In 1986, the government launched a structural adjustment program to liberalize prices, reduce tariffs, and reorient Tunisia toward a market economy.

Tunisia's economic reform program has been lauded as a model by international financial institutions. The government has liberalized prices, reduced tariffs, lowered debt-service-to-exports and debt-to-GDP ratios, and extended the average maturity of its $10 billion foreign debt. Structural adjustment brought additional lending from the World Bank and other Western creditors. In 1990, Tunisia acceded to the General Agreement on Tariffs and Trade (GATT) and is a member of the World Trade Organization (WTO).

In 1996 Tunisia entered into an "Association Agreement" with the European Union (EU) which removes tariff and other trade barriers on most goods by 2008. In conjunction with the Association Agreement, the EU is assisting the Tunisian government's Mise A Niveau (upgrading) program to enhance the productivity of Tunisian businesses and prepare for competition in the global marketplace.

The government has totally or partially privatized around 160 state-owned enterprises since the privatization program was launched in 1987. Although the program is supported by the GATT, the government has had to move carefully to avoid mass firings. Unemployment continues to plague Tunisia's economy and is aggravated by a rapidly growing work force. An estimated 55% of the population is under the age of 25. Officially, 14% of the Tunisian work force is unemployed.

EXTERNAL TRADE AND INVESTMENT

In 1992, Tunisia re-entered the private international capital market for the first time in 6 years, securing a $10-million line of credit for balance-of-payments support. In January 2003 Standard & Poor's affirmed its investment grade credit ratings for Tunisia. The World Economic Forum 2002-03 ranked Tunisia 34th in the Global Competitiveness Index Ratings (two places behind South Africa, the continent's leader). In April 2002, Tunisia's first US dollar-denominated sovereign bond issue since 1997 raised $458 million, with maturity in 2012.

For additional analytical, business and investment opportunities information, please contact Global Investment & Business Center, USA at (703) 370-8082. Fax: (703) 370-8083. E-mail: ibpusa3@gmail.com Global Business and Investment Info Databank - www.ibpus.com

Tunisian export by geographical areas (2008)

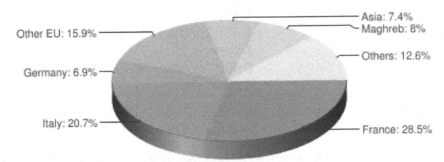

Geographical repartition of Tunisian export in 2008.

Tunisian import by geographical areas (2008)

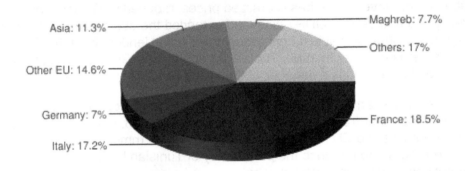

Geographical repartition of Tunisian import in 2008.

The Bourse de Tunis is under the control of the state-run Financial Market Council and lists over 50 companies. The government offers substantial tax incentives to encourage companies to join the exchange, and expansion is occurring.

The Tunisian government adopted a unified investment code in 1993 to attract foreign capital. More than 1,600 export-oriented joint venture firms operate in Tunisia to take advantage of relatively low labor costs and preferential access to nearby European markets. Economic links are closest with European countries, which dominate Tunisia's trade. Tunisia's currency, the dinar, is not traded outside Tunisia. However, partial convertibility exists for bonafide commercial and investment transaction. Certain restrictions still limit operations carried out by Tunisian residents.

The stock market capitalisation of listed companies in Tunisia was valued at $5.3 Billion in 2007, 15% of 2007 GDP, by the World Bank

For 2007, foreign direct investment totaled TN Dinar 2 billion in 2007, or 5.18% of the total volume of investment in the country. This figure is up 35.7% from 2006 and includes 271 new foreign enterprises and the expansion of 222 others already based in the country.

The economic growth rate seen for 2007, at 6.3% is the highest achieved in a decade.

Due to its limited natural resources, Tunisia has focused on developing its human resources: the bulk of the national budget has been allocated to education, health care, housing and social services, while a comparatively small amount was spent on defense. The private sector is encouraged to play a leading role in economic growth, and as a result, Tunisians have created a modern, diversified market-oriented economy based on an efficient agricultural sector, a growing manufacturing sector, and a thriving tourism industry.

TUNISIAN EXPORTS

The principal Tunisian exports are crude oil, minerals, clothing, and agricultural products, including its internationally-renowned olive oil. Tourism is a significant source of revenue and foreign exchange. Tunisia's primary trading partners are France, Italy, Germany, Belgium, Luxembourg, and the Maghreb countries.

A POLICY OF LIBERALIZATION

Liberalization measures and reforms have been introduced to promote economic efficiency and lay the groundwork for long-term growth. Improving the environment in which enterprises operate has been the main focus of government action.
Since 1988, Tunisia's economic policy has been resolutely outward-looking with the adoption of important reforms:

- Membership of GATT since 1990 and adoption of the provisions from the final Agreement.
- Liberalization of 92% of imports measured in terms of production.
- Regulation by market mechanisms of 87% of production prices and 80.5% of distribution prices.
- Association Agreement with the European Union (signed on July 17, 1995)

Tunisia's economy is also characterized by a rigorous financial policy reflected through:

- A gradual reduction in the budget deficit to 3.2 % of GDP in 1997.
- An increase in savings to 23.5 % of GNP in 1997.
- Lower inflation: 3.7 % in 1997.
  Debt control: Tunisia has never rescheduled its debt and has always honored its financial obligations. Debt servicing totals less than 17.3 % of current export earnings.

FINANCIAL SYSTEM

Through the dynamism of its banking system and the stability of its financial markets, Tunisia has, in only a few years, become a financial center of prime importance. It has been ranked by foreign experts as the first banking center in North Africa and one of the largest in the Arab World. This reputation has won Tunisia the confidence of leading banks such as CITIBANK, LINK, and ALUBAF International which, among others, have set up operations in Tunisia. The banking system is centered around the Central Bank of Tunisia (BCT) and consists of:

☐

For additional analytical, business and investment opportunities information, please contact Global Investment & Business Center, USA at (703) 370-8082. Fax: (703) 370-8083. E-mail: ibpusa3@gmail.com Global Business and Investment Info Databank - www.ibpus.com

- 13 Deposit Banks
- 8 Development Banks
- 8 Offshore Banks
- 2 Merchant Banks
- 8 Leasing Institutions

☐
The Tunisian banking system has managed to establish a vast network of representations and agencies. There are currently 765 banking agencies spread all over the country, averaging one agency per 12,000 inhabitants (about the same average as in the developed countries).

AGRICULTURE

Tunisia has a total land area of 16.4 million hectares. The country's arable lands are estimated at five million hectares, and 340,000 hectares of land are irrigated.

☐
The main agricultural products are: olive oil, citrus fruits, cereals and dates. Tunisia's water resource potential is 4,800 million cubic meters per year. Nearly 65% of the country's ground water is being tapped. Agriculture accounts for 16.5% of the GDP and 22% of exports of goods, and provides work for 22% of the active population.

☐
Large-scale actions undertaken since 1990 include implementation of a ten-year plan for water mobilization, through the building of 21 large dams, 203 hillside stream dams, and 1,000 hillside lakes, 1,760 wells and 98 water purification stations.
State-owned lands are being restructured.
Investments in the sector of agriculture reached 2,784.4 million dinars between 1992 and 1996. They are estimated to reach 5,383 million dinars during the next 5 years (1997-2001)

INDUSTRY

Tunisia has an important industrial basis. New growth sectors, such as electronics, automotive components, chemicals and service activities, are rapidly developing alongside the more traditional ones.

☐
Textiles, shoes and leather are the most important industries, followed by food processing, mechanical, electrical, building, chemicals and rubber industries.

☐
Over a third of manufacturing operations are located in Tunis, while the remaining are spread between the coastal areas and the north-western and southern regions.

☐
Approximately 2,000 manufacturing companies have already set up in the country and are either totally or partially producing for the European, American and African markets among others.

☐
Fifty per cent of these manufacturing companies are joint-ventures or foreign-owned, and have reinforced the transfer of technology and know-how, contributing to the country's efforts at economic and social development. The

service industries, notably those linked to industry, are also experiencing an important evolution. They contribute to 47% of total investments, 51.3% of GDP growth and 44% of job creations.

INFRASTRUCTURE

Tunisia has devoted considerable efforts to the establishment of an adequate infrastructure.

□
The railway network totals 2,475 km (1,500 miles) and covers the country from North to South. It is connected to both the Algerian and Moroccan railway networks.

□
The road network stretches over 31,000 km (18,600 miles). A 150 km (90 miles) highway system links Tunis, Hammamet and M'Saken, and plans for further extensions to the South and North of the country are underway.

TELECOMMUNICATIONS

Tunisia benefits from the most modern telecommunication systems, with an automated telephone network covering the whole country and linked to the international network and direct dialing. Telex and Fax machines are widely used.

Relative to its area, Tunisia can boast one of the best telecommunication services in Africa. Telephone and telefax lines are available throughout the country. The Tunisian system is linked to the rest of the world and its quality is better than the African average. All hotels and business offices have telefax and telex facilities. The present telephone density for 5 sets per 100 inhabitants is expected to reach 10 sets per 100 by 1996.

ELECTRIFICATION

Electrification rate: 81 percent
Electricity generation capacity: 1400 MW installed, to be raised to 2050 MW by 1996.
Natural gas: a high pressure network of 500 km serving major economic centres.

AIR CONNECTIONS

Daily flights connect Tunisian airports to more than 50 international destinations and regular domestic flights ensure connections between national airports.

MARITIME CONNECTIONS

More than 95% of Tunisia's exchanges with the outside world are done by sea. Ship traffic in the main national harbors totals over 5,400 vessels.

TRADE AND INVESTMENT FRAMEWORK[2]

MAIN LAWS AND REGULATIONS

1.   The Constitution is Tunisia's supreme law. The other legal instruments are, in decreasing order of precedence and importance, laws, decree-laws, decrees, orders, and notices. Once ratified by Tunisia, all treaties take precedence over national laws. The WTO Agreements form an integral part of Tunisian domestic law by virtue of Law No. 95-06 of 23 January 1995 ratifying the results of the Uruguay Round. Consequently, these agreements can be invoked directly in the Tunisian courts, even in the absence of an implementing provision.

2.   The main legislation affecting international trade and investment is summarized in Table II.1. This legislation is described below in the various sections of Chapters III and IV. For example, Law No. 94-41 authorizes the Ministry of Trade to restrict merchandise imports and exports. The Customs Code contains all the provisions of interest to customs, including those relating to the customs tariff, customs valuation, clearance formalities, tariff concessions, drawback, customs warehousing procedures, and customs regulations and administration. It is supplemented by various decrees and orders concerning matters such as countervailing and anti-dumping duties, temporary admission formalities and the economic activity park (industrial estate) programme. Current payments have been liberalized since 1993; the Foreign Exchange and External Trade Code includes provisions restricting the export of capital (Chapter I) .

MAIN TRADE AND INVESTMENT LEGISLATION

Title and/or field	Text of law	Date of last amendment, entry into force
Customs Code	Order of 29 December 1955	29 December 1955
Customs valuation	Law No. 2001-92	7 August 2001
Tariff	Law No. 89-113	31 December 2004
Import and export prohibitions, licences and controls	Law No. 94-41	7 March 1994
Commercial Code	Law No. 59-129	3 November 2000
Exercise of commercial activities (by foreigners)	Decree-Law 61-14	30 August 1961
Foreign Exchange and External Trade Code (foreign exchange regime)	Law No. 93-48	3 May 1993

[2] Tunisia government and WTO materials

VAT	Law No. 88-61	31 December 2004
Investment Incentives Code	Law No. 93-120	27 December 1993
Measures directly affecting imports	Decree No. 2004-7	5 January 2004
Unfair import practices (anti-dumping and countervailing duty measures)	Law No. 99-9 Decree No. 2000-477	13 February 1999 21 February 2000
Safeguard measures	Law No. 98-106	18 December 1998
Standards	Various legal instruments	n.a.
Sanitary and phytosanitary measures	Various legal instruments	n.a.
Export prohibitions, licences and controls	Decree No. 94-1743	29 August 1994
Competition policy	Law No. 91-64	11 November 2003
Trademarks	Law No. 2001-36	17 April 2001
Geographical indications	Law No. 99-57	28 June 1999
Industrial designs	Law No. 2001-21	6 February 2001
Patents	Law No. 2000-84	24 August 2000
New plant varieties	Law No. 99-42	10 May 1999
Topographies of integrated circuits	Law No. 2001-20	6 February 2001
Copyright	Law No. 94-36	24 February 1994
Agriculture (WTO Agreement – tariff quotas)	Decree No. 96-1119	10 June 1996
Mining Code	Law No. 2003-30	28 April 2003
Hydrocarbons Code	Law No. 99-93	17 August 1999
Telecommunications Code	Law No. 95-36 Law No. 2004-30	17 April 1995 5 April 2004
Postal services	Law No. 98-38	2 June 1998
Land transport	Law No. 2001-67 Law No. 98-21 Law No. 2004-33	10 July 2001 19 April 2004 14 October 2004

Air transport	Law No. 2004-57	12 July 2004
Maritime Trade Code	Law No. 62-13	16 March 1998
Commercial Seaport Code	Law No. 99-25	18 March 1999
Insurance Code	Law No. 2002-37	1 April 2002
Banks	Law No. 99-92 Law No. 85-108	17 August 1999 6 December 1985
Accounting services	Law No. 2004-0088 Law No. 88-108 Law No. 2001-91	31 December 2004 18 August 1988 7 August 2001

Source: Information provided by the Tunisian authorities and Official Journal of the Tunisian Republic, available at:http://www.cnudst.rnrt.tn/wwwisis/jort.03/form.htm

The Republic of Tunisia was established in July 1957, shortly after the country became independent. The Constitution of 1959, as amended, is based on the principle of the sovereignty of the people and the separation of powers. [1] The President of the Republic is the Head of State. He is elected by universal suffrage for a renewable term of five years. The President of the Republic appoints the Prime Minister and the other members of the Government and presides over the Council of Ministers. The Government is responsible to the President; however, the Chamber of Deputies may, by a two-thirds majority, adopt a motion of censure, in which case the President must either dismiss the Government or dissolve the Chamber of Deputies.

There have been six constitutional amendments since Tunisia's last Trade Policy Review in 1994. [2] One of the main changes was the introduction, in 2002, of a bicameral legislative system (to be installed in June 2005) comprising both a Chamber of Deputies (Majlis al-Nuwaab) and a Chamber of Counsellors (Majlis al-Mustasharin) . [3] A Constitutional Council [4] was created in 2002 and given responsibility for ensuring that legislative elections and referenda are properly conducted and that all laws are constitutional. Other constitutional amendments deal with political rights, other fundamental human rights, and the election of the President of the Republic.

The Chamber of Deputies has 189 members elected for a five-year term by direct and secret universal suffrage. Of these, 152 are directly elected in 26 electoral districts by a simple-majority party list system – all the seats reserved for each district going to the list which obtains the most votes, on the basis of one seat per 65 000 inhabitants. The other 37 seats are allocated *pro rata* to the losing lists. [5]

The Chamber of Counsellors has a maximum membership equal to two thirds of the number of members of the Chamber of Deputies. The members elected at regional level from among those elected to local authority bodies are divided up as follows: one member for each governorate with a population of less than 250 000, and two for each governorate with a population of 250 000 or more. One third of the members of the Chamber are elected nationally, in three groups of equal size representing employers, farmers and workers, respectively. Candidates are proposed by the trade associations and unions concerned. The President of the Republic appoints the remaining members of the Chamber of Counsellors from among people prominent in public life or expert in various fields.

The judicial system comprises the courts of ordinary law (commune courts, courts of first instance, appeal court, and court of cassation) and the special courts (real estate court, administrative court) . The commercial courts have jurisdiction over all commercial disputes, including those relating to intellectual property. Articles 197 to 309 of the Customs Code deal with disputes and provide for the possibility of appeal to the courts. In particular, Article 237 stipulates that the rules in force concerning appeals on points of law in civil and criminal cases are applicable to Customs disputes.

The Court of Auditors is the higher institution responsible for monitoring Tunisian public finances. Its task is to oversee the implementation of the Finance Acts and to assess the management of the organizations under its supervision. Its chairman is appointed by the President of the Republic. According to the authorities, the Court operates independently and is not answerable to any arm of government; from the administrative standpoint, its budget is linked with that of the Office of the Prime Minister. The Court reports directly to the President of the Republic and to the Chamber of Deputies. [6] Only extracts of its reports are published in the Official Journal. [7]

7.   The Economic and Social Council is a consultative body which can be asked to consider any draft economic or social legislation. [8] The Government, as well as the chambers, may consult the Council, which may also, on its own initiative, give opinions and make suggestions on any matter within its competence.

POLICY FORMULATION AND IMPLEMENTATION

The more important economic decisions must be incorporated in a law passed by the Chamber of Deputies and, since June 2005, by the Chamber of Counsellors as well. These include, in particular, the annual budget (Finance Act), the currency issuing regime, development plans, international trade treaties, and government borrowings and other financial commitments. [9] Draft legislation may be brought forward on the initiative of the President or originated by deputies; it is examined by the Council of Ministers before being submitted to Parliament. Legislation passed by the Chambers goes to the President for enactment and implementation. The President may return draft legislation for a second reading in the chambers, which may, by confirming their previous vote by a two thirds majority of their respective members, oblige the President to enact the law. Otherwise, the draft legislation is withdrawn or suitably amended. Once enacted, the law is published in the Official Journal, and then enters into force on the date prescribed.

The broad outlines of Tunisia's economic and social development are set out in a series of five-year development plans; the Tenth Plan ends in 2006. The plan lays down the objectives of macroeconomic (growth of GDP, employment, investment, savings, external accounts) and sectoral (production, investment, exports) development and establishes social development programmes (education, social security) .

However, the Tunisian plan has no binding force. The planning process is based on collaboration between the Government, the economic and social partners, civil society, the representatives of the regions, the state-owned enterprises and the private sector, often represented by trade associations such as the *Union tunisienne pour l'industrie, le commerce et l'artisanat* (UTICA – Tunisian Industry, Trade and Handicrafts Union) and the *Union tunisienne de l'agriculture et de la pêche* (UTAP – Tunisian Agriculture and Fishery Union), and the research institutes. The preparation of the plan, which often takes more than two years, is entrusted to three types of committees composed of representatives of the government, employers and labour.

Coordination is ensured by the Higher Council of the Plan presided over by the President of the Republic. The Ministry of Development and International Cooperation (MDCI) compiles all the documentation and reports to the Higher Council. The draft Plan is adopted by the Chamber of Deputies in the same way as draft legislation. The Plan is implemented by means of annual economic budgets which evaluate any new social or economic developments and establish programmes for the following year.

Chart II.1
Principal entities involved in the formulation of trade
and investment policies

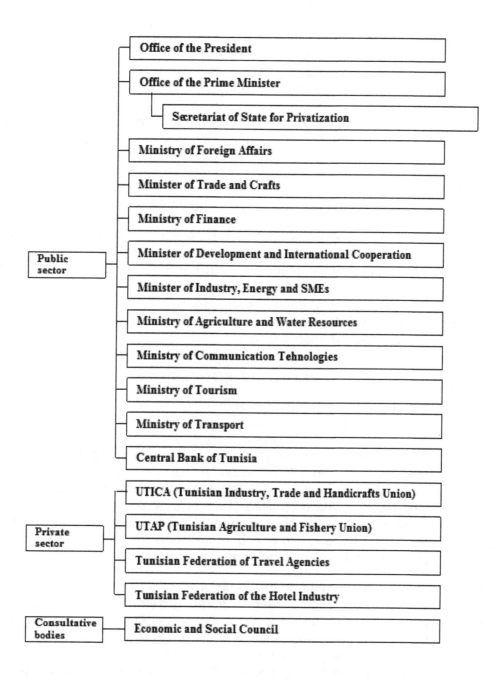

Source: Information provided by the Tunisian authorities.

As trade policy is part of macroeconomic policy, its broad outlines are formulated in the process of preparing the plan. In addition to the Ministry of Foreign Affairs, a number of ministries participate in the formulation of trade policy (Chart II.1) . The task of the Ministry of Trade and Crafts is to draw up and implement government policy in the areas relating to trade, crafts, consumer protection, economic and trade cooperation, small businesses, and trade-related services. The Ministry of Trade is also responsible for relations with the WTO and related matters. The financial aspects of external trade are the concern of the Ministry of Finance, in cooperation with the Central Bank of Tunisia (BCT); this ministry is also responsible for budgetary and fiscal matters, as well as for the customs administration. Other ministries also have an interest in trade policy, in particular, the Ministry of Agriculture and the Ministry of Industry, Energy, and SMEs. The MDIC plays a key role in the formulation of FDI policy.

The National Foreign Trade Council was set up in 1994 to advise the Minister responsible for trade on export promotion strategy and trade policy in general; it monitors trade measures and draws up programmes for fairs and other events. It brings together the directors general of all the competent ministries and public institutions and representatives of trade associations such as UTICA and UTAP. The Council meets at least twice a year under the chairmanship of the Minister for Trade. The Higher Export and Investment Council (CSEI) is responsible, in particular, for setting objectives and formulating strategy in these areas and evaluating and monitoring the results. The CSEI meets once a year. It consists of the ministers concerned (Chart II.1), the chairman of UTICA, the chairman of UTAP and the chairman of the *Union générale des travailleurs tunisiens* (General Union of Tunisian Workers) .

POLICY OBJECTIVES

1.   Job creation is undoubtedly the fundamental objective of Tunisian economic policy. Another aim is the fair distribution of the fruits of development among the various social groups, regions and generations. Since the early 80s, export promotion has been regarded as the best means of creating jobs and raising living standards. The promotion of private direct investment, through privatization, concessions and facilitation of the procedures for establishing businesses, is a Government priority. The priority sectors are manufacturing and tourism. The objectives of agricultural policy are food security and self-sufficiency and social stability. In the area of services, traditionally reserved for nationals or the Tunisian State, more and more activities are in process of being gradually incorporated into Tunisia's export promotion strategy.

2.   After having been the engine of the Tunisian economy during the 80s and 90s, manufactured exports have recently seen their real growth rate diminish. Despite the promotion measures adopted, the Tunisian economy has been facing increased world competition in its main export sector – textiles and clothing – and in its principal market – the European Union – following the decision, within the context of the WTO, to abolish import quotas for these products altogether by 2004. Tunisia has now begun to consider ways of safeguarding the sector's exports and increasing the share of other more dynamic sectors, such as the electronics industry, agri-food, and services, especially those related to the new information and communications technologies, as well as transport, financial, health, education and training, and environmental services.

For additional analytical, business and investment opportunities information, please contact Global Investment & Business Center, USA at (703) 370-8082. Fax: (703) 370-8083. E-mail: ibpusa3@gmail.com Global Business and Investment Info Databank - www.ibpus.com

TRADE AGREEMENTS AND ARRANGEMENTS

1. Tunisia has concluded trade agreements with about 60 countries, some of which provide for preferential trade arrangements. [10] Since its last TPR in 1994, Tunisia has signed some particularly important agreements, including the WTO Agreement, the bilateral Agreement with the EU, bilateral and plurilateral agreements with the members of the Arab League, and an agreement with Turkey.

(i) World Trade Organization (WTO)

2. Tunisia is an original Member of the WTO and grants at least MFN treatment to all its trading partners. It is not party to any of the plurilateral agreements concluded under WTO auspices. Tunisia has not participated in the Information Technology Agreement and has not signed the Pharmaceutical Understanding. As of April 2005, Tunisia had not been directly involved, as complainant or defendant, in any trade dispute settlement proceeding.

3. Tunisia has fulfilled most of its WTO notification obligations (Table AII.1) . The missing notifications relate to agriculture for export subsidies (after 2002); quantitative import restrictions (after 2001); subsidy programmes (after 2001); and state trading (after 2002) .

4. At the Doha (2001) [11] and Cancun (2003) [12] Ministerial Conferences, Tunisia stressed the need for globalization to be managed on the basis of fair rules and a more consistent commitment to development on the part of the international community. A rules-based multilateral trading system as a vehicle of economic development must, according to Tunisia, work for the integration of the developing countries (DCs) and help eliminate poverty. The provisions concerning DCs should be adapted to their actual capacity to implement them. Special and differential treatment remained, according to Tunisia, a fundamental principle of the multilateral trading system, but the rules should be strengthened to allow DCs to participate more fully in international trade. Tunisia stressed the need for a negotiating programme that enabled all DCs to obtain better access to developed country markets.

5. Tunisia has emphasized the special economic and social importance of the agricultural sector for the DCs and least developed countries (LDCs) . It recommends arrangements that would make it possible to support small farmers so as to prevent small-scale agriculture from being adversely affected by trade liberalization. Tunisia has also called for the scaling back of support measures that are distorting agricultural trade and hindering the development of agriculture in the DCs.

6. Tunisia considers that greater attention should also be paid to those countries, such as itself, that are net food importers, in case the reduction in export subsidies were to aggravate the adverse effects of liberalization on the food bill, the current food aid arrangements no longer being appropriate. Accordingly, Tunisia has called for the establishment of the special short-term food financing facility designed to implement the Marrakesh Ministerial Decision in favour of the LDCs and net food-importing developing countries. [13]

7. With regard to non-agricultural market access, the elimination of tariff peaks and tariff escalation is, according to Tunisia, crucial for ensuring improved access to export

markets. However, Tunisia fears that the proposals aimed at the total and sectoral dismantling of customs duties would deprive it of substantial export revenue by opening up the markets of its preferential partners (preferential destinations for its products) to greater competition. Tunisia has welcomed the WTO Declaration on Intellectual Property and Public Health. Nevertheless, it considers that there are other diseases that threaten human health and lives and that these also warrant special attention from the international community. In Tunisia, the importation of pharmaceuticals is a state monopoly (Chapter IV(4)(iv)) .

8.   In the area of services, Tunisia has asked its trading partners for the mutual recognition of diplomas and professional qualifications and improved market access through liberalization of the movement of natural persons and the facilitation of travel. Tunisia has a pool of human resources with recognized skills in professional and business services. Services are mainly exported under sub-contracting arrangements with European enterprises or within the context of international financing granted to developing countries. However, the authorities have pointed out that the numerous obstacles to obtaining visas make the potential for exporting to the developed countries difficult to realize. These obstacles include, *inter alia*, the large number of documents to be provided, the waiting times, the high cost of visas and the policy of non-reimbursement in the event of an application being refused, the non-transparent criteria, the need in some cases for sponsorship by professional organizations, and the refusal to grant visas for the personnel of enterprises that have obtained contracts to supply services (an essential component of their competitiveness) and for international road transport workers. Moreover, the time requirements and other conditions relating to the granting of residence permits are particularly restrictive and foreign providers of professional services often have to re-sit examinations and tests in order to be able to practice.

(ii) Association Agreement with the European Union

1.   In July 1995, within the context of the Barcelona Declaration, one of whose main objectives is the establishment of a Euro-Mediterranean free trade area by 2010, Tunisia signed a bilateral Association Agreement with the European Communities and their Member States. The Agreement provides for the reciprocal liberalization of merchandise trade by 2008. [14] The prospect of duty-free admission of European products by 2008 has prompted reforms aimed at increasing the competitiveness of Tunisian products; it has also led to an effort to harmonize trade regulations and procedures with the European Union, particularly in the customs field.

2.   The Association Agreement was ratified by Tunisia on 20 June 1996. It provides for duty-free trade in most imported industrial products 12 years after its entry into force, i.e. in 2008. List 1 (12 per cent of the volume of imports from the EU in 1994) mainly covers capital goods and inputs, duties on which were dismantled in 1996. List 2 also concerns products not produced locally, primarily raw materials and intermediate products (28 per cent of total Tunisian imports from the EU in 1994), which have been entering duty-free since 2001.

3.   Lists 3 and 4 consist of locally manufactured goods. List 3 comprises products considered capable of facing up to outside competition. In this case protection will be removed over a 12-year transition period (1996-2007), with duty-free status in 2008.

These products represented about 30 per cent of Tunisian imports from the EU in 1994. Finally, list 4 also concerns industrial products manufactured locally, but in this case tariffs will be reduced over an 8-year period (2000-2007), following a 4-year transition period (1996-1999), with duty-free status in 2008. The products covered by this list accounted for 29 per cent of Tunisian imports from the EU in 1994.

4. The Agreement also provides for the progressive liberalization of certain agricultural and fishery products. Thus, Protocols 1 and 2 provide for tariff preferences for agricultural and fishery products originating in Tunisia, in particular, olive oil, meat, roses, cut flowers, spices, and fruit and vegetables (the latter only during specified periods of the year), preserved fruit and vegetables, wine, and preserved fish and crustaceans. [15]Altogether, the volumes of certain preferential tariff quotas seem rather limited, only about 100 tonnes in some cases. According to the authorities, Tunisia has been able to fulfil them for the following products: olive oil, citrus fruit, fishery products, and dates. In 2000, further negotiations ended in the conclusion of a new five-year agricultural protocol which began to be implemented in January 2001. This led to improved access for Tunisian products, including an increase in quotas, in particular for olive oil, where volume rose to 56 000 tonnes in 2005, an extension of the market access periods and the introduction of a number of new products. For its part, Tunisia granted the EU, for the first time, preferential tariff quotas for cereals and sugar.

5. The Agreement also contains non-tariff provisions. It prohibits the maintenance of quantitative restrictions and measures having equivalent effect on trade between Tunisia and the Community. At the same time, Tunisia and the EU reserve the right to take anti-dumping, countervailing and safeguard measures in their bilateral trade. The parties also undertake to "progressively adjust, without affecting commitments made under the GATT, any state monopolies of a commercial character so as to ensure that, by the end of the fifth year following the entry into force of this Agreement, no discrimination regarding the conditions under which goods are procured and marketed exists between nationals of the Member States and of Tunisia". Moreover, "any official aid which distorts or threatens to distort competition by favouring certain undertakings or the production of certain goods" will be incompatible with the Agreement; in this respect, Tunisia benefits from renewable transitional derogations (Article 36) .

(iii) Greater Arab Free Trade Area (GAFTA)

1. The executive programme of the Convention on the Facilitation and Development of Inter-Arab Trade entered into force in January 1998; it is currently being applied by 17 of the 22 members of the League of Arab States. [16] Its objective is to create a Greater Arab Free Trade Area within ten years, by reducing customs duties by 10 per cent a year. The main body responsible for ensuring the implementation of the programme is the Economic and Social Council of the Arab League. By 1 January 2005, 15 countries had completed the accelerated removal of their tariff barriers, namely: Bahrain, Egypt, Iraq, Jordan, Kuwait, Lebanon, Libya, Morocco, Oman, Palestine, Qatar, Saudi Arabia, Syria, Tunisia and the United Arab Emirates (as LDCs, Sudan and Yemen have been allowed more time) . Consequently, Tunisia has granted duty-free access to all products originating in these 17 countries. [17] This agreement has not been notified to the WTO.

(iv) Arab-Mediterranean Free Trade Agreement ("Agadir Agreement")

1. On 25 February 2004, Tunisia, together with Egypt, Jordan and Morocco, signed a free trade agreement known as the Arab-Mediterranean Free Trade Agreement (or "Agadir Agreement") . Like GAFTA, the Agreement provides for the elimination of almost all customs duties and charges having an equivalent effect on the bilateral trade between parties. The main objective of the Agadir Agreement is to make possible pan-Euro-Mediterranean cumulation in relation to rules of origin. The Agreement also provides for enhanced cooperation on customs procedures and technical standards. In addition, it covers government procurement, financial services, contingency trade measures and intellectual property and establishes a dispute settlement procedure. By May 2005 only Egypt and Tunisia had ratified the Agreement.

(v) Free Trade Agreement with EFTA

1. In December 2004, Tunisia signed bilateral free trade agreements on trade in non-agricultural products with the Member States of the European Free Trade Association (EFTA), namely, Iceland, Liechtenstein, Norway and Switzerland. Bilateral protocols of agreement with each of these countries on agriculture, fish farming and agri-food are annexed to these agreements. The agreements also include substantive provisions concerning intellectual property, competition and dispute settlement and cover certain aspects of services, investment and government procurement (to be liberalized progressively and reciprocally) . They provide for payments, without restrictions, for current transactions and guarantee the freedom of movement of capital linked with direct investment. Moreover, the parties have agreed to grant each other complete protection and security for investments. The agreement between Tunisia, on the one hand, and Switzerland and Liechtenstein, on the other, entered into force on 3 June 2005.

(vi) Other agreements and arrangements

1. The Maghreb Arab Union (UMA) was established in 1989 by Algeria, Libya, Morocco, Mauritania and Tunisia. [18] Its objectives are the free movement of goods and persons and the harmonization of legislation with a view to the creation of a free trade area. However, UMA appears not to be operational where international trade or investment is concerned.

2. Tunisia is also signatory to a series of bilateral agreements providing for tariff preferences (immediate abolition for certain products, accelerated phase-out for others) with Egypt (1998), Jordan (1998), Morocco (1999), Libya (2001), Iraq (2001), and Syria (2003) . At present, the GAFTA regime is more favourable than that offered by these various agreements. Tunisia has also signed, on 25 November 2004, an association agreement establishing a free trade area with Turkey. The agreement has been ratified by the two parties. It is scheduled to enter into force in July 2005. It provides for tariff exemption for three lists of non-agricultural originating products. Tariff preferences are granted on a reciprocal basis to certain agricultural and fishery products. The agreement also includes provisions on the protection of intellectual property, services, dispute settlement, anti-dumping duties, countervailing duties and safeguards.

3. Tunisia benefits, on a non-reciprocal basis, from concessions granted under the Generalized System of Preferences (GSP) by countries such as Australia, Belarus, Bulgaria, Canada, the Czech and Slovak Republics, the European Union, Hungary, Japan, New Zealand, Poland, Russia, Switzerland, and the United States. Thus, in these

countries Tunisian exports of products covered by the GSP are granted total or partial exemption from customs duties.

4. In February 1989, Tunisia became one of the first developing countries to ratify the Agreement on the Global System of Trade Preferences (GSTP) among Developing Countries. Products originating in the 48 countries signatory to the agreement benefit from tariff preferences on a reciprocal basis. The agreement also provides for special treatment for LDCs. The authorities have pointed out that Tunisia did not participate in the second round of negotiations but is still fulfilling the commitments it made at the end of the first round.

FOREIGN INVESTMENTS

INVESTMENT REGIME

1. For more than 30 years, the Government has been pursuing a policy of encouraging private, especially foreign, investment. In view of the decline in private investment in relation to GDP since 2002 (Table I.2), the promotion of investment remains one of its current priorities. Investment policy is based on a complex system of laws and regulations, whose application depends on whether the investment is in a "resident" ("general regime") or "non-resident" enterprise, is direct or portfolio, relates to "wholly exporting" activities (Chapter III(3)), or involves sectors covered by the Investment Incentives Code (CII) . [19] The authorities claim that, in practice, the regime is flexible and based on statements made by the investors themselves and poses no problems of implementation. There are numerous benefits, including tax exemptions, direct subsidies, and exemptions from the foreign exchange legislation, particularly for industrial export activities (Chapter III(3)(iv)) . An estimate of the budgetary cost of the measures covered by Article 25.1 of the Agreement on Subsidies and Countervailing Measures indicates a total of 557 million dinars for the year 2000. [20]

2. The main role of the *Commission supérieur des investissements* (CSI – Investment Commission) [21] is to approve the acquisition of shares in Tunisian enterprises by foreigners and to approve foreign direct investment in sectors subject to its prior authorization. [22] The CSI is responsible to the Prime Minister who acts as its chairman. Approval is granted if the investment "is of special importance or interest to the national economy".

3.   Where portfolio investment is concerned, foreigners are currently authorized to acquire shares in Tunisian enterprises, whether or not listed on the Tunis Stock Exchange, up to a limit of 50 per cent of the company capital, without the authorization of the CSI. Investments of 50 per cent or more are subject to CSI approval, except for acquisitions which do not confer voting rights. [23]

4.   Direct investment in most manufacturing industries, as well as in certain service activities, is eligible for the CII, which specifies, in a positive list, the sectors eligible and the incentives. The non-eligible manufacturing industries include, for example, oil-refining and investment in the production of pharmaceuticals also produced by the state-owned enterprise SIPHAT. Certain other activities are subject to prior authorization or specifications. These include the manufacture of arms and ammunition and parts thereof; mechanical carpet weaving; brewing, malting and winemaking; flour and meal

For additional analytical, business and investment opportunities information,
please contact Global Investment & Business Center, USA
at (703) 370-8082. Fax: (703) 370-8083. E-mail: ibpusa3@gmail.com
Global Business and Investment Info Databank - www.ibpus.com

milling; edible oil refining; the fabrication of bars, sections and reinforcing rods; teasing; and tobacco production. Most service activities covered by the CII, unless wholly exporting, are also subject to the prior authorization of the CSI when the foreign holding exceeds 50 per cent of the company capital. [24]

5. The CII provides for "common benefits" and "specific benefits". The common benefits consist mainly of tax exemptions (Chapter III(4)(i)), including the deduction of the sums invested from taxable profits up to a limit of 35 per cent of the latter; a reducing-balance depreciation regime; and exemption from customs duties and (in some cases) VAT on plant essential to the investment. The specific benefits are fixed in accordance with horizontal objectives, in particular, export promotion (Chapter III(3)(vi)) . The other horizontal objectives include regional and agricultural development and the promotion of technology and small and medium-sized enterprises (Chapter III(4)(i)) .

6. Some of the activities not covered by the Code are also open to foreign participation but subject to authorization in relation to the conditions under which it is permissible to engage in them, irrespective of the status or nationality of the investor. This applies, for example, to the activities of banks and investment companies. Other activities are subject to authorization when the level of foreign participation is 50 per cent or more; these include the activities of insurance companies, stock market intermediaries and forwarding agents, and transport and port activities. In practice, authorization is granted, except in certain sectors reserved for the State or nationals, for example, fixed telephony and all postal and courier, distribution (wholesale and retail), electricity, gas and water services.

7. With respect to international investment, Tunisia has acceded to a number of international conventions, in particular, those of the Multilateral Investment Guarantee Agency (MIGA) and the International Centre for the Settlement of Investment Disputes (ICSID) . Tunisia has signed investment protection and double taxation agreements with most of the OECD countries. It has signed bilateral mutual investment protection agreements with some 50 countries.

Tunisia's thriving economy creates an attractive atmosphere for investors from the European Community, Japan and the United States. More than 1,600 foreign firms have direct investments in or joint ventures with Tunisian companies. Many of these firms were attracted by Tunisia's proximity and preferential trading relations with the European Community and the Arab Maghreb Union, as well as by the newly revised Investment Code which offered tax and customs concessions to foreign investors and reduced the administrative "red tape" required for project approval. A particular incentive for U.S. Investors is the *Tunisian-U.S. Bilateral Investment Treaty* (BIT), signed in January 1993, that guarantees the safety of investments and profit repatriation.

Since 1987, Tunisia has made considerable progress in its efforts to liberalize foreign trade and reduce price controls and consumer subsidies. With the assistance of the International Monetary Fund (IMF) and the World Bank, Tunisia engaged in a series of structured economic reforms. The tax code was simplified and the banking and financial sectors were partially liberalized and restructured. A number of public companies were privatized and trade and domestic prices were decontrolled. The government has also sought to make the dinar convertible, and adopt a unified code that will simplify investment and ensure that it goes toward high priority activities.

Early indications show that Tunisia's reforms are reaping rewards. Exports have been driven up while imports have been maintained at steady rates. Because of ongoing privatization and marketing programs, the economy has grown at an average rate of 5.6% while inflation averaged just 6%. The country's free zone has also received much international attention.
The site at Bizerte recently received applications from 200 companies seeking to set up in the free zone.

Tunisia's economy should be boosted by a July 17, 1995 association agreement signed with the European Union (EU). Under the terms of the agreement, duty free access will be given to Tunisian industrial products in European markets and all restrictions and duties on 60% of European industrial products will be eliminated over the coming five years. For the remaining 40%, restrictions and duties will gradually be eliminated before the end of a twelve-year time schedule. This will allow Tunisia time to introduce its industries to foreign competition. Liberalization of the agriculture sector is also a provision of the accord. The European Union and Tunisia have both agreed to eliminate all duties during the twelve-year period. In addition, the agreement also includes in its proviso cooperation in the fields of education, scientific research, professional training, technology transfer, and communications. With 80% of its exports already going to the EU, Tunisia should expect increased international trade in 1997.

Tunisia has continued in its efforts to privatize its industrial base. In 1995, about twenty public companies were privatized. For 1996, the government is aiming to privatize about 30 more companies. State companies that are expected to be sold include: Tunis Air, CTN (the state maritime company), two hotels, a ceramics manufacturer, a mineral water company, a cloth factory, and a fabric finishing company. World Bank officials would like to see Tunisia's privatization program proceed more rapidly.

BUSINESS AND INVESTMENT CLIMATE

Lying at the meeting point of the eastern and western Mediterranean, only 140 km (87 miles) from Europe, across the Strait of Sicily, Tunisia occupies a strategic geographic position. Its proximity to Europe, coupled with its place in Africa and in the Arab world, make the country an attractive site for investment and business.

POLITICAL LIFE

Since attaining independence in 1956, Tunisia has undergone a profound political and social transformation based on sound human development policies. Since 1987, under the leadership of President Ben Ali, major reforms have been introduced to liberalize the economy, promote democracy and establish the rule of law.

Tunisia has a republican system of government. The President of the Republic is elected for five years by universal suffrage, and can be re-elected for two further consecutive terms. The legislative power is exercised by the Chamber of Deputies, whose members are elected by universal suffrage for a five-year term. There are seven political parties. Respect of the constitutionality of laws is ensured by the Constitutional Council. The Constitution guarantees the independence of the judiciary and freedom of expression and faith.
Tunisia adheres to all international conventions on human rights and the rights of

For additional analytical, business and investment opportunities information,
please contact Global Investment & Business Center, USA
at (703) 370-8082. Fax: (703) 370-8083. E-mail: ibpusa3@gmail.com
Global Business and Investment Info Databank - www.ibpus.com

women and children.

HISTORY

The history of Tunisia goes back more than 3,000 years. A succession of civilizations : Berber, Punic, Roman, Byzantine, Arab, Spanish, Turkish, and others, have created a mixture which has shaped the Tunisian personality, imbuing it with a spirit of tolerance and openness.

Numerous cultural and artistic events are organized every year in Tunisia, including the international festivals of Carthage, Hammamet and Douz. These events reflect the cultural richness and diversity of a country that has contributed to universal thought through the achievements of such leaders and thinkers as Hannibal, Magon, Saint Augustine, Ibn Khaldun, Imam Sahnun, Kheireddine, Tahar Haddad, and others.

INFRASTRUCTURE

* 6 international airports : Tunis-Carthage, Skanes- Monastir, Djerba-Zarzis, Tozeur, Sfax, Tabarka
* 8 commercial ports : Bizerte, La Goulette, Rades, Sousse, Sfax, Gabès, Zarzis, Skhira.
* A 20,000-km (12,500-mile) road system including 150 km (90 miles) of highway.
* Power capacity of 1,680 megawatts, with plans to add one 300-megawatt power station every two years.
* A 790-km (494-mile) distribution network of high-pressure natural gas
* 62 industrial zones in operation, and two developed, serviced off-shore zones (Bizerte, Zarzis).
* 26 industrial zones under development

TELECOMMUNICATIONS

* 6 telephone lines per 100 inhabitants
* Proportion of digital telephone lines : 85%
* Satellite links: INTELSAT- ARABSAT- IMMARSAT- EUTELSAT
* Connections to :

THE INTERNET

The Videotex and Audiotex networks according to X 500 international standards.
* Possibility of X25 data transmission: 1,500 access points, now being extended to 4,800.
* Undersea optical fiber cable link to the American continent, Southeast Asia, the Middle East, and Europe.
* Establishment of a business center, TelecomExpress, to deal with the telecommunications needs of all those involved in business and investment.

The Tunisian economy is a liberal economy, open to the outside world.

The development process Tunisia has pursued since 1960 has brought about major changes in the country's economic structures, a transformation which has been marked by three stages:

1960-1970: Large public investments in the basic sectors.

1970-1985: Development of national entrepreneurship by the establishment of a liberal policy of openness and by the encouragement of private initiative.

1986 to date: Integration of the Tunisian economy into the world market, through GATT membership and the signing of the agreement to establish a Free-Trade Zone between

For additional analytical, business and investment opportunities information, please contact Global Investment & Business Center, USA
at (703) 370-8082. Fax: (703) 370-8083. E-mail: ibpusa3@gmail.com
Global Business and Investment Info Databank - www.ibpus.com

Tunisia and the European Union.

A LIBERAL ECONOMY

Investment is free in most sectors. 96% of production is subject to international competition. 87% of producer prices are governed by market mechanisms. Tunisian currency is convertible for current transactions.

An economy open to the outside world

Exchanges of goods and services with other countries represented 93% of GDP in 1995; of which 76% is accounted for by goods

A growing economy

Annual growth in the GDP was 4.2% (at constant prices) from 1987 to 1996, and is expected to reach 5.7% by 1997. Trends in GDP at 1990 constant prices

Export has been an important growth vector. Exports of goods and services increased by an average of 8.7% per year (at constant prices) from 1987 to 1996. The sectors making the greatest contribution were manufacturing industries (13% per year) and tourism (9% per year). In 1995, these two sectors represented nearly 76% of all exports.

FINANCIAL POLICY

The following factors have enhanced growth: Savings have been maintained at an average rate of 22% of GDP for the years 1991-1996. The budget deficit was brought down from 6% of GDP in 1991 to 3.8% in 1996. Inflation has been contained at around 4.7% per year for 1993-96, despite the effect of drought on food prices.
Debt service has been reduced, and amounted to only 18% of current revenues of the balance of payments in 1995.

INVESTMENT & LEGAL CLIMATE

OPENNESS TO FOREIGN INVESTMENT

The Tunisian Government actively encourages and places a priority on attracting foreign direct investment (FDI) in key industry sectors, such as call centers, electronics, aerospace and aeronautics, automotive parts and textile manufacturing. The Government encourages export-oriented FDI and screens any potential FDI to minimize the impact of the investment on domestic competitors and employment.

Foreign investment in Tunisia is regulated by Investment Code Law No. 93-120, dating from December 1993, and was last amended on January 26, 2009. It covers investment in all major sectors of economic activity except mining, energy, the financial sector and domestic trade.

The Tunisian Investment Code divides potential investments into two categories:

- Offshore, in which foreign capital accounts for at least 66 percent of equity and at least 80 percent of production is destined for the export market (with some exceptions for the agricultural sector), and

For additional analytical, business and investment opportunities information,
please contact Global Investment & Business Center, USA
at (703) 370-8082. Fax: (703) 370-8083. E-mail: ibpusa3@gmail.com
Global Business and Investment Info Databank - www.ibpus.com

- On-shore, in which foreign equity is limited to 49 percent in most non-industrial projects. On-shore industrial investment can have up to 100 percent foreign equity.

The legislation contains two major hurdles for potential FDI:

- Foreign investors are denied national treatment in the agriculture sector. Foreign ownership of agricultural land is prohibited, although land can be secured through long-term (up to 40 years) lease. However, the Government actively promotes foreign investment in agricultural export projects.

- For onshore companies outside the tourism sector, government authorization is required if the foreign capital share exceeds 49 percent and can be difficult to obtain.

Investment in manufacturing industries, agriculture, agribusiness, public works, and certain services requires only a simple declaration of intent to invest. Other sectors can require a series of Government of Tunisia authorizations.

The Government of Tunisia allows foreign participation in its privatization program and a significant share of Tunisia's FDI in recent years has come from the privatization of state-owned or state-controlled enterprises. Privatizations have occurred in telecommunications, banking, insurance, manufacturing, and petroleum distribution, among others. Major FDI entered the financial sector via the privatization of Banque du Sud, since renamed Attijari Bank, in late 2005. In 2006, TECOM Investments and Dubai Investment Group purchased a 35% stake, valued at US$2.25 billion, in state-owned Tunisie Telecom. In July 2008, French company Groupama won a bid to purchase 35 percent of the Société Tunisienne d'Assurances et de Reassurances (STAR) for 70 million Euro (around $100 million). In 2008, the French bank Caisse Générale d'Epargne purchased 60 percent of the Tunisian Kuwaiti Bank (BTK), valued at US$249 million.

Tunisia's investment promotion authorities have established a system of regulations that has received favorable feedback from established U.S. companies it has assisted.

Nevertheless, there are difficulties, particularly when U.S. companies have attempted to launch projects in sectors that the Government of Tunisia does not actively promote. Until recently the Government discouraged foreign investment in service sectors such as restaurants, real estate, and retail distribution. Many of these issues are expected to be addressed in the context of ongoing negotiations between Tunisia and the European Union over liberalization of services sector under the EU/Tunisia Association Agreement.

Indeed, FDI in retail distribution is gradually expanding. French multinational retail chain Carrefour opened its first store in 2001, followed by the entry of French retail company Géant in 2005. Until then, Monoprix, a French grocery franchise, dominated the retail grocery market. In August 2009, the Tunisian Government adopted a new law to regulate domestic trade, which includes a new legislative framework for franchising – until recently franchise status was only granted to businesses on a case-by-case basis. Thanks to this new law, franchises now have the ability to set up shop like any other business serving the Tunisian market. Although some issues still need to be clarified through the upcoming implementation decree, such as the details of royalty repatriation, the law will likely encourage investment, create additional jobs and boost knowledge transfer. Many Tunisian business groups have already started looking for international franchisors and are confident the market exists for franchises to thrive.

Since 2007, there have been numerous announcements of significant Arabian Gulf company investments in the real estate sector but due to the international economic crisis, some investments have been postponed and possibly cancelled. Sama Dubai, which was set to build the Mediterranean Gate mega-construction project, has halted their operations. Investment has not come to a complete standstill, however: Another such investment, the Bukhatir Group's Tunis Sports City, a sports and recreational complex, is moving forward as planned,

FDI in certain state monopoly activities (electricity, water, postal services) can be carried out following establishment of a concession agreement. There are also certain restrictions on trade activities. With few exceptions, domestic trading can only be carried out by a company set up under Tunisian law, in which the majority of the share capital is held by Tunisians and management is Tunisian. An additional barrier to non-EU investment results from Tunisia's Association Agreement with the European Union. The EU is providing significant funding to Tunisia for major investment projects, but clauses in the agreement prohibit non-EU member countries from participation in many EU-funded projects.

Each year in June, the Ministry of Development and International Cooperation and the Foreign Investment Promotion Agency (FIPA) hosts an investment promotion event called the Carthage Investment Forum. The purpose of the event is to introduce visiting foreign investors to the Tunisian investment environment and local business opportunities.

CONVERSION AND TRANSFER POLICIES

The Tunisian Dinar is not a fully convertible currency, and it is illegal to take dinars in or out of the country. Although it is convertible for current account transactions (i.e., most bona fide trade and investment operations), Central Bank authorization is needed for some foreign exchange operations. The Government of Tunisia has publicly committed to full convertibility of the dinar by 2014.

Non-residents are exempt from most exchange regulations. Under foreign currency regulations, non-resident companies are defined as having:

- Non-resident individuals who own at least 66 percent of the capital, and

- Capital financed by imported foreign currency.

Foreign investors may transfer returns on direct or portfolio investments at any time and without prior authorization. This applies to both principal and capital in the form of dividends or interest. U.S. companies have generally praised the speed of transfers from Tunisia, but lamented that long delays may occur in some operations.

There is no limit to the amount of foreign currency that visitors can bring into Tunisia and exchange for Tunisian Dinars. Amounts exceeding the equivalent of 25,000 Tunisian Dinars (approximately US$19,250) must be declared at the port of entry. Non-residents must also report foreign currency imports if they wish to re-export or deposit more than

For additional analytical, business and investment opportunities information,
please contact Global Investment & Business Center, USA
at (703) 370-8082. Fax: (703) 370-8083. E-mail: ibpusa3@gmail.com
Global Business and Investment Info Databank - www.ibpus.com

5,000 Tunisian Dinars (roughly US$3,850). Tunisian customs authorities may require production of currency exchange receipts on exit.

The dinar is traded on an intra-bank market. Trading operates around a managed float established by the Central Bank (based upon a basket of the Euro, the U.S. dollar and the Japanese yen). In 2009 (up to November 25), the Tunisian Dinar appreciated 2.8 percent against the USD and depreciated 3.1 percent against the Euro.

EXPROPRIATION AND COMPENSATION

The Tunisian Government has the right to expropriate property by eminent domain; there is no evidence of consistent discrimination against U.S. and foreign companies or individuals. There are no outstanding expropriation cases involving U.S. interests and such cases are rare. No policy changes on expropriation are anticipated in the coming year.

DISPUTE SETTLEMENT

There is no pattern of significant investment disputes or discrimination involving U.S. or other foreign investors. However, to avoid misunderstandings, contracts for trade and investment projects should always contain an arbitration clause detailing how eventual disputes should be handled and the applicable jurisdiction. Tunisia is a member of the International Center for the Settlement of Investment Disputes and is a signatory to the 1958 New York Convention on the Recognition and Enforcement of Foreign Arbitral Awards.

The Tunisian legal system is based upon the French Napoleonic code. There are adequate means to enforce property and contractual rights. Although the Tunisian constitution guarantees the independence of the judiciary, the judiciary is not fully independent of the executive branch. Local legal experts assert that courts are susceptible to political pressure.

The Tunisian Code of Civil and Commercial Procedures does allow for the enforcement of foreign court decisions under certain circumstances. Commercial disputes involving U.S. firms are relatively rare. In cases were disputes have occurred, U.S. firms have generally been successful in seeking redress through the Tunisian judicial system.

PERFORMANCE REQUIREMENTS AND INCENTIVES

Performance requirements are generally limited to investment in the petroleum sector or in the newer area of private sector infrastructure development. These requirements tend to be specific to the concession or operating agreement (e.g., drilling a certain number of wells or producing a certain amount of electricity). More broadly, the preferential status (offshore, free trade zone) conferred upon some investments is linked to both percentage of foreign corporate ownership and limits on production for the domestic market.

The Tunisian Investment Code and subsequent amendments provide a broad range of incentives for foreign investors, which include tax relief on reinvested revenues and profits, limitations on the value-added tax on many imported capital goods, and optional depreciation schedules for production equipment.

In order to encourage employment of new university graduates, the Government will bear the full cost of the employee's salary for the first two years of employment, and then a portion of the salary for the next five years. The Government will also pay initial training costs for new graduates. On December 23, 2008, the GOT announced that it would bear 50 percent of employers' contributions to the National Social Security Fund (CNSS) during period of partial layoffs due to the international financial crisis.

Large investments with high job creation potential may benefit, under certain conditions determined by the Higher Commission on Investment, from the use of state-owned land for a symbolic Tunisian dinar (less than one U.S. dollar). Investors who purchase companies in financial difficulty may also benefit from certain clauses of the Investment Code, such as tax breaks and social security assistance; these advantages are determined on a case-by-case basis.

Additional incentives are available to promote investment in designated regional investment zones in economically depressed areas of the country, and throughout the country in the following sectors: health, education, training, transportation, environmental protection, waste treatment, and research and development in technological fields.

Further benefits are available for investments of a specific nature. For example, companies producing at least 80 percent for the export market receive tax exemptions on profits and reinvested revenues, duty-free import of capital goods with no local equivalents, and full tax and duty exemption on raw materials and semi-finished goods and services necessary for the business.

Foreign companies resident in Tunisia face a number of restrictions related to the employment and compensation of expatriate employees. Tunisian law limits the number of expatriate employees allowed per company to four. There are lengthy renewal procedures for annual work and residence permits. Although rarely enforced, legislation limits expatriate work permit validity to a total of two years. Central Bank regulations impose administrative burdens on companies seeking to pay for temporary expatriate technical assistance from local revenue. For example, a foreign resident company that has brought in an accountant would have to document that the service was necessary, fairly valued, and unavailable in Tunisia before it could receive authorization to transfer payment from its operations in Tunisia. This regulation prevents a foreign resident company from paying for services performed abroad.

For U.S. passport holders, a visa is not necessary for stays of up to four months; however, a residence permit is required for longer stays.

RIGHT TO PRIVATE OWNERSHIP AND ESTABLISHMENT

Tunisian Government actions clearly demonstrate a strong preference for offshore, export-oriented FDI. Investors in that category are generally free to establish and own business enterprises and engage in most forms of remunerative activity. Investment which competes with Tunisian firms or on the Tunisian market or which is seen as leading to a net outflow of foreign exchange may be discouraged or blocked.

Acquisition and disposal of business enterprises can be complicated under Tunisian law and depend on the nature of the contract specific to the proposed transaction.

Disposal of a business investment leading to reductions in the labor force may be challenged or subjected to substantial employee compensation requirements. Acquisition of an on-shore company may require special authority from the Government if it is an industry subject to limits on foreign equity shareholding (such as in the services sector).

PROTECTION OF PROPERTY RIGHTS

Secured interests in property are both recognized and enforced in Tunisia. Mortgages and liens are in common use. Tunisia is a member of the World Intellectual Property Organization (WIPO) and has signed the United Nations (UNCTAD) Agreement on the Protection of Patents and Trademarks. The agency responsible for patents and trademarks is the National Institute for Standardization and Industrial Property (INNORPI - Institut National de la Normalisation et de la Propriete Industrielle). Foreign patents and trademarks should be registered with INNORPI.

Tunisia's patent and trademark laws are designed to protect only owners duly registered in Tunisia. In the area of patents, U.S. businesses are guaranteed treatment equal to that afforded to Tunisian nationals. Tunisia updated its legislation to meet the requirements of the WTO agreement on Trade-Related aspects of Intellectual Property (TRIPS). Copyright protection is the responsibility of the Tunisian Copyright Protection Organization (OTPDA - Organisme Tunisien de Protection des Droits d'Auteur), which also represents foreign copyright organizations. New legislation now permits customs officials to inspect and seize goods if copyright violation is suspected.

The new Customs Code, which went into effect on January 2009, allows customs agents to seize suspect goods in the entire country for products under foreign trademarks registered at INNORPI. Tunisian Copyright Law (No. 94-36, dated February 24, 1994) has been amended by law No. 2009-33, dated June 23, 2009, and includes literary works, art, scientific works, new technologies and digital works. However, its application and enforcement have not always been consistent with foreign commercial expectations. Print audio and video media are considered particularly susceptible to copyright infringement, and there is evidence of significant retail sale of illegal products in these media. Illegal copying of software and entertainment CDs/DVDs is widespread.

Although the concept and application of intellectual property protection is still in the early stages, the Government is making an effort to build awareness and has increased its enforcement efforts in this area. These efforts have led a major supermarket chain to halt the sale of pirated audio and video goods. A U.S. Government-backed initiative, operated by the Department of Commerce in conjunction with United States Patent and Trademark Office (USPTO) provides training for Tunisian officials in the field of IPR regulation enforcement. The Government of Tunisia has announced that new IPR legislation is being drafted which will improve enforcement capabilities and strengthen punishment for offenders.

TRANSPARENCY OF REGULATORY SYSTEM

While the Tunisian Government has adopted policies designed to promote foreign investment, it continues to enact legislation and implement protectionist measures to safeguard domestic industry. Some amendments to the Investment Code have substantially improved, standardized, and codified incentives for foreign investors. However, some aspects of existing tax and labor laws remain impediments to efficient business operations.

Tunisia's ranking improved from 73 to 69 of 183 economies regarding the ease of doing business in the World Bank's Doing Business 2010 report. That said, some bureaucratic procedures, while slowly improving in some areas, remain cumbersome and time-consuming. Foreign employee work permits, commercial operating license renewals, infrastructure-related services, and customs clearance for imported goods are usually cited as the lengthiest and most opaque procedures in the local business environment. Investors have commented on inconsistencies in the application of regulations. These cumbersome procedures are not limited to foreign investment and also affect the domestic business sector.

EFFICIENT CAPITAL MARKETS AND PORTFOLIO INVESTMENT

The mobilization and allocation of investment capital are still hampered by the underdeveloped nature of the local financial system. Tunisia's stock market "Bourse de Tunis" is under the control of the state-run Financial Market Council and lists 51 companies. The Government offers substantial tax incentives to encourage companies to join the exchange, and expansion is occurring. In September 2009, the stock market capitalization of listed companies in Tunisia was valued at TND 11.209 billion.

(US$8.689 billion), approximately 21% of 2009 GDP, up from TND 8.301 billion (US$6.723 billion) in December 2008. Over the first nine months of 2009, Tunindex, the stock market's benchmark index, grew by 40.5 percent, up from 28.6 percent growth in 2008 for the same period. Capital controls are still in place. Foreign investors are permitted to purchase shares in resident firms (through authorized brokers) or to purchase indirect investments through established mutual funds.

The banking system is considered generally sound and is improving as the Central Bank has begun to enforce adherence to international norms for reserves and debt. Given the current pace of reforms, the banking sector actually weathered the international economic crisis and resisted serious adverse effects visible in other countries. Reform is underway, however. Recent measures include actions to strengthen the reliability of financial statements, enhance bank credit risk management, and improve creditors' rights. Revisions to banking laws tightened the rules on investments and bank licensing, and increased the minimum capital requirement. The required minimum risk-weighted capital/asset ratio has been raised to 8 percent, consistent with the Basel Committee capital adequacy recommendations. Despite the strict new requirements, many banks still have substantial amounts of non-performing or delinquent debt in their portfolios. The Government has established debt recovery entities (sociétés de recouvrement de créances) to buy the non-performing loans (NPLs) of commercial banks. The current ratio of NPLs to total loans is around 15 percent although the Presidential electoral program, announced in October 2009, targets a 7 percent ratio by 2014. Although in recent years the Government has undertaken a number of banking privatizations and consolidations, the Government is the controlling shareholder in 10 of the 20 major banks. The estimated total assets of the country's five largest banks are about TND 24.482 billion (roughly US$19.83 billion). Foreign participation in their capital has risen significantly and is now well over 20 percent.

In the last five years regulatory and accounting systems have been brought more in line with required international standards. Most of the major global accounting firms are represented in Tunisia. Tunisian firms listed on the stock exchange are required to publish semiannual corporate reports audited by a certified public accountant.

On June 12, 2009 the GOT passed legislation addressing access to financial services for non-residents (law No. 2009-64). Financial authorities aimed essentially to address regulatory gaps in the existing system by giving an appropriate framework for financial transactions between non-residents, introducing new financial tools attractive to foreign investors, defining new rules for monitoring and supporting the creation of the Tunis Financial Harbor project (a US$3 billion Bahraini project inaugurated on June 12, 2009 and envisioned to include banks, real estate firms, investment companies, commercial centers, housing units and tourism areas). The code allows non-resident individuals or companies to use financial products and services as well as perform other relevant financial operations. Non-resident financial service providers may, in some cases and under certain conditions, provide services to residents. Regarding financial products, the code distinguishes between two types: securities and financial contracts. Both must be issued in Tunisia or negotiated on a foreign regulated market member of the International Securities Commissions Organization.

Concerning financial services providers, the code established two categories of status regarding activities: banking (deposits, loans, payments and exchange operations, acquisition of capital in operating companies or companies in current creation) and investment services (reception, transmission, orders execution and portfolio management). Non-resident financial entities, namely lending institutions authorized to act as banks, investment companies and portfolio management companies are considered by the code non-resident investment service providers.

Among the conditions required, non-resident financial service providers must present initial minimum capital (fully paid up at subscription) in convertible currency equivalent in dinars to 25 million for a bank (US$19.25 million), 10 million (US$7.7 million) for a financial institution, 7.5 million (US$5.775 million) for an investment company and 250,000 (US$192,500) for a portfolio management company.

COMPETITION FROM STATE OWNED ENTERPRISES

Since the implementation of the IMF Adjustment Program in the end of 1986, Tunisia has undertaken many reforms aimed at limiting the State's intervention in economic activities in the domestic market. These reforms have centered on:

- Re-structuring of the national economy as part of the program for the comprehensive upgrading of private and public enterprises.

- Trade liberalization through the removal of import and export licenses, dismantling customs duties on imported goods in line with the Tunisia's international commitments (especially within the World Trade Organization and the European Union), and establishing bilateral and/or multilateral free-trade agreements with Arab countries such as Morocco, Egypt, Jordan, Libya and Algeria. However, imports of the most basic products such as cereals, sugar, oil and steel have remained under the control of State-Owned Enterprises (SOE) due to their socio-economic impact and to protect against inflation.

- Providing incentives to the private sector through a unified investment code for public and private enterprises, reforms in financial and tax systems, trade policy reforms, and privatization in a number of sectors, such as telecommunications.

SOEs are active in many sectors and compete alongside private enterprises (such as the telecom and insurance sectors). However, SOEs retain monopoly control in other sectors considered sensitive by the government, such as rail road transportation, water and electricity distribution, postal services and ports logistics. In these companies, senior management is appointed by the GOT and reports to the respective minister. The board of directors is mainly formed by representatives from other ministries and public shareholders. Like private companies, SOEs are required by law to publish independently-audited annual reports whether their capital is publicly traded on the stock market or not. Tunisia does not have a Sovereign Wealth Fund (SWF).

CORPORATE SOCIAL RESPONSIBILITY

The concept of corporate social responsibility is developing progressively through governmental campaigns but has not yet taken firm hold in Tunisia. The most successful campaigns to date have focused on preserving the environment, energy conservation and combating counterfeiting.

To date, most corporate social responsibility initiatives come from foreign multinationals that incorporate Tunisia into worldwide campaigns. Examples include supporting an educational program related to children's nutrition, supporting a clean water initiative, and creation of a program aimed at discouraging emigration of skilled workers from Tunisia. Such programs are viewed favorably by the GOT.

POLITICAL VIOLENCE

Tunisia is a stable country, and incidents involving politically-motivated damage to economic projects or infrastructure are extremely rare. In April 2002, Al-Qa'ida took responsibility for at an attack at the synagogue on the island of Djerba that claimed 20 victims, 14 of them German tourists. This resulted in a significant reduction in the number of European visitors in the immediate aftermath of the attack, but the sector has now recovered. In December 2006 and January 2007, Tunisian security forces disrupted a terrorist group, killing or capturing many individuals who reportedly planned to carry out acts of violence in Tunisia. The U.S. Embassy in Tunis was reportedly among the group's intended targets. In February 2008 Al-Qa'ida in the Islamic Maghreb claimed responsibility for kidnapping two Austrian tourists along Tunisia's southern border with Algeria. They were released in Mali in September, reportedly after payment of a ransom.

CORRUPTION

Tunisia's penal code devotes 11 articles to defining and classifying corruption and to assigning corresponding penalties (including fines and imprisonment). Several other legal texts also address broader concepts of corruption including violations of the commercial or labor codes, which range from speculative financial practices to giving or accepting bribes. Detailed information on the application of these laws or their effectiveness in combating corruption is not publicly available. There are no statistics specific to corruption. The Tunisian Ministry of Commerce publishes information on cases involving the infringement of the commercial code, but these incidents range from non-conforming labeling procedures to price/supply speculation. The print media report abuses of fiduciary authority by public officials only on rare occasions. Anecdotal reports from the Tunisian business community and U.S. businesses with regional experience suggest that corruption exists, but is not as pervasive as that found in neighboring countries. After several years of steady improvement, Tunisia's ranking on Transparency International's (TI) Corruption Index dropped from 43 in 2005 with a CPI score of 4.9 to 65, in 2009 with a score of 4.2. At the regional level, Tunisia is ranked 8th among MENA countries, before its direct competitor, Morocco (10), and its neighbors Algeria (11) and Libya (15). According to the TI Corruption Index scale, a score of ten indicates extremely little corruption and a score of zero means very serious corruption.

Most U.S. firms involved in the Tunisian market have not identified corruption as a primary obstacle to foreign direct investment. Some potential investors have asserted that unfair practices and corruption among prospective local partners have delayed or blocked specific investment proposals, or there has been an appearance that cronyism or influence peddling has affected some investment decisions. Some analysts believe corruption, or the perception of corruption, has affected domestic investment rates.

The Government's recent efforts to combat corruption have concentrated on ensuring that price controls are respected, enhancing commercial competition in the domestic market, and harmonizing Tunisian laws with those of the European Union. Since 1989, the public sector is governed by a comprehensive law designed to regulate each phase of public procurement and established the Higher Market Commission (CSM - Commission Supérieure des Marchés) to supervise the tender and award of major Government contracts. The Government publicly supports a policy of transparency and has called for it in the conduct of privatization operations. Public tenders require bidders to provide a sworn statement that they have not and will not, either themselves or through a third party, make any promises or give gifts with a view to influencing the outcome of the tender and realization of the project. Pursuant to the U.S. Foreign Corrupt Practices Act (FCPA), the U.S. Government requires that American companies requesting U.S. Government advocacy support with foreign states certify not to participate in corrupt practices.

BILATERAL INVESTMENT AGREEMENTS

A Trade and Investment Framework Agreement (TIFA) between Tunisia and the United States was signed in 2002 and three TIFA Council meetings have taken place, most recently in March 2008. A Bilateral Investment Treaty between Tunisia and the United States took effect in 1991. A 1985 treaty (and 1989 protocol) guarantees U.S. firms freedom from double taxation.

Tunisia has concluded bilateral trade agreements with approximately 81 countries. In January 2008, Tunisia's Association Agreement with the EU went into effect eliminating tariffs on industrial goods with the eventual goal of creating a free trade zone between Tunisia and the EU member states. In addition, Tunisia is signatory of the multilateral agreements with the Multilateral Investment Guarantee Agency (MIGA). Tunisia has signed the Agreement on WTO, bilateral agreements with the Member States of the European Free Trade Association (EFTA), bilateral and multilateral agreements with Arab League members, and a bilateral agreement with Turkey.

OPIC AND OTHER INVESTMENT INSURANCE PROGRAMS

OPIC is active in the Tunisian market and provides political risk insurance and other services to a variety of U.S. companies. OPIC supports private U.S. investment in Tunisia and has sponsored several reciprocal investment missions. The 1963 OPIC agreement with Tunisia was revised and signed in February 2004.

LABOR

Tunisian labor is readily available. Tunisia has a labor force of approximately 3.5 million and a national literacy rate of about 75 percent. About 90 percent of the work force under 35 is literate. The official unemployment rate is 14.1 percent (although this is considerably higher in some regions). The figure does not include many who are underemployed.

Nearly 80,000 new jobs must be created each year to keep unemployment at current levels, while sustained annual GDP growth of about 7 percent would be required in order to make significant inroads into the chronic unemployment figure. The structure of the workforce has remained stable over the past 20 years (19 percent agriculture, 32 percent industry, and 49 percent commerce and services).

The right to form a labor union is protected by law. There is only one national labor confederation, the General Union of Tunisian Workers (UGTT - Union General des Travailleurs Tunisiens). The UGTT claims about one third of the labor force as members, although more are covered by UGTT-negotiated contracts. Wages and working conditions are established through triennial collective bargaining agreements between the UGTT, the national employers' association (UTICA - Union Tunisienne de l'Industrie, du Commerce et de l'Artisanat), and the Government of Tunisia. These agreements set industry standards and generally apply to about 80 percent of the private sector labor force, whether or not individual companies are unionized. The most recent wage agreements were completed on August 3, 2009, although negotiations on sectoral wages are still underway. The official minimum monthly wage in the industrial sector is 225.160 TND (about US$173.37) for a 40 hour week and 260.624 TND (about US$200.68) for a 48 hour week.

FOREIGN TRADE ZONES/FREE TRADE ZONES

Tunisia has two free trade zones, one in the north at Bizerte, and the other in the south at Zarzis. The land is state-owned, but the respective zones are managed by a private company. Companies established in the free trade zones, officially known as "Parcs d'Activités Economiques," are exempt from most taxes and customs duties and benefit from special tax rates. Goods are allowed limited duty-free entry into Tunisia for transformation and re-export. Factories are considered bonded warehouses and have their own assigned customs personnel.

However, companies do not necessarily have to be located in one of the two designated free trade zones to operate with this type of business structure. In fact, the majority of offshore enterprises are situated in various parts of the country. Regulations are strict, and operators must comply with the Investment Code.

FOREIGN DIRECT INVESTMENT STATISTICS

Total foreign investment during the first 10 months of 2009 was TND 1.77 billion (US$1.36 billion), which represents a 36.4 percent drop (when calculated in USD, the drop is 39.55 percent) compared to the same period last year. This decline in foreign investment is the result of 34.4 percent decrease in foreign direct investment (TND 1.7 billion (US$1.3 billion) down from TND 2.6 billion (US$1.36 billion), and a 63.72 percent drop in portfolio investment (TND 70.7 million (US$54.43 million) down from TND 194.9 million (US$157.869 million). Over the third quarter of 2009, foreign investment in portfolio was marked by an ongoing withdrawal of foreign investors from the Tunis Stock Market as well as flat volume of transactions on their behalf. This withdrawal was likely due to the liquidity squeeze in foreign financial markets. The downward trend in FDI is attributable to a drop in investment flows for the sectors of energy and services as well as well as the effect of the international economic crisis. Some decline is attributable to a delay in disbursement of the investment announced by the Divona/Orange France Telecom consortium, which won the third telecom operator license valued at TND 257.251 million (US$198.08 million). Although this investment occurred during 2009, the consortium only disbursed a first tranche, TND 92 million (US$70.84 million), in August and has yet to disburse the rest.

Over 2,966 foreign or joint capital companies are operational in Tunisia and employ 303,142 people. Foreign investments generate about one-third of exports and one-fifth of total employment. In recent years, however, FDI in real estate, infrastructure, and the energy sector has been a significant source of growth.

Tunisia's largest single foreign investor is British Gas, which has developed the Miskar offshore gas field (US$650 million) and is investing a further US$500 million for new development. The largest single foreign investment was Turkish company TAV's 550 million euro (US$792 million) construction of the Enfidha International Airport, which is operating on a 40-year concession. Major foreign presence in other key sectors includes telecommunications and electronics (Lucent, Lacroix Electronique, Sagem, Alcatel, Stream, Siemens, Philips, Thomson), the automotive industry (Lear Corporation, Draxlmaier, Valeo, Toyota Tsusho, Pirelli), food products (3 Suisses, Danone) and aeronautics (Zodiac Aerospace, Eurocast, SEA Latelec).

Major U.S. company presence in Tunisia includes: Citibank, Cisco, Coca-Cola, Crown Cork, Eurocast (a joint venture with Palmer), Hewlett-Packard, Johnson Controls, Lear Corporation, Pioneer Natural Resources, Microsoft, Pfizer, Sara Lee (represented in Tunisia under the name of Essel Tunisie / DBA), and Stream. JAL Group, originally part of an Italian-owned group producing safety footwear for the export market, was recently purchased by U.S. investors and, with a staff of over 4,600, is now the largest U.S.

For additional analytical, business and investment opportunities information, please contact Global Investment & Business Center, USA at (703) 370-8082. Fax: (703) 370-8083. E-mail: ibpusa3@gmail.com Global Business and Investment Info Databank - www.ibpus.com

employer in Tunisia. Over the past few years, Pioneer Natural Resources continued to expand its oil and gas drilling and production operations in Tunisia, bringing its total investments in Tunisia to approximately US$160 million.

Web Resources

Foreign Investment Promotion Agency (FIPA) www.investintunisia.com
Central Bank of Tunisia www.bct.gov.tn
General Information about Tunisia www.tunisie.com
Tunisian Industrial Promotion Agency www.tunisieindustrie.nat.tn
Bizerte Free Zone www.bizertaeconomicpark.com.tn
Zarzis Free Zone www.zfzarzis.com.tn

Stock Exchange www.bvmt.com.tn

Privatization www.privatisation.gov.tn
National Statistic Institute (INS) www.ins.nat.tn

INVESTMENT INCENTIVES

Entered into force in January 1994, the Investment Incentives Code is the law that governs both national and foreign investment. It confirms the freedom to invest in most fields and reinforces the Tunisian economy openness to the global world.

There are numerous incentives, in the form of tax exemption, investment bonuses, no-cost infrastructure, and assumption of employer's share of social costs.

COMMON INCENTIVES

Tax relief on reinvested profits and income up to 35% of the income or profits subject to tax.
→ Customs duties exemption for capital goods that have no locally made counterparts.
→ VAT limited on capital goods imports (1999 Finance Act provisions).

SPECIFIC INCENTIVES

Advantages to fully-exporting companies
→ Full tax exemption on exports-derived profits for the first 10 years and taxation at a low rate of 10% after this periode of ten years for the life of the company.
→ Full exemption on reinvested profits and income.
→ Duty free profits for capital goods including merchandise transport vehicles, raw materials, semi-finished products and services needed by the business.
→ Possibility of selling on the local market: 30% of production for industrial goods and agricultural products, along with payment of applicable duty and levies. (This rate is set at 50% until June 30th, 2010 by virtue of act 2009 - 35 of June 30th 2009 as amended by Act 2009-82).

Zones being encouraged in the context of regional development

Tax and related breaks
The investment incentives code provides benefits for investments in zones being encouraged in the context of regional development.
→ Full tax exemption on reinvested profits and income.

For additional analytical, business and investment opportunities information,
please contact Global Investment & Business Center, USA
at (703) 370-8082. Fax: (703) 370-8083. E-mail: ibpusa3@gmail.com
Global Business and Investment Info Databank - www.ibpus.com

→ Deduction from the tax base for individual or corporate tax of income or profits on investments in industry, tourism, handicrafts or certain service activities, as follows:

- 100% for the first five years dating from effective start up of activity for companies located in zones being encouraged in the context of regional development that are part of the first group (law n°2007-69 of 27/12/2007).
- 100% for the first 10 years dating from effective start up of activity for companies located in zones being encouraged in the context of regional development that are part of the second group (law n°2007-69 of 27/12/2007).
-100% for the first 10 years and up to 50% of such income for the next 10 years for companies located in priority zones being encouraged in the context of regional development (law n°2007-69 of 27/12/2007).
→ Assumption by the State of the employer's contribution to the legally-constituted social security system as part of the wage package for Tunisian staff financed by investments in industry, tourism, handicrafts and certain service activities, as follows:

1-Zones being encouraged in the context of regional development in tourism :
- 100% for the first five years dating from effective start up of activity
- 100% for the first five years dating from effective start up of activity, then for an additional period of five years for investments in Saharan tourism in zones being encouraged in the context of regional development.

2- Zones being encouraged in the context of regional development in industry, handicrafts, and certain service activities
- partial (varying between 100% and 20%) for the first five years for companies located in zones being encouraged in the context of regional development as part of the first group.
- 100% for the first five years for companies located in zones being encouraged for regional development as part of the second group.
- 100% for the first five years, then partial (varying from 80% to 20%) for an additional period of five years for companies located in priority zones being encouraged in the context of regional development.

→ exemption from contribution to the fund to provide housing for wage earners (FOPROLOS) for the first five years dating from effective start up of activity for investments in tourism, industry, handicrafts, and certain service activities figuring in the second group of zones being encouraged in the context of regional development and priority zones being encouraged in the context of regional development as per the list attached to the decree
→   Possibility that the State takes part to infrastructure expenses as folows:
→ 25% of such expenditure, when located in the first group of zones being encouraged in the context of regional development
→ 50% of such expenditure, when located in the second group of zones being encouraged in the context of regional development
→ 75% of such expenditure, when located in priority zones being encouraged in the context of regional development
But this premium does not cover infrastructure tied to normal activities, for which relevant national structures are responsible.

For additional analytical, business and investment opportunities information, please contact Global Investment & Business Center, USA at (703) 370-8082. Fax: (703) 370-8083. E-mail: ibpusa3@gmail.com Global Business and Investment Info Databank - www.ibpus.com

State assumption of infrastructure work is available for investments located in approved or developed industrial zones that are in line with approved development plans.

FINANCIAL INCENTIVES
a. Industries, handicrafts and certain service activities

Investment in manufacturing industries and services as well as investments made by handicraft companies that employ at least 10 people are eligible for an investment premium at the following rates:

→ 8% of the cost of investment exclusive of working capital (the premium not to exceed 320,000 dinars), for activities located in the first group of zones being encouraged in the framework of regional development, listed as follows:

First group of zones being encouraged in the context of regional development

governorate	delegations
Béja	Medjez el Bab
Sfax	Agareb, Djebeniana, El Amra, El Hancha, El Ghraiba,
Skhira	
Sousse	Sidi El Hani
Zaghouan	Zaghouan, Bir M'cherga

→ 15% of the cost of investment exclusive of working capital (the premium not to exceed 600,000 dinars), for activities located in the second group of zones being encouraged in the framework of regional development, listed as follows:

Second group of zones being encouraged in the context of regional development

governorate	delegations
Béja	Béja nord, Béja sud, Testour, Teboursouk, Goubellat, Tibar
Bizerte	Djoumine, Ghezala
Gabès	Mareth
Kairouan	Kairouan nord, Kairouan sud, Hajeb el Ayoun, Echebika,
Sbikha, Haffouz, Nasrallah, Bouhajla, Cherarda	
Mahdia	Ouled Chamekh, Hébira, Essouassi, Chorbane
Médenine	Médenine nord, Médenine sud, Sidi Makhlouf, Ben
Guerdane	
Sfax	Bir Ali ben Khélifa, Menzel Chaker
Sidi Bouzid	Sidi Bouzid Ouest, Sidi Bouzid Est, Mezzouna, Regueb,
Ouled Haffouz	
Siliana	Bou Arada, Gaâfour, el Krib, El Aroussa
Zaghouan	Ez-Zriba, el Fahs, Saouaf

→ 25% of the cost of investment exclusive of working capital (the premium not to exceed 1000,000 dinars), for activities located in the priority zones being encouraged in the context of regional development, listed as follows:

Priority zones being encouraged in the context of regional development

governorate	delegations
Beja	Nefza, Amdoun, Testour, Teboursouk, Goubellat, Tibar
Bizerte	Djoumine, Sejnane, Ghezala
Gabes	Old Matmata, New Matmata , El Hamma, Menzel el Habib
Gafsa	All delegations
Jendouba	All delegations
Kairouan	El Ala, Hajeb el Ayoun, Echebika, Sbikha, Haffouz, Nasrallah, Oueslatia, Bouhajla, Cherarda
Kasserine	All delegations
Kebili	All delegations
Le Kef	All delegations
Mahdia	Ouled Chamekh, Hebira, Essouassi, Chorbane
Medenine	Northern Medenine, southern Medenine, Sidi Makhlouf, Ben Guerdane, Beni Khedeche
Sfax	El Ghraiba, El Amra, Agareb, Djebeniana, Bir Ali ben Khelifa, Skhira, Kerkennah
Sidi Bouzid	All delegations
Siliana	All delegations
Sousse	Sidi el Hani
Tataouine	All delegations
Tozeur	All delegations
Zaghouan	Ez-Zriba, Ennadhour, Saouaf

b. Tourism

→ A premium of 8% is available for lodgings, entertainment facilities, and spas.

governorate	delegations
Saharan tourism	
Gabes	El hamma, Menzel habib
Tozeur	-
Kebili	-
Tataouine	Remada, Dhehiba
Gafsa	Northern Gafsa , Sidi aïch, Ksar, gafsa Sud, Guetar, Belkhir and Snad
Zaghouan	Zaghouan, El Fahs, Bir M'cherga
Mountain tourism	
Tataouine	Bir lahmar, Tataouine North, Tataouine Southern, Ghomrassen, Smar
Medenine	Beni khedeche
Gabes	new Matmata , Matmata old
Tourism along the northern coast	
Jendouba	Tabarka, Aïn Drahem
Beja	Nefza
Spa tourism	
Zaghouan	Zaghouan, Bir M'charga (Jebel-Ouest), Ez-Zriba
El Kef	Western Kef (Hammam Mellègue)
« Green »/Ecological tourism	

Bizerte	Tinja (Parc of Ichkeul)
Gasfa	Mezzouna (Parc of Bou Hedma)
Kasserine	Park of Chaâmbi
Sfax	Kerkennah
Kairouan	El Oueslatia (Djbel Oueslet)

→ A 25% premium is available for projects in areas being reconverted from mining activities.

Gafsa	Om laâres, Métlaoui of redeyef and M'dhilla

PRACTICAL AND LEGAL INFORMATION FOR CONDUCTING BUSINESS

DOING BUSINESS IN TUNISIA

MARKET OVERVIEW

* Tunisia is a small and politically stable country on the North African coast. It has the most diversified economy in the region. With a population of slightly over 10 million, it has one of the highest standards of living on the continent. The country does not have vast reserves of hydrocarbons like its neighbors Algeria and Libya, but has prospered under long-standing government policies to develop manufacturing, tourism, and agriculture. At the same time, social programs limit population growth, provide a high standard of education, and ensure a relatively decent standard of living for all. The 74.3% national literacy rate is one of the highest in North Africa and the Middle East, and the 2008 average annual income per capita reached $4,022. The International Monetary Fund projected that the 2008 GDP based on Purchasing Power Parity (PPP) per capita was $8,020.

* The Tunisian economy, which has maintained a steady average annual growth rate of about 5.4% between 2004 and 2007, grew by 5.1% in 2008. Government of Tunisia (GOT) planners predict GDP will grow at an annual average rate of 6.1% over the coming five years although this may be reduced in light of the economic crisis. The average inflation rate in 2008 reached 5%. Hard currency reserves reached $9.570 Million (11.687 Million TD) in December 2008.

* Manufacturing industries, producing largely for export, are the motor of Tunisia's economic growth and a major source of foreign currency revenue, accounting for about 69% of exports. Labor-intensive plants, historically producing textiles and, more recently, automobile components, create much-needed jobs. Textiles and mechanical and electrical equipment sales are the primary sources of foreign currency revenue, but both sectors are currently suffering due to the international economic crisis. The GOT export promotion center CEPEX (Centre de Promotion des Exportations) is responsible for identifying new export markets in all sectors.

* Tourism is the next largest source of foreign currency revenue. About 7 million tourists visited Tunisia in 2008 bringing in nearly $2.7 billion in convertible currency.

* Agriculture also plays a major role in Tunisia and employs approximately one-fifth of the population. Agriculture accounts for nearly 10.5% of GDP and comprises about 9.1% of exports. In 2008, Tunisia exported nearly $1.7 billion of agricultural products, mainly olive oil, seafood, dates and citrus.

* The government still retains control over certain "strategic" sectors of the economy (finance, hydrocarbons, the national airline, electricity and gas

distribution, telecommunications, and water resources), but the role of the private sector is increasing. The Government of Tunisia is currently studying the economic impact of liberalization of petroleum product price controls. Most of Tunisia's electricity is produced from natural gas (85%) and heavy fuel oil (15%). Electricity demand is growing 5.4% each year, and will reach about 22 billion KWH by 2020. The GOT plans to produce 900 MW of nuclear power by 2020. Tunisia has signed the Treaty on the Non-Proliferation of Nuclear Weapons and a Comprehensive Safeguards Agreement with the International Atomic Energy Agency (IAEA).

* Accessing the Tunisian market can be a challenge for U.S. companies. Geographically part of Africa but culturally more Mediterranean and Middle Eastern, this former French protectorate has extremely close ties with Europe. These ties have been reinforced by Tunisia's Association Agreement with the European Union (EU), which created a free trade zone for industrial products in January 2008. Over 70% of Tunisia's foreign trade is with Europe. Tunisia's other major trading partner is Libya. In 2008, total Tunisian imports were $24.7 billion and exports totaled $19.3 billion.

* Tunisia is a founding member of the World Trade Organization (WTO) and is publicly committed to a free trade regime and export-led growth. The government would like to expand trade and investment ties beyond Europe, but the European presence in the economy remains strong. The EU Association Agreement is backed by significant European funding to support the Tunisian economy through the transition period to an open market. Over 3600 Tunisian companies have taken part in the "Mise à Niveau" program so far. Tunisia's Association Agreement with the EU bars non-EU countries from certain major tenders receiving EU financing.

* Tunisia is a member of the Arab Maghreb Union (UMA - Union du Maghreb Arabe), a political-economic grouping of Tunisia, Algeria, Morocco, Mauritania, and Libya. It is also a signatory to several bilateral and multilateral trade agreements, including the Agadir Agreement. This agreement, a framework for a free trade area with Egypt, Jordan, and Morocco, will create a potential market of over 100 million people. Tunisia's commercial ties with the United Arab Emirates (UAE) have taken a leap forward since 2006 with the announcement of plans by

several Dubai-based companies to invest some $20 billion in real estate, tourism, and commerce in Tunisia over the next few years. Tunisia attracts about $750 million in Foreign Direct Investment (FDI) annually, two-thirds of which comes from Europe. However, in 2006, FDI flow rose to $3.522 billion (of which $2.377 billion came from the 35% participation of Tecom Dig in Tunisie Telecom), making the UAE contribution around 68% of total FDI. In 2007 and 2008 total FDI flows respectively reached $1.617 billion and $2.561 billion. Total U.S. FDI flows in 2008 were $94.26 million.

* In order to assist U.S. companies in gaining access to the Tunisian market, the United States signed a Trade and Investment Framework Agreement (TIFA) in October 2002 to formally discuss bilateral trade and investment issues. Follow-on TIFA Councils were held in October 2003, June 2005, and March 2008.

* The United States is not a major goods supplier to Tunisia. U.S. Department of Commerce trade statistics for the first eleven months of 2008 show Tunisian imports from United States at $471.7 million and Tunisian exports to the United States at $626.2 million.

* For many years the United States was Tunisia's fourth leading goods supplier, after France, Italy and Germany, but it dropped to 8th position in 2008. In the first eleven months of 2008, U.S. exports to Tunisia grew by 37.3% compared to the same period of 2007.

* Although initial U.S. investment in Tunisia was primarily in the hydrocarbons sector, U.S. companies now successfully invest in offshore manufacturing industries and are present in both textile production and electrical/mechanical equipment manufacturing. Offshore companies can be established under an attractive regime that offers significant tax incentives to export-oriented investors. In the tourism industry, only two of Tunisia's 800+ hotels are affiliated with U.S. groups. Currently, total U.S. investment in Tunisia is estimated at about $1.040 billion and has contributed to the creation of more than 18,175 jobs.

MARKET CHALLENGES

* Doing business in Tunisia can be challenging for U.S. companies, who may perceive the Tunisian bureaucracy as cumbersome and slow and may find that the regulatory environment lacks coherence and consistency. The decision-making process can be opaque and at odds with the government's official pro-business stance, which emphasizes transparency. However, with adequate planning and longer lead times, favorable results can be obtained.

* Imports from the EU enjoy a considerable price advantage over other countries' products, as many EU products are now totally exempt from

import duties. U.S. products generally enjoy widespread acceptance among consumers, although their perceived edge in quality and technology can be offset by the additional costs associated with their distribution by European intermediaries and the recent depreciation of the Tunisian Dinar against the Euro.

* The EU and many European countries offer excellent financing terms for trade. Tunisian companies are familiar with these opportunities but are generally unfamiliar with financing opportunities available when purchasing U.S. goods. The U.S. Embassy in Tunis works closely with the Ex-Im Bank, OPIC, and other U.S. organizations to promote awareness of U.S. financing sources.

* Despite difficulties, U.S. firms are able to successfully compete against better-established European companies and win significant Tunisian government contracts, especially in fields demanding cutting-edge U.S. technology. The U.S. Embassy in Tunis actively promotes these sectors as being the most attractive for U.S. companies.

* U.S. exporters to Tunisia should be aware that Tunisian law prohibits the export of currency as payment for imports before documents are presented to the bank

confirming that the merchandise has entered the country. This is usually in the form of Tunisian customs authority documents. U.S. exporters have used confirmed, irrevocable letters of credit and letters of credit authorizing "payment against documents" in past transactions.

* U.S. companies should also be extremely careful to verify with Tunisia's Central Bank (Banque Centrale de Tunisie) whether they are permitted to receive payment in foreign currency for services to customers resident in Tunisia. This issue has been the source of confusion and occasional difficulty for some U.S. companies in Tunisia.

MARKET OPPORTUNITIES

* For U.S. companies, the best investment opportunities are in sectors that will benefit from U.S. technology (hydrocarbons, power generation, transportation, and telecommunications) or to a lesser extent, in the more labor-intensive offshore, export-oriented industries such as the manufacture of textiles and mechanical or electrical equipment.

* Due to its moderate Mediterranean climate, Tunisia has a developing tourism industry, but niche travel is under-developed in areas away from the coasts. Investment possibilities in hotels include cultural or historical tours, golf packages, and desert tours.

* Agricultural opportunities for U.S. producers remain bulk commodities, such as wheat, corn and some intermediate products such as soybean

meal and planting seeds. The U.S. market share, currently hovering around 10% of overall agricultural imports, has room for growth despite a price competitiveness gap with the EU caused by substantially higher freight costs and preferential access granted to the EU.

* There is a sizable market for agricultural equipment in Tunisia. A government decision to privatize grain storage has created demand for grain silos and elevators. These represent good opportunities for U.S. suppliers.

* There is a significant market for U.S. medical equipment in Tunisia. The government decision to upgrade hospitals and the increase in the number of private clinics has created a large demand for medical equipment.

MARKET ENTRY STRATEGY

* A company planning to invest in offshore or export-oriented operations in Tunisia faces few obstacles. The Government of Tunisia's investment promotion authority has established a generous package of incentives for such operations.

* Entering the domestic market, particularly in the services sector, is more difficult. Unless the company is working on a project actively solicited by the Tunisian government or is closely associated with one of the country's well-connected business groups, the process can be fraught with obstacles. Currently, a new law regulating the services sector is being drafted. This law will

regulate distribution channels and establish a framework for commercial franchising.

* U.S. companies are strongly advised to obtain written confirmation from the Tunisian authorities of any exceptional conditions granted to a particular trade or investment operation.

* The U.S. Embassy strongly encourages all U.S. companies to visit Tunisia prior to entering into a business relationship with a local partner.

TRADE AND PROJECT FINANCING

THE BANKING SYSTEM

The Tunisian banking system is a mixture of private and state-owned institutions with varying ranges of financial instruments and services. The banks are strictly regulated by the Central Bank of Tunisia, which has increasingly insisted upon prudential norms for bank reserves and balance sheets close to international standards in recent years. In 1993, nearly 37 percent of overall bank portfolios were considered non-performing, but this rate has been reduced to under 25 percent. During this same period, the rate of non-performing loans at commercial banks was cut from 34 percent to well below 20 percent. These rates remain far higher than U.S. banking regulations would allow, but they are showing steady progress in reducing the level of bad loans.

Tunisian commitments under the WTO and its EU free trade agreement to begin liberalizing its banking sector will probably force more serious reform measures over the coming years.

FOREIGN EXCHANGE CONTROLS AFFECTING TRADE

The Tunisian dinar is convertible for current account transactions. Companies or individuals engaging in foreign trade can apply to the Central Bank for a convertible currency account. Foreign investors may freely repatriate profits and proceeds from the sale of equity, but other transfers may be subject to Central Bank authorization. Most trade-related transactions are conducted through letters of credit without difficulty. However, as mentioned above, Tunisian law strictly prohibits the flow of currency out of Tunisia as payment for imports before documents are presented to the issuing bank which establishes that the merchandise is in the custody of Tunisian customs. U.S. exporters have successfully used confirmed, irrevocable letters of credit and letters of credit authorizing "payment against documents" in past transactions. U.S. companies should be extremely careful in verifying their authority to receive payment in foreign currency from customers resident in Tunisia. This issue has been the source of confusion and occasional difficulty for some U.S. companies in Tunisia.

Royalty payments must be approved by relevant government ministries in consultation with the Central Bank on a case-by-case basis. Approval of royalty payments has been rare in recent years. Rates reflect the estimated value of the technology involved and the duration of the particular contract.

For additional analytical, business and investment opportunities information,
please contact Global Investment & Business Center, USA
at (703) 370-8082. Fax: (703) 370-8083. E-mail: ibpusa3@gmail.com
Global Business and Investment Info Databank - www.ibpus.com

GENERAL FINANCING AVAILABILITY

Financing is generally available. Tunisian banks are conservative and often reluctant to deal with newer firms, but it is rare to have a trade fail because of the unavailability of financing. Bankers have described the Tunisian market as one where the supply of short-term commercial credit has exceeded demand. This excess liquidity is not present on medium-to-long term credit.

HOW TO FINANCE EXPORTS / METHODS OF PAYMENT

Tunisian firms are prohibited from paying cash in advance and generally rely upon letters of credit. U.S. exporters should be aware that letters of credit are payable upon receipt of goods in Tunisia after passage through customs. Suppliers have experienced significant delays and losses in dealing with the Tunisian customs service.

TYPES OF AVAILABLE EXPORT FINANCING AND INSURANCE

Financing from the Export-Import Bank of the U.S. ("Ex-Im Bank") is available in Tunisia for American exporters. While lending has focused largely on transactions with state enterprises, Ex-Im Bank has expressed the desire to work more closely with the private sector in Tunisia. Companies competing for government tenders are advised to work closely with the Embassy and Ex-Im Bank once evidence of a foreign competitor's ability to obtain concessional financing becomes clear. Excellent financing terms offered by European suppliers remain an obstacle for U.S. companies but Ex-Im Bank will strive to match concessional financing from foreign competitors' governments, especially given new OECD requirements regarding concessional financing of commercially based projects. The U.S. Trade and Development Agency (TDA) has also played a role on behalf of U.S. firms seeking contracts in the Tunisian market. TDA's services in recent years have included feasibility study funding, conditional training grants, and trade development missions.

PROJECT FINANCING AVAILABILITY

The World Bank (IBRD - International Bank for Reconstruction and Development) and African Development Bank (AfDB) support a variety of projects in Tunisia. IBRD efforts are focused on several areas including the environment, the financial sector, privatization and industrial restructuring, the road network, and dams and irrigation. AfDB assistance includes major dam projects.

The European Investment Bank (EIB) and the Japanese Economic Development Fund are both involved in financing a variety of major infrastructure projects and vocational training. The EIB also finances imports of European capital goods.

BANKS WITH CORRESPONDENT U.S. BANKING RELATIONSHIPS

Citibank, the only American bank operating in Tunisia, has both onshore and offshore branches, with offices in Sfax and Tunis. Most Tunisian banks maintain a corresponding relationship with one or more U.S. banks.

For additional analytical, business and investment opportunities information, please contact Global Investment & Business Center, USA at (703) 370-8082. Fax: (703) 370-8083. E-mail: ibpusa3@gmail.com Global Business and Investment Info Databank - www.ibpus.com

THE FOREIGN EXCHANGE MARKET REGULATIONS

A. DEVELOPMENT OF THE TUNISIAN DINAR AGAINST THE MAIN FOREIGN CURRENCIES

The development of the dinar exchange rate was influenced in 1996 by appreciation of the US dollar on international exchange markets, an appreciation which gained momentum in the last quarter of the year, and by an improvement in Tunisia's inflation rate, which came down from 6.3% in 1995 to 3.7% in 1996.

Thus between 1995 and 1996 the dinar depreciated by approximately 5.2% with respect to the US dollar, 9.3% against the Italian lira, and 2.5% against the Spanish peseta. It appreciated with reference to the French franc, the Deutschmark and the Japanese yen by around 1.5%, 2.9% and 6.6% respectively.

TRANSACTIONS ON THE FOREIGN EXCHANGE MARKET

The volume of cash transactions on the foreign exchange market was down considerably, falling from TD6.269 billion in 1995 to 4.998 billion in 1996. This decline resulted from a number of factors taken together, particularly a deceleration in import and export growth, an increase in compensation on the level of the individual banks, and an increase in foreign currency-foreign currency transactions between Tunisian banks.

The amount represented by interbank exchange market transactions in 1996 was TD3.4 billion, 20.4% lower than the previous year's level, while their share in exchange transactions as a whole remained virtually the same, at 68.4% in 1996 against 68.5% in 1995. This share fluctuated greatly during the year, however, reaching a maximum of 84% in May and a minimum of 54% in February, compared with extreme values of 78% in May 1995 and 45% in March of that year. Analysis of this trend shows that the interbank market ensured greater liquidity in covering the economy's needs, and that it accomplished this despite a decline in total transactions.

The average monthly rate of coverage of business needs in foreign currency varied, depending upon the currency, from 64% to 96.7% for the US dollar, from 63.5% to 98.1% for the French franc, from 45.1% to 100% for the Italian lira, and from 40% to 92.6% for the Deutschmark. The range of variation was still greater in the case of the Japanese yen, ranging from 8% to 100%.

Broken down by currency, interbank transactions continued in 1996 to be characterized by a clear predominance of the US dollar, which accounted for 50.3% of total transactions, followed by the French franc (17.9%), the Italian lira (8.6%), and the Deutschmark (8.3%). The shares occupied by these currencies in total transactions in 1995 were 48%, 18.6%, 7.8% and 9.3% respectively.

Despite a lower volume of transactions on the interbank exchange market, both overall and by groups of banks, the share occupied by deposit banks in the total increased from 64.8% in 1995 to 70.2% in 1996. Offshore and development banks, on the other hand, accounted for reduced shares, that of the former dropping from 32.8% to 27.5% an that of development banks from 2.4% to 2.3%.

In addition to interbank transactions, the Central Bank intervened in 1996 for a total of TD1.58 billion, against TD1.973 billion the previous year, to adjust the liquidity of the interbank market, particularly for transactions for refinancing of offshore banks and transactions involving foreign exchange cover.

TUNISIA: INVESTMENT AND BUSINESS OPPORTUNITIES

GOVERNMENT TO SPEED UP PRIVATIZATION PROGRAM

About forty enterprises are to be privatized during the next months, said Secretary of State in charge of public participation and privatization Mohamed Rachid Kechich during the second day of the Carthage Investment Forum.

For the present and coming years, he added, the privatization program will continue with the same determination, with the privatization, notably, of three new cement factories, the complex of the mechanical construction and naval repair and certain important companies operating in the textile sector. Mr. Kechich announced that new studies would also be conducted on various units operating in the field of agriculture, real estate, trade and tourism and a specific program would be undertaken with the public banks for the privatization of their branches.

Mr. Kechich underlined that the fundamental aim of privatization is to guarantee the continuity of the enterprise and the safeguard of the largest number possible of jobs. It is a matter of consolidating the balances of the public finances, vitalizing the financial market and developing the public's shareholding.

Mr. Kechich emphasized the legal framework ruling the privatization program, which guarantees the transparency of this process. Concerning the privatization mode, the secretary of state said that as of 1995, the model of transfer per share bloc is dominant and that foreign investors have acquired a very important part in these privatization projects.

The Secretary of State mentioned the advantages granted to investors in the privatization program such as tax reduction, tax exemption on profits and the exemption of appraisal transfer. Other advantages are also set aside for employees of the enterprises to be privatized such as priority purchase of the company's shares at reduced price and free share distribution.

TRAVEL TO TUNISIA

US STATE DEPARTMENT SUGGESTIONS

COUNTRY DESCRIPTION: Tunisia is a presidential republic with a developing economy. Tourist facilities are widely available in the main tourist areas. The workweek is Monday to Friday, with government offices open on Saturday mornings. Most stores are closed on Sunday, except in resort areas, where many remain open.

ENTRY/EXIT REQUIREMENTS: A passport is required. A visa is not required for a stay up to four months. For longer visits, Americans are required to obtain a residence permit. A residence permit may be requested and obtained from the central police station of the district of residence. Americans born in the Middle East or with Arabic names have experienced delays in clearing immigration at airports upon arrival. American citizens of Tunisian origin are expected to enter Tunisia on their Tunisian passports. If a Tunisian-American succeeds in entering on an American passport, there is a high probability that a Tunisian passport will be required before exiting the country.

For further information concerning entry requirements for Tunisia, travelers may contact the Embassy of Tunisia at 1515 Massachusetts Avenue, N.W. Washington, D.C. 20005, tel. 202-862-1850, or the Tunisian Consulate General in New York, tel. 212-272-6962, or in San Francisco, tel. 415-922-9222. Prospective travelers to Tunisia may consult the Embassy's home page at http://usembassy.state.gov/posts/ts1/wwwhmain.html/

In an effort to prevent international child abduction, many governments have initiated procedures at entry/exit points. These often include requiring documentary evidence of relationship and permission for the child's travel from the parent(s) or legal guardian not present. Having such documentation on hand, even if not required, may facilitate entry/departure.

DUAL NATIONALITY: Tunisia expects American citizens of Tunisian origin to enter Tunisia on Tunisian passports. If a Tunisian-American succeeds in entering on an American passport, there is a high probability that a Tunisian passport will be required to exit the country.
In addition to being subject to all Tunisian laws affecting U.S. citizens, dual nationals may also be subject to other laws that impose special obligations on Tunisian citizens. For additional information, please see the Consular Affairs home page on the Internet at http://travel.state.gov for our Dual Nationality flyer.

SAFETY/SECURITY: Tunisia has open borders with Libya and Algeria. (Please refer to the Consular Information Sheets for those countries.) There have been no instances in which U.S. citizens or facilities have been subject to terrorist attacks, and the Government of Tunisia takes many security measures for the benefit of the many tourists who visit Tunisia. Security personnel may at times place foreign visitors under surveillance.

During the latter part of 2001, there were some incidents of soccer-inspired violence in Tunisia in which unhappy fans became unruly and damaged property and vehicles in the vicinity of stadiums. Although the U.S. Embassy has not recommended that Americans avoid the games or stay off the streets when the games are scheduled, these incidents illustrate the need to exercise caution in the areas around stadiums before and after scheduled matches. When possible, Americans should avoid crowds and not park their cars on a street near the stadium. They should be aware of when/where soccer games are scheduled, and unless attending the game, avoid the area of the stadium one hour before kickoff and one hour after the conclusion of the game. In addition, it is prudent for those who live or are staying near a stadium to park their vehicles in garages or carports rather than leaving them on the street.

Proselytizing: Islam is the state religion of Tunisia. The Tunisian government does not interfere with the public worship of the country's religious minorities. However, some activities such as proselytizing or engaging in other activities which the Tunisian authorities could view as encouraging conversion to another faith are prohibited under laws designed to prevent disturbances to the public order. In the past, Americans who have engaged in such activities have been asked to leave the country.

CRIME: Tunisia has a moderate crime rate in urban areas. Criminals have targeted tourists and business travelers for theft, pick-pocketing, and scams. Care should be taken with wallets and other valuables kept in handbags or backpacks that can be easily opened from behind in crowded streets or marketplaces. Harassment of unaccompanied females occurs rarely in hotels, but it occurs more frequently elsewhere. Dressing in a conservative manner can diminish potential harassment, but it is wise to travel in groups of two or more people. Violent crime is rare by U.S. standards, but it is not unknown.

The loss or theft abroad of a U.S. passport should be reported immediately to the local police and the nearest U.S. embassy or consulate. U.S. citizens may refer to the Department of State's pamphlet, *A Safe Trip Abroad*, for ways to promote a trouble-free journey. The pamphlet is available by mail from the Superintendent of Documents, U.S. Government Printing Office, Washington, D.C. 20402, via the Internet at http://www.access.gpo.gov/su_docs, or via the Bureau of Consular Affairs home page at http://travel.state.gov.

MEDICAL FACILITIES: Medical care in Tunisia is available, but it is limited; specialized care or treatment may not be available. Medical staff will most likely be unable to communicate in English. Immediate ambulance service may not be available, especially outside of urban areas. Doctors and hospitals expect immediate cash payment for health care services. Over-the-counter medications are available. However, travelers should bring with them a full supply of medications that are needed on a regular basis. Emergency prescriptions are provided through a list of doctors available at theU.S. Embassy.

MEDICAL INSURANCE: The Department of State strongly urges Americans to consult with their medical insurance company prior to traveling abroad to confirm whether their policy applies overseas and whether it will cover emergency expenses such as a medical evacuation. U.S. medical insurance plans seldom cover health costs incurred outside the United States unless supplemental coverage is purchased. Further, U.S. Medicare and Medicaid programs do not provide payment for medical services outside the United States. However, many travel agents and private companies offer insurance plans that will cover health care expenses incurred overseas, including emergency services such as medical evacuations.

When making a decision regarding health insurance, Americans should consider that many foreign doctors and hospitals require payment in cash prior to providing service and that a medical evacuation to the United States may cost well in excess of $50,000. Uninsured travelers who require medical care overseas often face extreme difficulties. When consulting with your insurer prior to your trip, please ascertain whether payment will be made to the overseas healthcare provider or if you will be reimbursed later for expenses that you incur. Some insurance policies also include coverage for psychiatric treatment and for disposition of remains in the event of death.

OTHER HEALTH INFORMATION: Information on vaccinations and other health precautions may be obtained from the Centers for Disease Control and Prevention's hotline for international travelers at 1-877-FYI-TRIP (1-877-394-8747); fax 1-888-CDC-FAXX (1-888-232-3299), or via the CDC's Internet site at http://www.cdc.gov.

TRAFFIC SAFETY AND ROAD CONDITIONS: While in a foreign country, U.S. citizens may encounter road conditions that differ significantly from those in the United States. The information below concerning Tunisia is provided for general reference only, and it may not be totally accurate in a particular location or circumstance.

Safety of public transportation: Fair
Urban road conditions: Fair
Rural road conditions: Fair
Availability of road assistance: Poor

Driving in Tunisia can be dangerous. It is recommended that visitors avoid driving after dark outside of Tunis or the major resort areas. Driving practices are poor. Drivers fail to obey the rules of the road without the presence of the police. Traffic signs and signals are often ignored, and sometimes vehicles drive on the wrong side of the road. Bicycles, mopeds and motorcycles are operated without sufficient lights or reflectors, making them difficult to see darting in and out of traffic. Pedestrians cause additional problems, by dodging traffic and not paying attention to vehicles. Defensive driving is a must when driving in Tunisia. Drivers may be stopped for inspection by police officers within cities and on highways.

For additional general information about road safety, including links to foreign government sites, please see the Department of State, Bureau of Consular Affairs home page at http://travel.state.gov/road_safety.html. For specific information concerning Tunisian driver's permits, vehicle inspection, road tax and mandatory insurance, please contact the Tunisian National Tourist Organization offices in New York via the Internet at http://www.tourismtunisia.com/.

AVIATION SAFETY OVERSIGHT: As there is no direct commercial air service by local carriers at present, nor economic authority to operate such service between the United States and Tunisia, the U.S. Federal Aviation Administration (FAA) has not assessed Tunisia's Civil Aviation Authority for compliance with international aviation safety standards for oversight of Tunisia's air carrier operations. For further information travelers may contact the U.S. Department of Transportation within the United States at tel. 1-800-322-7873, or visit the FAA Internet web site at http://faa.gov/avr/iasa. The U.S. Department of Defense (DOD) separately assesses some foreign air carriers for suitability as official providers of air services. For information regarding the DOD policy on specific carriers, travelers may contact the DOD at tel. (618) 229-4801.

CUSTOMS REGULATIONS: Tunisian customs authorities may enforce strict regulations concerning temporary importation into or export from Tunisia of items such as firearms, religious materials, antiquities, medications, business equipment and currency. It is advisable to contact the Embassy of Tunisia in Washington, D.C. for specific information regarding customs requirements.

CRIMINAL PENALTIES: While in a foreign country, a U.S. citizen is subject to that country's laws and regulations, which sometimes differ significantly from those in the United States and may not afford the protections available to the individual under U.S. law. Penalties for breaking the law can be more severe than in the United States for similar offenses. Persons violating Tunisian laws, even unknowingly, may be expelled, arrested or imprisoned. Penalties for possession, use, or trafficking in illegal drugs in Tunisia are strict, and convicted offenders can expect jail sentences and heavy fines.

SPECIAL CIRCUMSTANCES: Travelers checks and credit cards are accepted at some establishments in Tunisia, mainly in urban or tourist areas. The Tunisian dinar is not yet a fully convertible currency. Tunisian law prohibits the export or import of Tunisian bank notes or coins. Tunisian law permits the export of foreign currency declared when entering Tunisia. Tourists are expected to make foreign exchange transactions at authorized banks or dealers and to retain receipts for dinars obtained. Under foreign currency regulations, a tourist can reconvert to foreign currency 30 percent of what has been exchanged into dinars, up to a maximum of 100 dollars. Declaring foreign currency on entering Tunisia and obtaining a receipt for dinars purchased thereafter will facilitate reconverting dinars to U.S. dollars. Please keep all receipts of monetary transactions for presentation when leaving the country.

CHILDREN'S ISSUES: For information on international adoption of children and international parental child abduction, please refer to our Internet site at http://travel.state.gov/children's_issues.html or telephone (202) 736-7000.
REGISTRATION/EMBASSY LOCATION: U.S. citizens are encouraged to register at the Consular Section of the U.S. Embassy and to obtain updated information on travel and security within Tunisia. The U.S. Embassy is located at 144 Avenue de La Liberte, 1002 Tunis-Belvedere, in the capital city of Tunis, telephone 216-71-782-566, fax 216-71-789-719 or 216-71-789-923. The consular e-mail address is consulartunis@state.gov. Travelers are encouraged to consult the Embassy's Internet site at http://usembassy.state.gov/posts/ts1/wwwhmain.html/

BUSINESS TRAVEL

BUSINESS CUSTOMS

Tunisia is an open society that prides itself in being a bridge between the European and Arab worlds. Although the official language is Arabic, French is widely spoken and serves as the common business language. Many Tunisians also speak English, and some Italian and German. The Tunisian government has begun to place a greater emphasis on teaching English-language skills in the public schools and at a younger age, and the use of English is becoming more widespread.

TRAVEL ADVISORY AND VISAS

American business travelers do not need a visa if they plan on staying in Tunisia less than four months. Stays longer than four months require a visa. Residency and work permits are available from the Ministry of Interior and Ministry of Social Affairs, respectively. Applications for residency permits can now be made through the regional police headquarters (Directions Régionales de la Sécurité Nationale) instead of local police stations. The
Tunisian government instituted this change in response to complaints that the application and renewal procedures for residency permits were labor-intensive and time-consuming (sometimes taking up to eight months). The government also introduced an office in the Ministry of Development and International Cooperation to expedite this process for foreign investors. By law, these permits are valid for only one year, renewable for only one additional year upon application. In practice, this limitation is rarely enforced and expatriate residents routinely stay in Tunisia beyond the two-year maximum, renewing their permits annually.

HOLIDAYS

Major Tunisian secular holidays are as follows:

Tunisian Independence Day - March 20
Tunisian Youth Day - March 21
Martyr's Day - April 9
Labor Day - May 1
Republic Day - July 25
Women's Day - August 13
Anniversary of change of government - November 7

The following religious holidays are also observed. Actual dates are based on the lunar calendar and vary from year to year:

Aid Esseghir (El-Fitr)
Aid El Kebir (El-Idha)
Ras El Am El Hijri
Mouled

BUSINESS INFRASTRUCTURE

Tunisia's physical business infrastructure is improving. The main container port at Rades/Tunis handles most incoming and outgoing sea-freight traffic. Sfax, Tunisia's second largest city and a large commercial center, can also handle a limited amount of container traffic. The road network is fairly well developed, with major highways constructed or in the planning stages between major coastal population centers. Municipal power and water are generally reliable. Access to high quality telecommunications services, particularly high-speed / high-capacity data transmission and the Internet is becoming more widely available. International calling cards are not operational in Tunisia. The government has licensed five private companies to provide

For additional analytical, business and investment opportunities information,
please contact Global Investment & Business Center, USA
at (703) 370-8082. Fax: (703) 370-8083. E-mail: ibpusa3@gmail.com
Global Business and Investment Info Databank - www.ibpus.com

Internet access although these ISPs can only access the Internet via the state Internet agency. The government's policies in this area reflect an ongoing effort to balance its political and security concerns with the growing demand for Internet access and other new information technologies.

Expatriate housing is very comfortable, although prices have been rising. Houses in the Tunis neighborhoods of Mutuelleville, Notre Dame, Carthage, Sidi Bou Said, La Soukra, La Marsa, and Gammarth are comparable to or better than many suburban U.S. communities. Medical and dental services are adequate in the major cities. Tunis has several large, well-equipped private clinics. A project to establish an offshore clinic catering to the expatriate community is underway. Except for specialized care, most illnesses can be treated locally. Food standards are fair and the water in the coastal area is potable. For those who prefer bottled water, it is inexpensive and easily available. Expatriates generally equate the overall cost-of-living with that of major cities in the U.S.

Temporary entry of goods such as laptop computers and other personal business items brought by the visitor as luggage is allowed; such items are routinely checked through the customs control posts at airports. However, publicity and exhibit materials shipped into the country require customs clearance by the receiving party in Tunisia. Provision should be made in advance to avoid customs difficulties. U.S. business travelers are encouraged to consult the "Key Officers of Foreign Service Posts: Guide for Business Representatives" available for sale by the Superintendent of Documents, U.S. Government Printing Office, Washington, D.C. 20402; Tel (202) 512-1800; Fax (202) 512-2250. This information is also available for free on the Department of State's home page www.state.gov. Business travelers to Tunisia seeking appointments with U.S. Embassy Tunis should contact the Commercial Section in advance. The commercial section can be reached by telephone at (+216) 71-107-000 or fax at (+216) 71-962-115.

SUPPLEMENTS

U.S. AND COUNTRY CONTACTS

In case of difficulty or for assistance, please e-mail the U.S. Embassy Commercial Section in Tunisia at the following address:

TunisCommercial@state.gov

CHAMBER OF COMMERCE
Tunisian-American Chamber of Commerce (TACC)
5 Ave. Mosbah Jarbou
El Manar III 2092
Tunis
Tel: +216-71-889.780
Fax: +216-71-889.880

GOVERNMENT CONTACTS

Ministry of Development and International Cooperation
Place Ali Zouaoui
Tunis
Tel: +216-71-240.133
Fax: +216-71-799.069

Ministry of Industry
Rue 8010 Cite Montplaisir
Immeuble Ennouzha
1002 Tunis
Tel: +216-71-791.132
Fax: +216-71-351.666

Ministry of Tourism, Commerce and Handicrafts
37, Avenue Kheireddine Pacha
Tunis
Tel: +216-71-890.263
Fax: +216-71-781.324

Ministry of Finance
Place du Gouvernement
La Kasbah
Tunis
Tel: +216-71-566.210
Fax: +216-71-563.959
Ministry of Environment
Centre Urbain Nord
Tunis
Tel: +216-71-704.000
Fax: +216-71-703.286

Ministry of Agriculture
30 Rue Alain Savary
Tunis
Tel: +216-71-681.654
Fax: +216-71-890.391

Ministry of Communications Technologies and Transport
Rue d'Angleterre
Tunis
Tel: +216-71-359.000
Fax: +216-71-352.353

Foreign Investment Promotion Agency (FIPA)
Centre Urbain Nord
Tunis
Tel: +216-71-703.140
Fax: +216-71-702.600

Entreprise Tunisienne des Activitiés Pétrolières (ETAP)
27 bis Avenue Kheireddine Pacha
Tunis
Tel: +216-71-782.288
Fax: +216-71-784.092
(State Petroleum Company)

Agence de Promotion de l'Industrie (API)
Rue de Syrie
Tunis
Tel: +216-71-792.144
Fax: +216-71-782.482

Institut National de la Normalisation et de la
Propriété Industrielle (INNORPI)
Cite El Khadra
Tunis
Tel: +216-71-785.922
Fax: +216-71-781.563
(Industrial Standards and Copyright Authority)

Tunisian Gas and Electricity Company (STEG)
38, Rue Kamel Ataturk
Tunis
Tel: +216-71-341.311
Fax: +216-71-341.401

Office National d'Assainissment
32 Rue Hédi Nouira
Tunis

Tel: +216-71-343.200
Fax: +216-71-350.411
(State Sanitation Agency)

Tunisie Télécom
Rue Asdrubal
(En Face du Galaxie 2000)
Tunis
Tel: +216-71-801.011
Fax: +216-71-800.777
(Telecommunications Parastatal)

Tunisair
Boulevard du 7 Novembre
Tunis
Tel: +216-71-700.100
Fax: +216-71-700.008
(State Airline)

Central Bank of Tunisia
Rue Hédi Nouira
Tunis
Tel: +216-71-340.588
Fax: +216-71-340.615

Customs Bureau
Rue Ich-Bilia
Tunis
Tel: +216-71-333.600
Fax: +216-71-353.255

Tunisian Embassy
1515 Massachusetts Ave., N.W.
Washington D.C. 20005
U.S.A.
Tel: (202) 862-1850
Fax: (202) 862-1858

Market Research

GTN Tunisie (Global Technology Network)
Rym Bedoui, Representative
Rue du Lac Malaren
Le Palais du Golfe
Bloc D
Les Berges du Lac
Tunis
Tel: +216-71-963.437

For additional analytical, business and investment opportunities information,
please contact Global Investment & Business Center, USA
at (703) 370-8082. Fax: (703) 370-8083. E-mail: ibpusa3@gmail.com
Global Business and Investment Info Databank - www.ibpus.com

Fax: +216-71-963.598

Tunisian American Chamber of Commerce (See Above)

Tunisian American Association for Management Studies (TAAMS)
10, Rue Mosbah Jarbou
Manar III
Tunis
Tel: +216-71-889.566
Fax: +216-71-872.033

COMMERCIAL BANKS

Citibank
55, Avenue Jugurtha
Tunis
Tel: +216-71-790.066
Fax: +216-71-785.556
(Only U.S. Bank in Tunisia with
Onshore and Offshore Services)

Société Tunisienne de Banque
Rue Hedi Nouira
Tunis
Tel: +216-71-340.477
Fax: +216-71-348.400

Amen Bank
13 Avenue de France
Tunis
Tel: +216-71-340.511
Fax: +216-71-349.909

Banque International Arabe de Tunisie (BIAT)
70-72, Avenue Habib Bourguiba
Tunis
Tel: +216-71-340.722
Fax: +216-71-340.680

Banque Nationale Agricole (BNA)
Rue Hedi Nouira
Tunis
Tel: +216-71-791.200
Fax: +216-71-793.031

U.S. Embassy Trade Contacts

American Embassy Tunis
Zone Nord-Est des Berges du Lac

For additional analytical, business and investment opportunities information,
please contact Global Investment & Business Center, USA
at (703) 370-8082. Fax: (703) 370-8083. E-mail: ibpusa3@gmail.com
Global Business and Investment Info Databank - www.ibpus.com

Tunis
Tunisia
Tel: +216-71-107-000
Fax: +216-71-962-115

Amy Lenk, Commercial Attaché
Charlotte Joulak, Commercial Specialist
Mourad El Almi, Economic Specialist

Col. Brad Anderson, Chief
Office of Defense Cooperation

Merritt Chesley, Agricultural Counselor
Office of Agricultural Affairs
(Resident In Rabat, Morocco)

WASHINGTON-BASED U.S. GOVERNMENT COUNTRY CONTACTS

U.S. Department Of Commerce
David Roth
Office of The Near East
Herbert Hoover Building Room 2039
Washington D.C. 20230
Tel: (202) 482-1860
Fax: (202) 482-0878

U.S. DEPARTMENT OF STATE

Aimee Cutrona
Tunisia Desk Officer
NEA/ENA
Room 5250
Washington D.C. 20520
Tel: (202) 647-3614
Fax: (202) 736-4458

U.S. Department of State
Office of the Coordinator for Business Affairs
Tel: (202) 647-1625
Fax: (202) 647-3953
TPCC Trade Information Center
Washington, DC
Tel: 1 - 800 - U.S.A - Trade

U.S. Department of Agriculture
Foreign Agricultural Service
Trade Assistance And Promotion Office
Tel: (202) 720-7420

For additional analytical, business and investment opportunities information,
please contact Global Investment & Business Center, USA
at (703) 370-8082. Fax: (703) 370-8083. E-mail: ibpusa3@gmail.com
Global Business and Investment Info Databank - www.ibpus.com

TUNISIA: SELECTED GOVERNMENT & BUSINESS CONTACTS

PRIME MINISTER
Address: Place du Gouvernement,
La Kasbah, 1008 Tunis
Tel.: (216-1) 263-991
e-mail : prm@ministeres.tn

MINISTRY OF JUSTICE
Address: 31, Av. Bab Benat,
1006 Tunis - La Kasbah
Tel.: (216-1) 560-502
e-mail : mju@ministeres.tn

MINISTRY OF NATIONAL DEFENSE
Address: Boulevard Bab M'Nara,
1030 Tunis
Tel.: (216) (1) 560 244
e-mail : mdn@ministeres.tn

MINISTRY OF FOREIGN AFFAIRS
Address: Palais du Gouvernement
La Kasbah (Le Cabinet)

Other offices:
76, Bis Boulevard Bab Benat 1001 -
Tunis
Tel: (01) 560 760
41, Rue d'Iran, 1002 Tunis - Belvédère
Tel: (01) 833 300
Cité Dorra, El Manar 3
Tel: (01) 886 511/403
e-mail : mae@ministeres.tn

MINISTRY ON WOMEN AND FAMILY
AFFAIRS
(Prime minister)
    Addresses:
Prime Ministry
Place du Gouvernement
La Kasbah, 1008 Tunis

17, Rue Beyrouth - 1002 Tunis
Tel.: (216-1) 562-814
       (216-1) 785-321
       (216-1) 782-421
e-mail : mff@ministeres.tn

State Secretary for Scientific Research
and Technology
(Prime Ministry)
Address: 18, rue 8010,
Montplaisir - 1002 Tunis
Tel.: (216-1) 896-944
       (216-1) 796-827
e-mail : serst@ministeres.tn

State Secretary for Data Processing
(Prime Ministry)
Address: 16, rue 8010,
Montplaisir - 1002 Tunis
Tel.: (216 1) 840-867 / 849-455
e-mail : sei@ministeres.tn

MINISTRY OF INTERIOR

   Address: Av. Habib Bourguiba,
   1000 Tunis
   Tel.: (216-1) 333-000
   e-mail : mint@ministeres.tn

MINISTRY OF RELIGIOUS AFFAIRS

   Address: Av. Bab Benat,
   1009 Tunis - La Kasbah
   Tel.: (216-1) 570-147
          (216-1) 570-123
   e-mail : mar@ministeres.tn

MINISTRY OF SOCIAL AFFAIRS

   Address: 25, Bld Bab Benat,
   1006 Tunis - La Kasbah
   Tel.: (216-1) 567-502
   e-mail : mas@ministeres.tn

MINISTRY OF FINANCE

For additional analytical, business and investment opportunities information,
please contact Global Investment & Business Center, USA
at (703) 370-8082. Fax: (703) 370-8083. E-mail: ibpusa3@gmail.com
Global Business and Investment Info Databank - www.ibpus.com

Address: Place du Gouvernement,
1008 Tunis - La Kasbah
Tel.: (216 1) 571 888
e-mail : mfi@ministeres.tn

MINISTRY OF INTERNATIONAL COOPERATION AND EXTERIOR INVESTMENTS

Address: 98, Avenue Mohamed V,
1002 Tunis Belvédère
Tel.: (216-1) 798-522
e-mail : mciie@ministeres.tn

MINISTRY OF EDUCATION

Address: Blvd. Bab Benat, 1030 Tunis
Tel.: (216-1) 263-336
e-mail : med@ministeres.tn

MINISTRY OF STATE DOMAINS AND LAND AFFAIRS

Address:19, av. de Paris
1000 Tunis
Tel.: (216-1) 341-644
       (216 1) 344 387
       (216 1) 341 174
e-mail : mdeaf@ministeres.tn

MINISTRY OF PROFESSIONAL FORMATION AND EMPLOYMENT

Address: 10 Av, Ouled Haffouz
1005 Tunis
Tel.: (216-1) 790-838
       (216-1) 792-727
e-mail : mfpe@ministeres.tn

MINISTRY OF PUBLIC HEALTH

Address: Bab Saadoun
1006 Tunis
Tel.: (216-1) 560-545
e-mail : msp@ministeres.tn

MINISTRY OF SUPERIOR EDUCATION

Address: Av. Ouled Haffouz
1030 Tunis
Tel.: (216-1) 786-300
e-mail : mes@ministeres.tn

MINISTRY OF THE ENVIRONMENT AND REGIONAL PLANNING

Address: Centre Urbain Nord,
Imm ICF - 2080 Ariana - Tunisie
Tel.: (216-1) 704 000
e-mail : meat@ministeres.tn

MINISTRY OF COMMUNICATIONS

Address: 3, bis rue d'Angleterre, 1000 Tunis
Tel.: (216-1) 359-000
(216-1) 324 948/ 1854 (bureau des relations avec le citoyen)
e-mail : mcom@ministeres.tn

MINISTRY OF EQUIPMENT AND HOUSING

Address: Avenue HABIB CHRITA
Cité Jardin 1002 -Tunis-Belvédère
Tel.: (216-1) 842-244
e-mail : meh@ministeres.tn

MINISTRY OF COMMERCE

Address: 37, av. Keireddine Pacha,
1002 Tunis
Tel.: (216-1) 892-313
e-mail : mcmr@ministeres.tn

MINISTRY OF INDUSTRY

Address: 37, Av. Kheireddine Pacha,
1002 Tunis
Tel.: (216 1) 289-368
e-mail : mind@ministeres.tn

MINISTRY OF TOURISM AND CRAFT INDUSTRY

Address: Av. Mohamed V,
1001 Tunis
Tel: (216 1) 341 077
e-mail : mta@ministeres.tn

MINISTRY OF ECONOMIC
DEVELOPMENT

Address: Place de la monnaie,
1000 Tunis
Tel.: (216 1) 351 515, (216 1) 350 847
e-mail : mde@ministeres.tn

MINISTRY OF CULTURE

Address: 8, rue du 2 mars 1934,
La Kasbah - 1006 Tunis
Tel.: (216 1) 562 661
        (216 1) 563 006
e-mail : mcu@ministeres.tn

MINISTRY OF AGRICULTURE

Address: 30, rue Alain Savary
1002 - Tunis

Tel.: (216 1) 786 833
e-mail : mag@ministeres.tn

MINISTRY OF YOUTH AND
CHILDHOOD

Address: Av. Ali Akid, Cité Nationale
Sportive -
1004 El Menzah - Tunis
Tel.: (216-1) 841 433
e-mail : mje@ministeres.tn

Union of Tunisian Chambers of
Commerce & Industry
103, Avenue De La Liberte, Tunis
1002 Belvedere Tunisie
Tunis, Tunisia
Tel: (0216) 1-780366/892457
Tx : (0409) 13982 UTICA TN

Chamber de Commerce de Tunis
P.O. Box 7943
6, Rue de Entrepreneurs,
Tunis, Tunisia
Tel: (0216) 1-242872/247669

TUNISIA: LARGEST LAW FIRMS

Adly Bellagha and Associates, 126 Rue de Yougoslavie, Tunis, 1000, Tunisia, Tel: (2161) 327.116 or (2161) 329.117, Fax: (2161) 323.746, Contact: Adly Bellagha
Al-Namouchi & Associates, 5 Rue De Russie, Tunis, 1000, Tunisia, Tel:(216)1-323-402, Fax:(216)1-321-910, Contact: Mokhtar Namouchi
Ammar & Associes Avocats, 9 Rue de Jerusalem, Tunis, 1002, Tunisia, Tel:(216)1-784-275, Fax:(216)1-793-851, Contact: Yadh Ammar
Annabi, Samir El & Associates, 11 Rue Azzouz Rebai, Impasse 7, El Manar 2, Tunis, 2092, Tunisia, Tel:(216)1-886181, Fax:(216)1-886182, Contact: Samir El Annabi
Kallel & Associates, 2 Rue de Marseille, Tunis, 1001, Tunisia, Tel:(216)1-241-167, Fax:(216)1-339-584, Contact: Sami Kallel
Malouche Law Firm, Immeuble Galaxie 2000, Tour D, Rue d'Arabie Saoudite, Tunis, 1002, Tunisia, Tel:(216)1-791-793, Fax:(216)1-790-513, Contact: Elyes Malouche
Noureddine Ferchiou et Associes, 34, Place du 7 Novembre 1987, Tunis, 1001, Tunisia, Tel:(216)1-345373, Fax:(216)1-350028, Contact: Noureddine Ferchiou
Salaheddine Caid Essebsi and Associates, 14 Avenue Alain Savary, Tunis, 1002, Tunisia, Tel:(216)1-785611, Fax:(216)1-783913, Contact: Salaheddine Caid Essebi
Samir El Annabi, 11, Rue Azzouz Rebai, Impasse 7 2092 El Manar 2, Tunis, Tunisia, Tel:(216)1-88-61-81, Fax:(216)1-88-6182, Samir El Annabi

TUNISIA : ASSOCIATIONS AND NGO ORGANIZATIONS

□
There are today more than 6,000 associations in Tunisia. About 90% of these associations were created after 1987.
The various categories of associations are:

□
Cultural and artistic associations
Athletic associations
Humanitarian and social associations
Women's associations
Friendship associations
Development associations
Scientific associations
Associations of general character
Major national associations and labor organizations include:

□
The Tunisian General Labor Union (UGTT)
The Tunisian Union for Industry, Trade and Handicrafts (UTICA)
The National Union of Tunisian Women (UNFT)
The Tunisian Union of Agriculture and Fisheries (UTAP)
The General Union of Tunisian Students (UGET)
Human Rights Associations:

□
The Tunisian League for Human Rights
The Tunisian Association for the Defense of Human Rights and Public Liberties
The Tunisian Chapter of Amnesty International

□
A higher Committee on Human Rights and Basic Freedoms was also created on 7 January 1991, with the task of assisting the President of the Republic in strengthening and promoting human rights and basic freedoms.

TUNISIA: RESEARCH AND TECHNOLOGY CONTACTS

Research in Tunisia is organized into management, coordination and execution structures.

MANAGEMENT AND COORDINATION STRUCTURES:
An important step in the organization and structuring of research in Tunisia was accomplished in 1991 with the creation for the first time of the Secretariat of State for Scientific Research and Technology.

The Secretariat plays a central role in the management of the national science and technology programs. It collaborates with other ministries in the formulation of national science and technology policies and plans. The mission of the Secretariat of State is to promote the development of research and technology. It is also responsible for the coordination and evaluation of national research activities.

THE HIGHER COUNCIL FOR SCIENTIFIC RESEARCH AND TECHNOLOGY

The task of the Higher Council for Scientific Research and Technology is to suggest policy options for research and technology.

The Council is headed by the Prime Minister with the membership of relevant ministries. A technical committee, attached to the Council, is headed by the Secretariat of State for Scientific Research and Technology. It insures the follow-up of the council decisions.

THE MINISTRY OF HIGHER EDUCATION

The Ministry of Higher Education plays an important role in the national research and technology activities. It coordinates university research through its General Director for Scientific Research and Technology.

THE MINISTRY OF AGRICULTURE

The Ministry of Agriculture coordinates agricultural research and higher education through the Institute for Agricultural Research and Agricultural Higher Education (IRESA). IRESA insures both financial and administrative management for its research centers.

OTHER MINISTRIES

Other ministries have recently created research institutions each in its field of interest.

Research in the medical and health fields takes place essentially at university hospitals.

EXECUTION STRUCTURES
Research programs have recently created research institutions and university labs.

RESEARCH INSTITUTIONS

The National research network is composed of twenty five institutions:

Private institution:

The Center for Ottoman and Moorish Studies for Documentation and Information, with two associated institutions, the Center of Maghrebi Studies of Tunis, and the Center for the Contemporary Maghreb.

Information and Documentation:

The National Academic Center for Scientific and Technical Documentation.

Science and Technology:

The Regional Institute for Informatics and Telecommunication
The National Institute for Scientific and Technical Research
The Biotechnology Center of Sfax
The National Center for Nuclear Sciences and Technologies
The National Center for Remote Detection

Humanities and Social Sciences:

The Higher Institute of the History of National Movement
The Center for Islamic Studies
The Center for Research, Studies and Publications
Economic and Social Research Center
The Center of Legal Studies
National Heritage Institute
Center for Youth and Sports Studies and Research
Center for Women Studies

Agriculture:

The National Agronomic Research Institute
The Center for Rural Engineering Research
The Arid Areas Institute
The National Oceanography and Fishery Institute
The Veterinary Research Institute
The Olive Institute
The National Aquaculture Center

Health:

The Pasteur Institute
The National Institute for Nutrition and Food Technology
Radiation Protection Center

EDUCATION

Tunisian higher education counts 85 institutions with 208 research laboratories in various scientific and technical fields:

National Institute for Scientific
and Technical Research
Borj-Cedria
B.P. 95
Hammam-Lif - 2050 Tunis
Tel: (216-1) 430-215

Regional Institute for Informatics
and Telecommunications
2 Rue Ibn Nadim
Montplaisir - Tunis
Tel: (216-1) 800-122

Center of Biotechnology of Sfax
B.P. "W"3038
Sfax
Tel: (216-4) 275-373

National Center for Nuclear
Sciences and Technologies

Immeuble Maghrebia
Boulevard du 7 Novembre
1060 Tunis
Tel: (216-1) 707-772

National Center for Remote Sensing
B.P. 200
1080 Tunis
Tel: (216-1) 761-210

HUMANITIES AND SOCIAL SCIENCES

Institute of the History of National
Movement
17 rue de Tolede
El Manar 1
2092 Tunis
Tel: (216-1) 881-607

Center for Islamic Studies

209 Avenue Beit El Hikma
3100 Kairouan
Tel: (216-7) 224-844

Center for Research Studies and
Publications
Campus Universitaire
Boulevard du 7 Novembre
1060 Tunis
Tel: (216-1) 518-914

Economic and Social Research Center
23 Rue d'Espagne
1000 Tunis
Tel: (216-1) 343-237

Center of Legal Studies
Impasse Virgile Boulevard Bab Bnat
1006 Tunis
Tel: (216-1) 568-802

National Patrimony Institute
4 Place du Chateau
1008 Tunis
Tel: (216-1) 286-296

Center for Youth and Sports
Studies and Research
7 Rue Tahar Haddad
Montfleury - Tunis
Tel: (216-1) 247-038

Center for Women Studies
Avenue du Roi Abdelaziz Al Saoud
Rue 7131, El Manar II
2092 Tunis
Tel: (216-1) 885-322
Fax: (216-1) 887-436

The National Agronomic
Research Institute
2049 Ariana - Tunis
Tel: (216-1) 230-024

The Center for Rural
Engineering Research
B.P. 10
2080 Ariana - Tunis
Tel: (216-1) 717-811

The Arid Areas Institute
El Fej
Medenine - Tunisie
Tel: (216-5) 640-687

The National Oceanography
and Fishery Institute
28 Rue 2 Mars 1934
2025 Salammbo - Tunis
Tel: (216-1) 730-548

The Veterinary Research Institute
Rue Djebel Lakhdar
La Rabta 1006 - Tunis
Tel: (216-1) 562-602

The Olive Institute
Route de l'aeroport Km 1,5
3029 Sfax
Tel: (216-4) 241-240

Institute of Forestry Research
B.P. No. 2
2080 Ariana - Tunis
Tel: (216-1) 230-039

HEALTH
The Pasteur Institute
Rue Ernest Conseil
1002 Tunis Belevedere
Tel: (216-1) 789-608

UNIVERSITES
University of Ezzitouna
(Theology and Religious Studies)
29 Rue Asdrubal
Lafayette - Tunis
Tel: (216-1) 788-424

University of Tunis I
(Humanities and Social Sciences)
29 Rue Asdrubal
Lafayette - Tunis
Tel: (216-1) 788-068

University of Tunis II
(Sciences, Engineering & Medical
Studies)

For additional analytical, business and investment opportunities information,
please contact Global Investment & Business Center, USA
at (703) 370-8082. Fax: (703) 370-8083. E-mail: ibpusa3@gmail.com
Global Business and Investment Info Databank - www.ibpus.com

29 Rue Asdrubal
Lafayette - Tunis
Tel: (216-1) 789-312

University of Tunis III
(Management, Economics, Law)
29 Rue Asdrubal
Lafayette - Tunis
Tel: (216-1) 787-502

The Central University
(Multi-disciplinary)

43 Avenue Mohamed Karoui
4002 Sousse
Tel: (216-3) 234-011

The Southern University
(Multi-disciplinary)
Route de l'Aerodrome Km 1
3029 Sfax
Tel: (216-4) 240-678

BASIC TITLES ON TUNISIA
IMPORTANT!
All publications are updated annually!
Please contact IBP, Inc. at ibpusa3@gmail.com for the latest ISBNs and additional information

Title
Tunisia A "Spy" Guide - Strategic Information and Developments
Tunisia A Spy" Guide"
Tunisia Air Force Handbook
Tunisia Air Force Handbook
Tunisia Banking & Financial Market Handbook
Tunisia Banking & Financial Market Handbook
Tunisia Business and Investment Opportunities Yearbook
Tunisia Business and Investment Opportunities Yearbook
Tunisia Business and Investment Opportunities Yearbook Volume 1 Strategic Information and Opportunities
Tunisia Business Intelligence Report - Practical Information, Opportunities, Contacts
Tunisia Business Intelligence Report - Practical Information, Opportunities, Contacts
Tunisia Business Law Handbook - Strategic Information and Basic Laws
Tunisia Business Law Handbook - Strategic Information and Basic Laws
Tunisia Business Law Handbook - Strategic Information and Basic Laws
Tunisia Business Law Handbook - Strategic Information and Basic Laws
Tunisia Clothing & Textile Industry Handbook
Tunisia Company Laws and Regulations Handbook
Tunisia Constitution and Citizenship Laws Handbook - Strategic Information and Basic Laws
Tunisia Country Study Guide - Strategic Information and Developments
Tunisia Country Study Guide - Strategic Information and Developments
Tunisia Country Study Guide - Strategic Information and Developments Volume 1 Strategic Information and Developments
Tunisia Customs, Trade Regulations and Procedures Handbook

- 237 -

Title
Tunisia Customs, Trade Regulations and Procedures Handbook
Tunisia Diplomatic Handbook - Strategic Information and Developments
Tunisia Diplomatic Handbook - Strategic Information and Developments
Tunisia Ecology & Nature Protection Handbook
Tunisia Ecology & Nature Protection Handbook
Tunisia Ecology & Nature Protection Laws and Regulation Handbook
Tunisia Economic & Development Strategy Handbook
Tunisia Economic & Development Strategy Handbook
Tunisia Energy Policy, Laws and Regulation Handbook
Tunisia Energy Policy, Laws and Regulations Handbook
Tunisia Energy Policy, Laws and Regulations Handbook
Tunisia Export-Import Trade and Business Directory
Tunisia Export-Import Trade and Business Directory
Tunisia Foreign Policy and Government Guide
Tunisia Foreign Policy and Government Guide
Tunisia Immigration Laws and Regulations Handbook - Strategic Information and Basic Laws
Tunisia Industrial and Business Directory
Tunisia Industrial and Business Directory
Tunisia Insolvency (Bankruptcy) Laws and Regulations Handbook - Strategic Information and Basic Laws
Tunisia Internet and E-Commerce Investment and Business Guide - Strategic and Practical Information: Regulations and Opportunities
Tunisia Internet and E-Commerce Investment and Business Guide - Strategic and Practical Information: Regulations and Opportunities
Tunisia Investment and Business Guide - Strategic and Practical Information
Tunisia Investment and Business Guide - Strategic and Practical Information
Tunisia Investment and Business Guide - Strategic and Practical Information
Tunisia Investment and Business Guide - Strategic and Practical Information
Tunisia Investment and Trade Laws and Regulations Handbook
Tunisia Labor Laws and Regulations Handbook - Strategic Information and Basic Laws
Tunisia Mineral & Mining Sector Investment and Business Guide - Strategic and Practical Information
Tunisia Mineral & Mining Sector Investment and Business Guide - Strategic and Practical Information
Tunisia Mining Laws and Regulations Handbook
Tunisia Oil & Gas Sector Business & Investment Opportunities Yearbook
Tunisia Oil & Gas Sector Business & Investment Opportunities Yearbook
Tunisia Oil and Gas Exploration Laws and Regulation Handbook
Tunisia Recent Economic and Political Developments Yearbook
Tunisia Recent Economic and Political Developments Yearbook
Tunisia Recent Economic and Political Developments Yearbook

Title
Tunisia Starting Business (Incorporating) in....Guide
Tunisia Taxation Laws and Regulations Handbook
Tunisia Telecom Laws and Regulations Handbook
Tunisia Telecommunication Industry Business Opportunities Handbook
Tunisia Telecommunication Industry Business Opportunities Handbook
Tunisia Transportation Policy and Regulations Handbook
Tunisia: How to Invest, Start and Run Profitable Business in Tunisia Guide - Practical Information, Opportunities, Contacts

BASIC BUSINESS LAWS

Please contact IBP, Inc. at ibpusa3@gmail.com for additional information

COUTRY	LAW TITLE
Tunisia	Code of registration fees and stamp
Tunisia	Act 2005-56 of 18 July 2005 on the economic spin-off companies
Tunisia	Act 1992 to 1924 promulgating the Code of Insurance
Tunisia	Press Code
Tunisia	Post Code
Tunisia	Code of the film industry
Tunisia	Law 1997-1924 of 28 April 1997 relating to the inclusion in the Insurance Code, title IV on the insurance for export.
Tunisia	Telecommunications Code
Tunisia	Law Amending the 2008-08 insurance code
Tunisia	Insurance Code
Tunisia	Finance Act 2007
Tunisia	Law 2009-64 of 12 August 2009 promulgating the Code of delivering financial services to non-residents repealing Act No. 85-108 of 6 December 1985 on the encouragement of financial and banking organizations working mainly with non-residents
Tunisia	Act 2005-96 of 18 October 2005 on strengthening the security of financial relations.
Tunisia	Law 2010-18 Establishing the system of creativity and innovation incentives in the field of information and communication technologies.
Tunisia	of the Maritime Labor Code
Tunisia	Law 2005-96 of 18 October 2005 on the strengthening of the security of financial relations
Tunisia	Code of Maritime Commerce
Tunisia	Act 1997 to 1937 on the transport of dangerous goods by road
Tunisia	1996-1960 Act on the Organization of Land Transport
Tunisia	Act 1995 to 1973 on the maritime public domain.
Tunisia	On the establishment and organization of the Central Bank of Tunisia Act
Tunisia	Maritime Disciplinary and Penal Code
Tunisia	Highway Code
Tunisia	Code of Civil Aeronautics
Tunisia	Act 2002-46 of 7 May 2002, completing the telecommunications code promulgated by Law No. 2001-1 of 15 January 2001
Tunisia	Act Guidance No. 2007-13 dated February 19, 2007, on the establishment of the Digital Economy
Tunisia	2008-1 Act of 8 January 2008 telecommunications code

For additional analytical, business and investment opportunities information,
please contact Global Investment & Business Center, USA
at (703) 370-8082. Fax: (703) 370-8083. E-mail: ibpusa3@gmail.com
Global Business and Investment Info Databank - www.ibpus.com

COUTRY	LAW TITLE
	promulgated by Law No. 2001-1
Tunisia	Law 2006-85 of 25 December 2006 Finance Act 2007: fixing the base of stamp duty on transactions of electronic recharge the phone - Article 72 and 73 amend sections 117 and 126 of the Code of registration fees and stamp duties.
Tunisia	Act 2004-5 of 3 February 2004 on computer security.
Tunisia	Law 2004-30 of April 5, 2004, on the transformation of the legal form of the National Telecommunications Office
Tunisia	Law 2004-63 of 27 July 2004 on the protection of data personal.
Tunisia	Law 2003-49 of 25 June 2003 on purchase transactions commitment to resell the securities and commercial paper.
Tunisia	Law 2008-34 dated 2 June 2008 promulgating the customs' code
Tunisia	Act From 1988 to 1992 August 2, 1988 (1) On The Investment Societies
Tunisia	Code Collective Investment
Tunisia	Code of delivering financial services to non-resident
Tunisia	Investment Incentives Code
Tunisia	Law 2006-25 of 15 May 2006 on the tax amnesty
Tunisia	Decree No. 97-2462 of 22 December 1997 laying down the terms and conditions of issue and redemption Treasury bills equivalent (BTA).
Tunisia	Wearing enactment of Act 1988-61 tax code value Added
Tunisia	Decree No. 99-1782 of 9 August 1999 laying down the terms and conditions of issue and redemption of treasury bills in the short term BTC.
Tunisia	Human Rights Code and tax procedures.
Tunisia	Customs Code
Tunisia	Tax Code Added Value
Tunisia	code Tax on Personal Income and Corporation Tax
Tunisia	Tax Code on personal income and corporate tax
Tunisia	Locale Tax Code
Tunisia	2006-25 Act of 15 May 2006 on tax amnesty
Tunisia	Act 1989-9 of 1 February 1989 on investments, businesses and public institutions
Tunisia	Law 2001-65 of 10 July 2001 on credit institutions
Tunisia	Act 2000-35 of 21 March 2000 on the dematerialization of
Tunisia	Act 1999 -. 92 of 17 August 1999 on the recovery of the financial market
Tunisia	of Law from 1997 to 1924 April 28, 1997, regarding the insertion Insurance Code, title IV on export insurance.
Tunisia	from 1994 to 1989 Act of 26 July 1994 concerning the leasing
Tunisia	Code Foreign Exchange and Foreign Trade

For additional analytical, business and investment opportunities information,
please contact Global Investment & Business Center, USA
at (703) 370-8082. Fax: (703) 370-8083. E-mail: ibpusa3@gmail.com
Global Business and Investment Info Databank - www.ibpus.com

COUTRY	LAW TITLE
Tunisia	Act 1994 -. 117 of 14 November 1994 on the reorganization of financial market
Tunisia	Law 2001-65 of 10 July 2001 relating to credit institutions
Tunisia	from 1997 to 1937 Act relating to road transport of hazardous materials.
Tunisia	Act 1985-108 of 6 December 1985 encouraging financial and banking organizations working mainly with non-resident
Tunisia	2007-34 Act of June 4, 2007, on air quality.
Tunisia	Law 2010-29 Relating to the encouragement of the companies to the admission of Their shares to the stock exchange.
Tunisia	Law Relating to the 2009-71 appropriations law for the year 2010.
Tunisia	Law 2008-56 dated 4 August 2008, Amending Law No. 99-64 dated 15 July 1999 Relating to the excessive interest rates.
Tunisia	law 1994-117 of 14 November 1994 on the reorganization of financial market
Tunisia	Law 2009-29 dated June 9, 2009, Amending and Completing the territorial development and urbanism code.
Tunisia	1995-1970 Act on the conservation of water and soil.
Tunisia	Act 1997-34 Relative to the exercise of fishing
Tunisia	Act 1996-104 Relative to the Protection of Agricultural Land
Tunisia	1975-1917 Act promulgating the fisherman Code.
Tunisia	Law 2009-59 dated July 20, 2009, Simplifying the administrative procedures in the sector of agriculture and fishing.
Tunisia	1999 to 1930 Act Relative to agriculture Organic
Tunisia	Code of Ethics of the Veterinary Medical
Tunisia	Act 1999-1942 Relative to seeds, plants and plant varieties
Tunisia	Code homework architects
Tunisia	Code of Planning and Urban Development in 2009
Tunisia	Act 2008-23 on the concession system.
Tunisia	Act 2005-82 of 15 August 2005 establishing a system of energy management
Tunisia	2005-102 Act on Gas Transportation
Tunisia	Act 2004-72 relative to the mastery of energy
Tunisia	Law from 1999 to 1942 on Seeds, Seedlings and New Plant Varieties
Tunisia	Law 2000-83 of August 9th, 2000 related to the Electronic Exchanges and Electronic Commerce Bill
Tunisia	1993-1942 Act of 26 April 1993 promulgating the Code of Arbitration.
Tunisia	Arbitration Code
Tunisia	Orientation Law No. 2007-13 dated February 19, 2007 relating to the development of the digital economy

COUTRY	LAW TITLE
Tunisia	Act 2005-51 of 27 June 2005 on the Electronic Funds Transfer
Tunisia	Act 2004-5 Relative to computer security
Tunisia	1999 to 1924 Act Relative to health veterinary import controls and export
Tunisia	Act 2000-83 on trade and e-commerce
Tunisia	Law 2009-07 dated 9 February 2009 , Amending and Completing law No. 2004-72 dated 2 August 2004 Relating to the energy management.
Tunisia	Decree no. 2000-2331 of 10 October 2000 setting out the administrative and financial organization and operating methods of the National Digital Certification Agency
Tunisia	Decree No. 2008-2639 dated 21 July 2008 fixing the terms and procedures of the import and commercialization of encryption means clustering of services and through the telecommunications network.
Tunisia	Act 2005-95 on livestock and animal products
Tunisia	Act 2005-94 on mutual agricultural service companies
Tunisia	Act 1999-74 Relative to the exercise of fishing
Tunisia	Act 1999-1957 of 28 June 1999 relating to appellations of origin and indications of agricultural products from the
Tunisia	Law 2000-83 of 9 August 2000 relating to trade and Electronic Commerce
Tunisia	Law 2009-17 dated March 16, 2009, Relating to the biologic system of rest in the field of fishing and Its Financing.
Tunisia	Law 2000-84 of August 24, 2000, Patents
Tunisia	Law 1999-42 of May 10, 1999, Seeds, Seedlings and New Plant Varieties
Tunisia	Law 1994-36 of February 24, 1994, Literary and Artistic Property
Tunisia	Law 2004-90 of 31 December 2004 Finance Act 2005
Tunisia	Law 2001-14 of 30 January 2001 on the simplification administrative procedures related to permits issued by the Ministry of Environment and Spatial Planning in the areas of its competence.
Tunisia	Act 1991 to 1945 relative to petroleum products.
Tunisia	1988-1991 Act of 2 August 1988 on the establishment of a national agency for environmental protection.
Tunisia	Law 2009-33 dated 23 June 2009, Amending and Completing law n ° 94-36 dated 24 February1994, Relating to the literary and artistic property.
Tunisia	Forest Code
Tunisia	Code fisherman
Tunisia	Water Code
Tunisia	Act Relative to 1998-1974 railways.

For additional analytical, business and investment opportunities information,
please contact Global Investment & Business Center, USA
at (703) 370-8082. Fax: (703) 370-8083. E-mail: ibpusa3@gmail.com
Global Business and Investment Info Databank - www.ibpus.com

COUTRY	LAW TITLE
Tunisia	Act 1998-1921 on the International Multimodal Transport of Goods
Tunisia	Act 1997-69 on the organization of the Merchant Navy professions
Tunisia	Act 2005-17 on precious metals
Tunisia	2001-20 Act of 6 February 2001 on Protection of Layout Designs of Integrated Circuits
Tunisia	1997-1956 Act on the organization of the activity of road haulage
Tunisia	Law 1990-56 Dated June 18, 1990 Promoting Exploration And Production Of The Liquid And Gaseous Hydrocarbons
Tunisia	Decree No. 2004-2145 of 2 September 2004 on the labeling of equipment, appliances and household materials.
Tunisia	Decree-law No. 85-9 Dated September 14th, 1985 Establishing Special Provisions With Regard To The Exploration And Production Of Liquid And Gaseous Hydrocarbons
Tunisia	Hydrocarbons Code
Tunisia	Act 2007-68 of 27 December 2007 relating to designations of origin, geographical indications and indications of source handicrafts
Tunisia	Law of 2001-20 February 6, 2001 on the Protection of the Layout-Designs of Integrated Circuits
Tunisia	Act 2001-21 of 6 February 2001 on the Protection of Industrial Designs
Tunisia	Law 2001-21 of February 6, 2001 on the Protection of Industrial Designs
Tunisia	Patents Act 2000-84 to
Tunisia	Law 2000-84 of 24 August 2000 relating to patents
Tunisia	Act Relative to the 2000-84 patents.
Tunisia	Law 1999-42 of 10 May 1999 on seeds, plants and plant varieties
Tunisia	1994-1936 Act of 24 February 1994 on Literary and Artistic Property
Tunisia	1991-1945 Act on Petroleum Products
Tunisia	Act 2001-36 of 17 April 2001 on the protection of trade marks, trade and services
Tunisia	Law 2007-54 Relating to anti-doping in spoirts
Tunisia	Act 1960-1930 of 14 December 1960 on the organization of social security schemes, as amended and supplemented by subsequent texts
Tunisia	Act Relative to 1960-1930 the organization of social security
Tunisia	Law No. 2010-26 dated 21 May 2010, voluntary activities.
Tunisia	Law Relating to the 2010-23 Youth Parliament.

COUTRY	LAW TITLE
Tunisia	Law 2009-64 promulgating the code provision of financial services to the non-residents.
Tunisia	Decree No. 2008-2471 dated 05 July 2008 Amending and Completing decree No. 2002-3158 dated 17 December 2002 Regulating the public procurements
Tunisia	2008-19 Law Relating to Higher Education
Tunisia	1975-1940 Act of 14 May 1975 on passports and travel documents (almondy 1998)
Tunisia	Education Act 2002
Tunisia	Decree No. 2009-3018 of 19 October 2009 19 October 2009 amending and supplementing Decree No. 2002-3158 of 17 December 2002 regulating public procurement.
Tunisia	Order No. 2009-2861 of 5 October 2009 05 October 2009 laying down the terms and conditions for the award of negotiated steps supplies of goods and services with the spin-off companies
Tunisia	Decree No. 2009-2617 of 14 September 2009 regulating the construction of civil buildings
Tunisia	Decree No. 2008-3505 dated November 21, 2008 Amending decree No. 2002-3158 dated 17 December 2002, the-governing public procurements
Tunisia	Penal Code (almondy 1995)
Tunisia	Law 2008-19, February 25, 2008 on Higher Education
Tunisia	Act 2009-11 March 2, 2009, promulgating the code of safety and prevention of fire, explosion and panic in buildings.
Tunisia	Maritime Disciplinary and Penal Code
Tunisia	Code of Administrative Police Maritime
Tunisia	Code of Military Justice
Tunisia	Code of Criminal Procedure
Tunisia	Penal Code
Tunisia	Reglamentation procurement
Tunisia	Act 1968-198 of 22 June 1968 regulating conditions of entry and residence of foreigners in Tunisia (almondy 1992)
Tunisia	957-3 Law of 1 August 1957, regulating civil status
Tunisia	1975-1940 Act Relative to passports and travel documents.
Tunisia	Act 2001 -118 relative to the code of archaeological, historical heritage and traditional arts
Tunisia	Act Relative to the 1999-1932 national statistical system
Tunisia	Act Relative to the 1999-1918 National Identity Card
Tunisia	from 1997 to 1980 Act of 1 December 1997 on promulagation code decorations
Tunisia	Act 1988 -95 2 ao t 1988 on archives
Tunisia	Decree No. 2007-1330 dated 04 June 2007 fixing the list of public enterprises Whose orders for goods and services are

COUTRY	LAW TITLE
	excluded from the supply scope of implementation public procurements règlements of
Tunisia	Nationality Act Tunisia
Tunisia	Act 1988-1912 7 March 1988 relating to the Economic and Social Council
Tunisia	1969-1925 Act of 8 April 1969 on the Electoral Code
Tunisia	Law 1997-48, dated 21 July 1997, public Funding of Political Parties.
Tunisia	Election Code
Tunisia	Law 2004-52 of 12 July 2004 on the Constitutional Council
Tunisia	Law 2003-70 on the tribunal
Tunisia	Decree No. 2008-2472 dated 05 July 2008 Relating to the review of the Exceptional prices of the public procurements works of
Tunisia	Act 1995-29 on the organization of the profession of Bailiffs
Tunisia	Act of 6 November 1998 amending and supplementing certain provisions of the Electoral Code
Tunisia	Act 1968-8 of 8 March 1968 on the organization of the Audit
Tunisia	Act 1967 to 1929 of 14 July 1967 on judicial organization, the High Council of the Judiciary and Status of Judges
Tunisia	Act 1957-52 Relative to the creation of a High Court Justice
Tunisia	Law 1968-8, dated 8 March 1968 related to the organization of the Court of Accounts
Tunisia	Decree 2004-1562 of 14 July 2004 relating to the special outfit members of the Constitutional Council
Tunisia	Constitution of the Republic of Tunisia
Tunisia	Act 1998-1965 Relative to professional law firms
Tunisia	Code of registration fees and stamp
Tunisia	Decree No. 2007-1329 dated 04 June 2007 Amending and Completing decree No. 2002-3158 dated 17 December 2002, public procurements Regulating
Tunisia	Code archaeological, historical and traditional arts
Tunisia	Code mutual funds
Tunisia	Code decorations
Tunisia	Code to provide financial services to non-resident
Tunisia	Code of Tunisian nationality
Tunisia	Act 1988- 33 of 3 May 1988 relating to tax benefits in favor of political parties
Tunisia	Organic Law No. 2009-19 dated 13 April 2009, Amending and Completing the elections code.
Tunisia	Act of 21 July 1997 on the public financing of political parties
Tunisia	Act 2006-7 of 15 February 2006 amending Law No. 97-48
Tunisia	Act 2005-58 18 July 2005 on seed fund

COUTRY	LAW TITLE
Tunisia	Act 2003-58 August 4, 2003, amending and supplementing the Electoral Code
Tunisia	Act 2001-2 of 23 January 2001 amending Law No. 97-48
Tunisia	Act 2000-32 of 21 March 2000 amending certain provisions of the Electoral Code
Tunisia	Organic Law No. 88-32 of May 3, 1988 organizing political parties
Tunisia	Code of public accounting
Tunisia	Law 2009-1 dated January 5 2009 Amending the Commercial companies code.
Tunisia	Wearing Act 2000-93 promulgation of the Code of Commercial Companies.
Tunisia	Act 1996-112 of 30 December 1996 relating to the corporate accounting system.
Tunisia	Law 1995-1988 of 30 October 1995 on tax provisions related to investment companies
Tunisia	Act 1992 to 1952 of 12 April 1992 on Associations
Tunisia	from 1991 to 1964 Act of 29 July 1991 relating to the Competition
Tunisia	Act 2004-76 on the exercise of trade in liquor to take
Tunisia	Law 2009-16 dated 16 March 2009, Amending and Completing the Commercial Companies. Code
Tunisia	Code Labor
Tunisia	Decree No. 2006-1546 of 6 June 2006 on the application of Articles 13, 13a, 13b, 13c and 256 bis of the Code of Commercial Companies
Tunisia	Code of Commercial Companies
Tunisia	Law 2007-69 of 27 December 2007 relating to economic initiative
Tunisia	2007-37 Act of June 4, 2007, amending and supplementing certain provisions of the Commercial Code.
Tunisia	Law 2006-75 of 30 November 2006 on Chambers of Commerce and Industry
Tunisia	on Act 2005-50 has the exclusive economic zone off the coast Tunisian
Tunisia	Act 1988 to 1992 of 2 August 1988 on the investment company
Tunisia	Act 1973-1955 Organizing pharmaceutical professions
Tunisia	Act 2006-31 22 May 2006 amending certain provisions of the Electoral Code
Tunisia	Law 2008-58 dated 4 August 2008 Relating to the prisoner pregnant or breast feeding mother.
Tunisia	Mining Code
Tunisia	Act 2005-83 on the promotion and protection of persons with

COUTRY	LAW TITLE
	disabilities
Tunisia	Act 2002-54 on medical analysis laboratories
Tunisia	from 1999 to 1973 Act to regulate the manufacture and registration of drugs for human medicine
Tunisia	Act 2000-93 Wearing enactment of the Commercial Companies Code.
Tunisia	Act 1992-1950 on communicable diseases
Tunisia	Code of Personal Status
Tunisia	Law No. 2010-30 Amending law 73-55 dated August 3, 1973, organizing the pharmaceutical professions.
Tunisia	Medical Ethics Code
Tunisia	Code of Veterinarian Ethics
Tunisia	From 1974 to 1946 Act May 22, 1974 From On Organisation On the Architectural Profession in Tunisia
Tunisia	Law Relating to 2008-10 Vocational Training
Tunisia	Law 2009-39 dated 8 July 2009, on the retirement Before the lawful age.
Tunisia	from 1998 to 1917 Act on the prevention of harm of smoking
Tunisia	Act 1998-101 Relative to narcotics.
Tunisia	Investment Incentives Code
Tunisia	Law 2010-39 relating to the unification of the age of majority.
Tunisia	Act Relative to the 1994-1989 leasing
Tunisia	Code of Obligations and Contracts
Tunisia	Code of the Child Protection
Tunisia	Code on Private International Law
Tunisia	Commercial Code
Tunisia	Law 2003-75 of 10 December 2003 on support international efforts against terrorism and the laundering of monies.
Tunisia	Code of Civil Procedure and Commercial
Tunisia	Act 1993-112 supplementing the Criminal Code
Tunisia	1992-1952 Act of 18 May 1992, on narcotics
Tunisia	Law 2003-74 of 11 November 2003 amending and completing them the Law No. 91-64 of 29 July 1191 on competition and prices
Tunisia	Act 1996-101 on the social protection of workers
Tunisia	Law 2009-68 Relating to the establishment of the award of criminal compensation and modernization of the alternate to the Processes s doing.
Tunisia	Law 2009-06 dated 26 January 2009, Amending and Completing law No. 92-52 dated 18 May 1992 Relating to narcotics.
Tunisia	2010-40 to amend the provisions of section 319 of the code criminal.

COUTRY	LAW TITLE
Tunisia	Act 1995- 44 of 2 May 1995 on the Commercial Register
Tunisia	Act 2002-62 of 9 July 2002 on the promotional games.
Tunisia	2008-58 Act of August 4, 2008, relating to the pregnant and lactating mother owned
Tunisia	Code Exchange and Foreign Trade
Tunisia	Act 2000-83 of 9 August 2000 on trade and electronic commerce.
Tunisia	1998 to 1940 Act Relative to sales techniques and commercial advertising
Tunisia	2003-43 Act of 9 on the code of public accounting
Tunisia	Act 1998 to 1914 on the exercise of trade in alcoholic drinks to go
Tunisia	Act 1993-120 of 27 December 1993 promulgating the Code of the Investment Incentives
Tunisia	Act 1992 to 1952 on narcotics
Tunisia	Act 1992-117 Consumer Protection
Tunisia	from 1991 to 1964 Act of July 29, 1991 and No. 93-83 of 26 July 1993 on competition and prices
Tunisia	Law 2009-69 dated 12 August 2009, Relating to the distribution trade
Tunisia	Decree No. 2008-562 dated 04 March 2008 fixing the terms and conditions of the contracts of the finding of the supply of goods and services expanded with the enterprises
Tunisia	Law 2009-38 dated 30 June 2009, Relating to the national system of Standardization.

For additional analytical, business and investment opportunities information,
please contact Global Investment & Business Center, USA
at (703) 370-8082. Fax: (703) 370-8083. E-mail: ibpusa3@gmail.com
Global Business and Investment Info Databank - www.ibpus.com

WORLD TELECOM & INTERNET INVESTMENT AND BUSINESS LIBRARY

Price: $149.95 Each

1.	Albania Internet and E-Commerce Investment and Business Guide: Regulations and Opportunities
2.	Algeria Internet and E-Commerce Investment and Business Guide: Regulations and Opportunities
3.	Angola Internet and E-Commerce Investment and Business Guide: Regulations and Opportunities
4.	Argentina Internet and E-Commerce Investment and Business Guide: Regulations and Opportunities
5.	Armenia Internet and E-Commerce Investment and Business Guide: Regulations and Opportunities
6.	Australia Internet and E-Commerce Investment and Business Guide: Regulations and Opportunities
7.	Austria Internet and E-Commerce Investment and Business Guide: Regulations and Opportunities
8.	Azerbaijan Internet and E-Commerce Investment and Business Guide: Regulations and Opportunities
9.	Bangladesh Internet and E-Commerce Investment and Business Guide: Regulations and Opportunities
10.	Belarus Internet and E-Commerce Investment and Business Guide: Regulations and Opportunities
11.	Belgium Internet and E-Commerce Investment and Business Guide: Regulations and Opportunities
12.	Bermuda Internet and E-Commerce Investment and Business Guide: Regulations and Opportunities
13.	Bolivia Internet and E-Commerce Investment and Business Guide: Regulations and Opportunities
14.	Bosnia and Herzegovina Internet and E-Commerce Investment and Business Guide: Regulations and Opportunities
15.	Botswana Internet and E-Commerce Investment and Business Guide: Regulations and Opportunities
16.	Brazil Internet and E-Commerce Investment and Business Guide: Regulations and Opportunities
17.	Bulgaria Internet and E-Commerce Investment and Business Guide: Regulations and Opportunities
18.	Cambodia Internet and E-Commerce Investment and Business Guide: Regulations and Opportunities
19.	Cameroon Internet and E-Commerce Investment and Business Guide: Regulations and Opportunities
20.	Canada Internet and E-Commerce Investment and Business Guide: Regulations and Opportunities
21.	Chile Internet and E-Commerce Investment and Business Guide: Regulations and Opportunities
22.	China Internet and E-Commerce Investment and Business Guide: Regulations and Opportunities
23.	Colombia Internet and E-Commerce Investment and Business Guide: Regulations and Opportunities
24.	Cook Islands Internet and E-Commerce Investment and Business Guide: Regulations and Opportunities
25.	Costa Rica Internet and E-Commerce Investment and Business Guide: Regulations and Opportunities
26.	Croatia Internet and E-Commerce Investment and Business Guide: Regulations and Opportunities
27.	Cuba Internet and E-Commerce Investment and Business Guide: Regulations and Opportunities
28.	Cyprus Internet and E-Commerce Investment and Business Guide: Regulations and Opportunities
29.	Czech Republic Internet and E-Commerce Investment and Business Guide: Regulations and

For additional analytical, business and investment opportunities information,
please contact Global Investment & Business Center, USA
at (202) 546-2103. Fax: (202) 546-3275. E-mail: rusric@erols.com

	Opportunities
30.	Denmark Internet and E-Commerce Investment and Business Guide: Regulations and Opportunities
31.	Dominican Republic Internet and E-Commerce Investment and Business Guide: Regulations and Opportunities
32.	Dubai Internet and E-Commerce Investment and Business Guide: Regulations and Opportunities
33.	Ecuador Internet and E-Commerce Investment and Business Guide: Regulations and Opportunities
34.	Egypt Internet and E-Commerce Investment and Business Guide: Regulations and Opportunities
35.	El Salvador Internet and E-Commerce Investment and Business Guide: Regulations and Opportunities
36.	Equatorial Guinea Internet and E-Commerce Investment and Business Guide: Regulations and Opportunities
37.	Estonia Internet and E-Commerce Investment and Business Guide: Regulations and Opportunities
38.	Fiji Internet and E-Commerce Investment and Business Guide: Regulations and Opportunities
39.	Finland Internet and E-Commerce Investment and Business Guide: Regulations and Opportunities
40.	France Internet and E-Commerce Investment and Business Guide: Regulations and Opportunities
41.	Georgia Republic Internet and E-Commerce Investment and Business Guide: Regulations and Opportunities
42.	Germany Internet and E-Commerce Investment and Business Guide: Regulations and Opportunities
43.	Greece Internet and E-Commerce Investment and Business Guide: Regulations and Opportunities
44.	Guatemala Internet and E-Commerce Investment and Business Guide: Regulations and Opportunities
45.	Guernsey Internet and E-Commerce Investment and Business Guide: Regulations and Opportunities
46.	Guyana Internet and E-Commerce Investment and Business Guide: Regulations and Opportunities
47.	Haiti Internet and E-Commerce Investment and Business Guide: Regulations and Opportunities
48.	Honduras Internet and E-Commerce Investment and Business Guide: Regulations and Opportunities
49.	Hungary Internet and E-Commerce Investment and Business Guide: Regulations and Opportunities
50.	Iceland Internet and E-Commerce Investment and Business Guide: Regulations and Opportunities
51.	India Internet and E-Commerce Investment and Business Guide: Regulations and Opportunities
52.	Indonesia Internet and E-Commerce Investment and Business Guide: Regulations and Opportunities
53.	Iran Internet and E-Commerce Investment and Business Guide: Regulations and Opportunities
54.	Iraq Internet and E-Commerce Investment and Business Guide: Regulations and Opportunities
55.	Ireland Internet and E-Commerce Investment and Business Guide: Regulations and Opportunities
56.	Israel Internet and E-Commerce Investment and Business Guide: Regulations and Opportunities
57.	Italy Internet and E-Commerce Investment and Business Guide: Regulations and Opportunities
58.	Jamaica Internet and E-Commerce Investment and Business Guide: Regulations and Opportunities
59.	Japan Internet and E-Commerce Investment and Business Guide: Regulations and Opportunities
60.	Jordan Internet and E-Commerce Investment and Business Guide: Regulations and Opportunities
61.	Kazakhstan Internet and E-Commerce Investment and Business Guide: Regulations and Opportunities
62.	Kenya Internet and E-Commerce Investment and Business Guide: Regulations and Opportunities
63.	Korea, North Internet and E-Commerce Investment and Business Guide: Regulations and Opportunities
64.	Korea, South Internet and E-Commerce Investment and Business Guide: Regulations and Opportunities
65.	Kuwait Internet and E-Commerce Investment and Business Guide: Regulations and Opportunities

For additional analytical, business and investment opportunities information,
please contact Global Investment & Business Center, USA
at (202) 546-2103. Fax: (202) 546-3275. E-mail: rusric@erols.com

66.	Kyrgyzstan Internet and E-Commerce Investment and Business Guide: Regulations and Opportunities
67.	Laos Internet and E-Commerce Investment and Business Guide: Regulations and Opportunities
68.	Latvia Internet and E-Commerce Investment and Business Guide: Regulations and Opportunities
69.	Lebanon Internet and E-Commerce Investment and Business Guide: Regulations and Opportunities
70.	Libya Internet and E-Commerce Investment and Business Guide: Regulations and Opportunities
71.	Lithuania Internet and E-Commerce Investment and Business Guide: Regulations and Opportunities
72.	Macao Internet and E-Commerce Investment and Business Guide: Regulations and Opportunities
73.	Macedonia, Republic Internet and E-Commerce Investment and Business Guide: Regulations and Opportunities
74.	Madagascar Internet and E-Commerce Investment and Business Guide: Regulations and Opportunities
75.	Malaysia Internet and E-Commerce Investment and Business Guide: Regulations and Opportunities
76.	Malta Internet and E-Commerce Investment and Business Guide: Regulations and Opportunities
77.	Mauritius Internet and E-Commerce Investment and Business Guide: Regulations and Opportunities
78.	Mauritius Internet and E-Commerce Investment and Business Guide: Regulations and Opportunities
79.	Mexico Internet and E-Commerce Investment and Business Guide: Regulations and Opportunities
80.	Micronesia Internet and E-Commerce Investment and Business Guide: Regulations and Opportunities
81.	Moldova Internet and E-Commerce Investment and Business Guide: Regulations and Opportunities
82.	Monaco Internet and E-Commerce Investment and Business Guide: Regulations and Opportunities
83.	Mongolia Internet and E-Commerce Investment and Business Guide: Regulations and Opportunities
84.	Morocco Internet and E-Commerce Investment and Business Guide: Regulations and Opportunities
85.	Myanmar Internet and E-Commerce Investment and Business Guide: Regulations and Opportunities
86.	Namibia Internet and E-Commerce Investment and Business Guide: Regulations and Opportunities
87.	Netherlands Internet and E-Commerce Investment and Business Guide: Regulations and Opportunities
88.	New Zealand Internet and E-Commerce Investment and Business Guide: Regulations and Opportunities
89.	Nicaragua Internet and E-Commerce Investment and Business Guide: Regulations and Opportunities
90.	Nigeria Internet and E-Commerce Investment and Business Guide: Regulations and Opportunities
91.	Norway Internet and E-Commerce Investment and Business Guide: Regulations and Opportunities
92.	Pakistan Internet and E-Commerce Investment and Business Guide: Regulations and Opportunities
93.	Panama Internet and E-Commerce Investment and Business Guide: Regulations and Opportunities
94.	Peru Internet and E-Commerce Investment and Business Guide: Regulations and Opportunities
95.	Philippines Internet and E-Commerce Investment and Business Guide: Regulations and Opportunities
96.	Poland Internet and E-Commerce Investment and Business Guide: Regulations and Opportunities
97.	Portugal Internet and E-Commerce Investment and Business Guide: Regulations and Opportunities
98.	Romania Internet and E-Commerce Investment and Business Guide: Regulations and Opportunities
99.	Russia Internet and E-Commerce Investment and Business Guide: Regulations and Opportunities
100.	Saudi Arabia Internet and E-Commerce Investment and Business Guide: Regulations and Opportunities
101.	Scotland Internet and E-Commerce Investment and Business Guide: Regulations and Opportunities

For additional analytical, business and investment opportunities information,
please contact Global Investment & Business Center, USA
at (202) 546-2103. Fax: (202) 546-3275. E-mail: rusric@erols.com

102. Singapore Internet and E-Commerce Investment and Business Guide: Regulations and Opportunities
103. Slovakia Internet and E-Commerce Investment and Business Guide: Regulations and Opportunities
104. Slovenia Internet and E-Commerce Investment and Business Guide: Regulations and Opportunities
105. South Africa Internet and E-Commerce Investment and Business Guide: Regulations and Opportunities
106. Spain Internet and E-Commerce Investment and Business Guide: Regulations and Opportunities
107. Sri Lanka Internet and E-Commerce Investment and Business Guide: Regulations and Opportunities
108. Sudan Internet and E-Commerce Investment and Business Guide: Regulations and Opportunities
109. Suriname Internet and E-Commerce Investment and Business Guide: Regulations and Opportunities
110. Sweden Internet and E-Commerce Investment and Business Guide: Regulations and Opportunities
111. Switzerland Internet and E-Commerce Investment and Business Guide: Regulations and Opportunities
112. Syria Export Import & Business Directory
113. Taiwan Internet and E-Commerce Investment and Business Guide: Regulations and Opportunities
114. Tajikistan Internet and E-Commerce Investment and Business Guide: Regulations and Opportunities
115. Thailand Internet and E-Commerce Investment and Business Guide: Regulations and Opportunities
116. Tunisia Internet and E-Commerce Investment and Business Guide: Regulations and Opportunities
117. Turkey Internet and E-Commerce Investment and Business Guide: Regulations and Opportunities
118. Turkmenistan Internet and E-Commerce Investment and Business Guide: Regulations and Opportunities
119. Uganda Internet and E-Commerce Investment and Business Guide: Regulations and Opportunities
120. Ukraine Internet and E-Commerce Investment and Business Guide: Regulations and Opportunities
121. United Arab Emirates Internet and E-Commerce Investment and Business Guide: Regulations and Opportunities
122. United Kingdom Internet and E-Commerce Investment and Business Guide: Regulations and Opportunities
123. United States Internet and E-Commerce Investment and Business Guide: Regulations and Opportunities
124. Uruguay Internet and E-Commerce Investment and Business Guide: Regulations and Opportunities
125. US Internet and E-Commerce Investment and Business Guide: Regulations and Opportunities
126. Uzbekistan Internet and E-Commerce Investment and Business Guide: Regulations and Opportunities
127. Venezuela Internet and E-Commerce Investment and Business Guide: Regulations and Opportunities
128. Vietnam Internet and E-Commerce Investment and Business Guide: Regulations and Opportunities
129. Yugoslavia Internet and E-Commerce Investment and Business Guide: Regulations and Opportunities

For additional analytical, business and investment opportunities information,
please contact Global Investment & Business Center, USA
at (202) 546-2103. Fax: (202) 546-3275. E-mail: rusric@erols.com

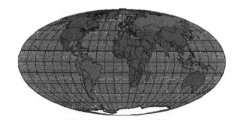

WORLD INVESTMENT AND BUSINESS LIBRARY

World Business Information Catalog, USA: http://www.ibpus.com
Email: ibpusa@comcast.net.

Price: $99.95 Each

TITLE
Abkhazia (Republic of Abkhazia) Investment and Business Guide Volume 1 Strategic and Practical Information
Afghanistan Investment and Business Guide Volume 1 Strategic and Practical Information
Aland Investment and Business Guide Volume 1 Strategic and Practical Information
Albania Investment and Business Guide Volume 1 Strategic and Practical Information
Algeria Investment and Business Guide Volume 1 Strategic and Practical Information
Andorra Investment and Business Guide Volume 1 Strategic and Practical Information
Angola Investment and Business Guide Volume 1 Strategic and Practical Information
Anguilla Investment and Business Guide Volume 1 Strategic and Practical Information
Antigua and Barbuda Investment and Business Guide Volume 1 Strategic and Practical Information
Antilles (Netherlands) Investment and Business Guide Volume 1 Strategic and Practical Information
Argentina Investment and Business Guide Volume 1 Strategic and Practical Information
Armenia Investment and Business Guide Volume 1 Strategic and Practical Information
Aruba Investment and Business Guide Volume 1 Strategic and Practical Information
Australia Investment and Business Guide Volume 1 Strategic and Practical Information
Austria Investment and Business Guide Volume 1 Strategic and Practical Information
Azerbaijan Investment and Business Guide Volume 1 Strategic and Practical Information
Bahamas Investment and Business Guide Volume 1 Strategic and Practical Information
Bahrain Investment and Business Guide Volume 1 Strategic and Practical Information
Bangladesh Investment and Business Guide Volume 1 Strategic and Practical Information
Barbados Investment and Business Guide Volume 1 Strategic and Practical Information
Belarus Investment and Business Guide Volume 1 Strategic and Practical Information
Belgium Investment and Business Guide Volume 1 Strategic and Practical Information
Belize Investment and Business Guide Volume 1 Strategic and Practical Information
Benin Investment and Business Guide Volume 1 Strategic and Practical Information
Bermuda Investment and Business Guide Volume 1 Strategic and Practical Information
Bhutan Investment and Business Guide Volume 1 Strategic and Practical Information
Bolivia Investment and Business Guide Volume 1 Strategic and Practical Information
Bosnia and Herzegovina Investment and Business Guide Volume 1 Strategic and Practical Information
Botswana Investment and Business Guide Volume 1 Strategic and Practical Information
Brazil Investment and Business Guide Volume 1 Strategic and Practical Information
Brunei Investment and Business Guide Volume 1 Strategic and Practical Information
Bulgaria Investment and Business Guide Volume 1 Strategic and Practical Information
Burkina Faso Investment and Business Guide Volume 1 Strategic and Practical Information
Burundi Investment and Business Guide Volume 1 Strategic and Practical Information
Cambodia Investment and Business Guide Volume 1 Strategic and Practical Information
Cameroon Investment and Business Guide Volume 1 Strategic and Practical Information
Canada Investment and Business Guide Volume 1 Strategic and Practical Information

For additional analytical, business and investment opportunities information,
Please contact Global Investment & Business Center, USA
at (202) 546-2103. Fax: (202) 546-3275. E-mail: rusric@erols.com

TITLE
Cape Verde Investment and Business Guide Volume 1 Strategic and Practical Information
Cayman Islands Investment and Business Guide Volume 1 Strategic and Practical Information
Central African Republic Investment and Business Guide Volume 1 Strategic and Practical Information
Chad Investment and Business Guide Volume 1 Strategic and Practical Information
Chile Investment and Business Guide Volume 1 Strategic and Practical Information
China Investment and Business Guide Volume 1 Strategic and Practical Information
Colombia Investment and Business Guide Volume 1 Strategic and Practical Information
Comoros Investment and Business Guide Volume 1 Strategic and Practical Information
Congo Investment and Business Guide Volume 1 Strategic and Practical Information
Congo, Democratic Republic Investment and Business Guide Volume 1 Strategic and Practical Information
Cook Islands Investment and Business Guide Volume 1 Strategic and Practical Information
Costa Rica Investment and Business Guide Volume 1 Strategic and Practical Information
Cote d'Ivoire Investment and Business Guide Volume 1 Strategic and Practical Information
Croatia Investment and Business Guide Volume 1 Strategic and Practical Information
Cuba Investment and Business Guide Volume 1 Strategic and Practical Information
Cyprus Investment and Business Guide Volume 1 Strategic and Practical Information
Czech Republic Investment and Business Guide Volume 1 Strategic and Practical Information
Denmark Investment and Business Guide Volume 1 Strategic and Practical Information
Djibouti Investment and Business Guide Volume 1 Strategic and Practical Information
Dominica Investment and Business Guide Volume 1 Strategic and Practical Information
Dominican Republic Investment and Business Guide Volume 1 Strategic and Practical Information
Ecuador Investment and Business Guide Volume 1 Strategic and Practical Information
Egypt Investment and Business Guide Volume 1 Strategic and Practical Information
El Salvador Investment and Business Guide Volume 1 Strategic and Practical Information
Equatorial Guinea Investment and Business Guide Volume 1 Strategic and Practical Information
Eritrea Investment and Business Guide Volume 1 Strategic and Practical Information
Estonia Investment and Business Guide Volume 1 Strategic and Practical Information
Ethiopia Investment and Business Guide Volume 1 Strategic and Practical Information
Falkland Islands Investment and Business Guide Volume 1 Strategic and Practical Information
Faroes Islands Investment and Business Guide Volume 1 Strategic and Practical Information
Fiji Investment and Business Guide Volume 1 Strategic and Practical Information
Finland Investment and Business Guide Volume 1 Strategic and Practical Information
France Investment and Business Guide Volume 1 Strategic and Practical Information
Gabon Investment and Business Guide Volume 1 Strategic and Practical Information
Gambia Investment and Business Guide Volume 1 Strategic and Practical Information
Georgia Investment and Business Guide Volume 1 Strategic and Practical Information
Germany Investment and Business Guide Volume 1 Strategic and Practical Information
Ghana Investment and Business Guide Volume 1 Strategic and Practical Information
Gibraltar Investment and Business Guide Volume 1 Strategic and Practical Information
Greece Investment and Business Guide Volume 1 Strategic and Practical Information
Greenland Investment and Business Guide Volume 1 Strategic and Practical Information
Grenada Investment and Business Guide Volume 1 Strategic and Practical Information
Guam Investment and Business Guide Volume 1 Strategic and Practical Information
Guatemala Investment and Business Guide Volume 1 Strategic and Practical Information
Guernsey Investment and Business Guide Volume 1 Strategic and Practical Information
Guinea Investment and Business Guide Volume 1 Strategic and Practical Information

For additional analytical, business and investment opportunities information,
Please contact Global Investment & Business Center, USA
at (202) 546-2103. Fax: (202) 546-3275. E-mail: rusric@erols.com

TITLE
Guinea-Bissau Investment and Business Guide Volume 1 Strategic and Practical Information
Guyana Investment and Business Guide Volume 1 Strategic and Practical Information
Haiti Investment and Business Guide Volume 1 Strategic and Practical Information
Honduras Investment and Business Guide Volume 1 Strategic and Practical Information
Hungary Investment and Business Guide Volume 1 Strategic and Practical Information
Iceland Investment and Business Guide Volume 1 Strategic and Practical Information
India Investment and Business Guide Volume 1 Strategic and Practical Information
Indonesia Investment and Business Guide Volume 1 Strategic and Practical Information
Iran Investment and Business Guide Volume 1 Strategic and Practical Information
Iraq Investment and Business Guide Volume 1 Strategic and Practical Information
Ireland Investment and Business Guide Volume 1 Strategic and Practical Information
Israel Investment and Business Guide Volume 1 Strategic and Practical Information
Italy Investment and Business Guide Volume 1 Strategic and Practical Information
Jamaica Investment and Business Guide Volume 1 Strategic and Practical Information
Japan Investment and Business Guide Volume 1 Strategic and Practical Information
Jersey Investment and Business Guide Volume 1 Strategic and Practical Information
Jordan Investment and Business Guide Volume 1 Strategic and Practical Information
Kazakhstan Investment and Business Guide Volume 1 Strategic and Practical Information
Kenya Investment and Business Guide Volume 1 Strategic and Practical Information
Kiribati Investment and Business Guide Volume 1 Strategic and Practical Information
Korea, North Investment and Business Guide Volume 1 Strategic and Practical Information
Korea, South Investment and Business Guide Volume 1 Strategic and Practical Information
Kosovo Investment and Business Guide Volume 1 Strategic and Practical Information
Kurdistan Investment and Business Guide Volume 1 Strategic and Practical Information
Kuwait Investment and Business Guide Volume 1 Strategic and Practical Information
Kyrgyzstan Investment and Business Guide Volume 1 Strategic and Practical Information
Laos Investment and Business Guide Volume 1 Strategic and Practical Information
Latvia Investment and Business Guide Volume 1 Strategic and Practical Information
Lebanon Investment and Business Guide Volume 1 Strategic and Practical Information
Lesotho Investment and Business Guide Volume 1 Strategic and Practical Information
Liberia Investment and Business Guide Volume 1 Strategic and Practical Information
Libya Investment and Business Guide Volume 1 Strategic and Practical Information
Liechtenstein Investment and Business Guide Volume 1 Strategic and Practical Information
Lithuania Investment and Business Guide Volume 1 Strategic and Practical Information
Luxembourg Investment and Business Guide Volume 1 Strategic and Practical Information
Macao Investment and Business Guide Volume 1 Strategic and Practical Information
Macedonia Investment and Business Guide Volume 1 Strategic and Practical Information
Madagascar Investment and Business Guide Volume 1 Strategic and Practical Information
Madeira Investment and Business Guide Volume 1 Strategic and Practical Information
Malawi Investment and Business Guide Volume 1 Strategic and Practical Information
Malaysia Investment and Business Guide Volume 1 Strategic and Practical Information
Maldives Investment and Business Guide Volume 1 Strategic and Practical Information
Mali Investment and Business Guide Volume 1 Strategic and Practical Information
Malta Investment and Business Guide Volume 1 Strategic and Practical Information
Man Investment and Business Guide Volume 1 Strategic and Practical Information
Marshall Islands Investment and Business Guide Volume 1 Strategic and Practical Information

For additional analytical, business and investment opportunities information,
Please contact Global Investment & Business Center, USA
at (202) 546-2103. Fax: (202) 546-3275. E-mail: rusric@erols.com

TITLE
Mauritania Investment and Business Guide Volume 1 Strategic and Practical Information
Mauritius Investment and Business Guide Volume 1 Strategic and Practical Information
Mayotte Investment and Business Guide Volume 1 Strategic and Practical Information
Mexico Investment and Business Guide Volume 1 Strategic and Practical Information
Micronesia Investment and Business Guide Volume 1 Strategic and Practical Information
Moldova Investment and Business Guide Volume 1 Strategic and Practical Information
Monaco Investment and Business Guide Volume 1 Strategic and Practical Information
Mongolia Investment and Business Guide Volume 1 Strategic and Practical Information
Montserrat Investment and Business Guide Volume 1 Strategic and Practical Information
Montenegro Investment and Business Guide Volume 1 Strategic and Practical Information
Morocco Investment and Business Guide Volume 1 Strategic and Practical Information
Mozambique Investment and Business Guide Volume 1 Strategic and Practical Information
Myanmar Investment and Business Guide Volume 1 Strategic and Practical Information
Nagorno-Karabakh Republic Investment and Business Guide Volume 1 Strategic and Practical Information
Namibia Investment and Business Guide Volume 1 Strategic and Practical Information
Nauru Investment and Business Guide Volume 1 Strategic and Practical Information
Nepal Investment and Business Guide Volume 1 Strategic and Practical Information
Netherlands Investment and Business Guide Volume 1 Strategic and Practical Information
New Caledonia Investment and Business Guide Volume 1 Strategic and Practical Information
New Zealand Investment and Business Guide Volume 1 Strategic and Practical Information
Nicaragua Investment and Business Guide Volume 1 Strategic and Practical Information
Niger Investment and Business Guide Volume 1 Strategic and Practical Information
Nigeria Investment and Business Guide Volume 1 Strategic and Practical Information
Niue Investment and Business Guide Volume 1 Strategic and Practical Information
Northern Cyprus (Turkish Republic of Northern Cyprus) Volume 1 Strategic Information and Developments
Northern Mariana Islands Investment and Business Guide Volume 1 Strategic and Practical Information
Norway Investment and Business Guide Volume 1 Strategic and Practical Information
Oman Investment and Business Guide Volume 1 Strategic and Practical Information
Pakistan Investment and Business Guide Volume 1 Strategic and Practical Information
Palau Investment and Business Guide Volume 1 Strategic and Practical Information
Palestine (West Bank & Gaza) Investment and Business Guide Volume 1 Strategic and Practical Information
Panama Investment and Business Guide Volume 1 Strategic and Practical Information
Papua New Guinea Investment and Business Guide Volume 1 Strategic and Practical Information
Paraguay Investment and Business Guide Volume 1 Strategic and Practical Information
Peru Investment and Business Guide Volume 1 Strategic and Practical Information
Philippines Investment and Business Guide Volume 1 Strategic and Practical Information
Pitcairn Islands Investment and Business Guide Volume 1 Strategic and Practical Information
Poland Investment and Business Guide Volume 1 Strategic and Practical Information
Polynesia French Investment and Business Guide Volume 1 Strategic and Practical Information
Portugal Investment and Business Guide Volume 1 Strategic and Practical Information
Qatar Investment and Business Guide Volume 1 Strategic and Practical Information
Romania Investment and Business Guide Volume 1 Strategic and Practical Information
Russia Investment and Business Guide Volume 1 Strategic and Practical Information
Rwanda Investment and Business Guide Volume 1 Strategic and Practical Information
Sahrawi Arab Democratic Republic Volume 1 Strategic Information and Developments
Saint Kitts and Nevis Investment and Business Guide Volume 1 Strategic and Practical Information

For additional analytical, business and investment opportunities information,
Please contact Global Investment & Business Center, USA
at (202) 546-2103. Fax: (202) 546-3275. E-mail: rusric@erols.com

TITLE
Saint Lucia Investment and Business Guide Volume 1 Strategic and Practical Information
Saint Vincent and The Grenadines Investment and Business Guide Volume 1 Strategic and Practical Information
Samoa (American) A Investment and Business Guide Volume 1 Strategic and Practical Information
Samoa (Western) Investment and Business Guide Volume 1 Strategic and Practical Information
San Marino Investment and Business Guide Volume 1 Strategic and Practical Information
Sao Tome and Principe Investment and Business Guide Volume 1 Strategic and Practical Information
Saudi Arabia Investment and Business Guide Volume 1 Strategic and Practical Information
Scotland Investment and Business Guide Volume 1 Strategic and Practical Information
Senegal Investment and Business Guide Volume 1 Strategic and Practical Information
Serbia Investment and Business Guide Volume 1 Strategic and Practical Information
Seychelles Investment and Business Guide Volume 1 Strategic and Practical Information
Sierra Leone Investment and Business Guide Volume 1 Strategic and Practical Information
Singapore Investment and Business Guide Volume 1 Strategic and Practical Information
Slovakia Investment and Business Guide Volume 1 Strategic and Practical Information
Slovenia Investment and Business Guide Volume 1 Strategic and Practical Information
Solomon Islands Investment and Business Guide Volume 1 Strategic and Practical Information
Somalia Investment and Business Guide Volume 1 Strategic and Practical Information
South Africa Investment and Business Guide Volume 1 Strategic and Practical Information
Spain Investment and Business Guide Volume 1 Strategic and Practical Information
Sri Lanka Investment and Business Guide Volume 1 Strategic and Practical Information
St. Helena Investment and Business Guide Volume 1 Strategic and Practical Information
St. Pierre & Miquelon Investment and Business Guide Volume 1 Strategic and Practical Information
Sudan (Republic of the Sudan) Investment and Business Guide Volume 1 Strategic and Practical Information
Sudan South Investment and Business Guide Volume 1 Strategic and Practical Information
Suriname Investment and Business Guide Volume 1 Strategic and Practical Information
Swaziland Investment and Business Guide Volume 1 Strategic and Practical Information
Sweden Investment and Business Guide Volume 1 Strategic and Practical Information
Switzerland Investment and Business Guide Volume 1 Strategic and Practical Information
Syria Investment and Business Guide Volume 1 Strategic and Practical Information
Taiwan Investment and Business Guide Volume 1 Strategic and Practical Information
Tajikistan Investment and Business Guide Volume 1 Strategic and Practical Information
Tanzania Investment and Business Guide Volume 1 Strategic and Practical Information
Thailand Investment and Business Guide Volume 1 Strategic and Practical Information
Timor Leste (Democratic Republic of Timor-Leste) Investment and Business Guide Volume 1 Strategic and Practical Information
Togo Investment and Business Guide Volume 1 Strategic and Practical Information
Tonga Investment and Business Guide Volume 1 Strategic and Practical Information
Trinidad and Tobago Investment and Business Guide Volume 1 Strategic and Practical Information
Tunisia Investment and Business Guide Volume 1 Strategic and Practical Information
Turkey Investment and Business Guide Volume 1 Strategic and Practical Information
Turkmenistan Investment and Business Guide Volume 1 Strategic and Practical Information
Turks & Caicos Investment and Business Guide Volume 1 Strategic and Practical Information
Tuvalu Investment and Business Guide Volume 1 Strategic and Practical Information
Uganda Investment and Business Guide Volume 1 Strategic and Practical Information
Ukraine Investment and Business Guide Volume 1 Strategic and Practical Information
United Arab Emirates Investment and Business Guide Volume 1 Strategic and Practical Information

For additional analytical, business and investment opportunities information,
Please contact Global Investment & Business Center, USA
at (202) 546-2103. Fax: (202) 546-3275. E-mail: rusric@erols.com

TITLE
United Kingdom Investment and Business Guide Volume 1 Strategic and Practical Information
United States Investment and Business Guide Volume 1 Strategic and Practical Information
Uruguay Investment and Business Guide Volume 1 Strategic and Practical Information
Uzbekistan Investment and Business Guide Volume 1 Strategic and Practical Information
Vanuatu Investment and Business Guide Volume 1 Strategic and Practical Information
Vatican City (Holy See) Investment and Business Guide Volume 1 Strategic and Practical Information
Venezuela Investment and Business Guide Volume 1 Strategic and Practical Information
Vietnam Investment and Business Guide Volume 1 Strategic and Practical Information
Virgin Islands, British Investment and Business Guide Volume 1 Strategic and Practical Information
Wake Atoll Investment and Business Guide Volume 1 Strategic and Practical Information
Wallis & Futuna Investment and Business Guide Volume 1 Strategic and Practical Information
Western Sahara Investment and Business Guide Volume 1 Strategic and Practical Information
Yemen Investment and Business Guide Volume 1 Strategic and Practical Information
Zambia Investment and Business Guide Volume 1 Strategic and Practical Information
Zimbabwe Investment and Business Guide Volume 1 Strategic and Practical Information

For additional analytical, business and investment opportunities information,
Please contact Global Investment & Business Center, USA
at (202) 546-2103. Fax: (202) 546-3275. E-mail: rusric@erols.com